Wedding Kit For Dummies®

Cheat Sheet

D1515496

When, What, and Where for the Wedding

_____&_____

Ceremony Rehearsal

Date:_____ Time:_____

Place:_____

Address:_____

Phone:_____

Rehearsal Dinner

Date:_____ Time:_____

Place:_____

Address:_____

Phone:_____

Ceremony

Date:_____ Time:_____

Place:_____

Address:_____

Phone:_____

Reception

Date:_____ Time:_____

Place:_____

Address:_____

Phone:_____

Honeymoon

Dates:_____

Place:_____

Address:_____

Phone:_____ E-mail:_____

Flight info:_____

Car:_____ Other:_____

For Dummies: Bestselling Book Series for Beginners

Wedding Kit For Dummies®

Cheat Sheet

Everyone's 411 at a Glance

Key Player	Name	Contact Info	
Bride		Phone:	Cell:
		Beeper:	E-mail:
Groom		Phone:	Cell:
		Beeper:	E-mail:
Bride's parents		Phone:	Cell:
		Beeper:	E-mail:
Groom's parents		Phone:	Cell:
		Beeper:	E-mail:
Wedding Consultant		Phone:	Cell:
		Beeper:	E-mail:
Maid of Honor		Phone:	Cell:
		Beeper:	E-mail:
Best Man		Phone:	Cell:
		Beeper:	E-mail:
Officiant		Phone:	Cell:
		Beeper:	E-mail:
Ceremony Site		Phone:	Cell:
		Beeper:	E-mail:
Reception Site		Phone:	Cell:
		Beeper:	E-mail:
Caterer or Banquet Manager		Phone:	Cell:
		Beeper:	E-mail:

For Dummies: Bestselling Book Series for Beginners

Praise for Wedding Kit For Dummies

"This is the perfect gift for any bride to be. I wish I had it when I got married."

— Heidi Klum, supermodel

"Here is the one bridal accessory you simply must have, advice from Marcy Blum."

— Antonia van der Meer, Editor-in-Chief, *Modern Bride*

"The nitty gritty couples really need."

— Carley Roney, Editor-in-chief, *The Knot*

"Do you really want to enjoy your wedding celebration and then hear rave reviews afterward? Then give Marcy Blum all the work behind the scenes — you can't afford not to."

— Monica Hickey, Director – Custom/Couture Bridal Designs, Saks Fifth Avenue, NY

"Marcy Blum has created magical weddings for hundreds of engaged couples. Every bride-to-be who dreams of a beautiful, memorable wedding celebration will benefit from her boundless creativity, and the tricks of the trade she shares here."

— Millie Martini Bratten, Editor-in-chief, *Bride's Magazine*

"Sassy! Before you say 'I do,' you must read this book. An easy-to-use guide with practical tips and advice. Blum and Kaiser pull no punches to guide the betrothed through the minefield that is planning a weeding."

— Alan and Denise Fields, Authors, *Bridal Bargains* and *The Bridal Gown Guide*

"Anyone planning a wedding should read this book. The game rules, tip, and caution icons highlight practical advice that everyone can understand and follow."

— Adrienne Vittadini, Fashion Designer

"For those entering the wilderness of wedding planning, there is no better guide than Marcy Blum. She is funny, she is smart, she is cool, she's seen it all. No one knows more about flowers, centerpieces, diamond rings, wedding gowns, and life in general. From bridesmaid dresses to avoiding tacky trends, take her advice!"

— Lois Smith Brady, Wedding Columnist, *New York Times*

Praise for Weddings For Dummies

"In *Weddings For Dummies,* Marcy Blum and Laura Fisher Kaiser have revolutionized the wedding-planning process. Their book is worth buying for the budget tips alone. Their research into wedding logistics is equally impressive; who knew that each wedding guest requires exactly three square feet of space on the dance floor?"

— Nancy Marx Better, Senior Contributing Editor, *SmartMoney Magazine,* New York

"*Weddings For Dummies* will help you say 'I do' with confidence and a smile. Marcy offers straight talk that makes sense and all the information any couple needs to plan a great wedding."

— Maria McBride-Mellinger, Author of *The Perfect Wedding, The Wedding Dress, and Bridal Flowers*

"Brides- and grooms-to-be can rest easy! *Weddings For Dummies* is filled with lots of smart ideas — and all presented with wit, humor, and great common sense. Marcy Blum's expertise and savvy professionalism render this an incredibly detailed and fun-to-read wedding planning bible. She and Laura Fisher Kaiser outline everything you need to know to make planning your wedding a breeze. Getting married has never been easier!"

— Diane Forden, Editor-in-Chief, *Bridal Guide Magazine*

by Marcy Blum and Laura Fisher Kaiser

WILEY

Wiley Publishing, Inc.

Wedding Kit For Dummies®

Published by
Wiley Publishing, Inc.
111 River Street
Hoboken, NJ 07030
www.wiley.com

Copyright © 2002 by Wiley Publishing, Inc., Indianapolis, Indiana

Published by Wiley Publishing, Inc., Indianapolis, Indiana

Published simultaneously in Canada

For general information on our other products and services or to obtain technical support, please contact our Customer Care Department within the U.S. at 800-762-2974, outside the U.S. at 317-572-3993, or fax 317-572-4002.

Wiley also publishes its books in a variety of electronic formats. Some content that appears in print may not be available in electronic books.

Library of Congress Cataloging-in-Publication Data:

Library of Congress Control Number: 00-104225

ISBN: 978-0-7645-5263-2

Manufactured in the United States of America

10 9 8 7

3B/RV/QR/QV/IN

About the Authors

Photo Credit: Harold Hechler Associates Ltd.

Marcy Blum, one of the first female graduates of The Culinary Institute of America, is a highly respected expert on weddings and special events. She has appeared on a number of television shows including *Good Morning America, The Today Show, Weddings of A Lifetime,* The Food Channel, and on NBC Nightly News. Ms. Blum was named as a Best of New York in *New York* magazine, is a recipient of The Silver Spoon Award for professional excellence from *Food Arts* magazine and is a member of the prestigious Les Dames D'Escoffier. Marcy serves on the advisory boards of TheKnot.com and Disney Fairy Tale weddings. She is a contributing editor for *Modern Bride* magazine and a spokesperson for Things Remembered.

Photo Credit: Michael Edwards

Laura Fisher Kaiser is the co-author of *Weddings For Dummies* with Marcy Blum and *The Official eBay Guide to Buying, Selling, and Collecting Just About Anything* (Fireside) with her husband, Michael Kaiser. As a writer and editor, she has tackled a variety of subjects from fashion and design to health and home improvement. As editor of *eShopper* magazine and special projects editor of *Yahoo! Internet Life* magazine, she has covered the world of e-commerce and consumer affairs extensively. Prior to that, she served as editor in chief of *Avenue* magazine and deputy editor of *This Old House Magazine*.

Dedication

From Marcy: This book is dedicated to the memory of Gertrude and Harold Blum, my parents; I miss them every day.

From Laura: For Michael Bear.

Authors' Acknowledgments

This book, like most things in life, was not nearly as simple as it looks. We are thankful to everyone who helped us professionally, especially our friends and families who keep us safe and sane so we can attempt to do 300 things at once.

Our thanks must start with, Michael Kaiser: Laura's husband, Marcy's good friend and our anonymous third partner/co-author. Michael not only kept us beautifully fed and watered as we wrote, but also labored over the spreadsheets, technical details, and many of the Internet-related aspects of the book with laser-beam focus and his usual perspicacity. We are truly appreciative.

We are grateful to our agent, Mark Reiter, who, even though he is a superstar, returns our calls, eventually (and his marvelous assistant, Michelle Yung, who makes sure that he does). We thank our acquisitions editor, Stacy Collins who picked up after others dropped the ball and nurtured us appropriately, and the patient Linda Brandon — our project editor — for shepherding this project along and taking the time to figure out what we were trying to say.

Thanks also goes to Liz Kurtzman whose whimsical illustrations greatly enhance our book, the cartoonist Rich Tennant for his zany contributions, Meaghan O'Neill, who cheerfully typed in endless contracts and menus; Mary Goodwin for her diligent editing, and Kathy Ehrich, who fact checked this book in record time.

We are grateful to Barry Golson, editor in chief of *Yahoo! Internet Life,* for generously allowing Laura the time to finish this project.

Most of all we both thank from the bottom of our hearts the brides and grooms who made our first book, *Weddings For Dummies,* such a success.

From Marcy: I feel blessed for the many really special friendships I have and to some of those who support me, both professionally and personally, my gratitude: Maria McBride Mellinger — a remarkably talented woman and my patron saint; Rozanne Gold and her husband Michael Whiteman who have adopted me and are never too busy to give the most salient professional advice or simply hand hold; Sheila Lukins who I always learn something from;

Marianna and Jay Watnick — whose generosity overwhelms me; Laurie and Bruce Wolf and Leslie and Doug Murphy-Chutorian for always being there when it counts; Stacy Morrison of the golden mind; my brother Howard, sister-in-law Jenny and their children Dani, Anna and Tony for being proud of me and to Michael Liebowitz and Susan Burden — two consummate professionals who have never, ever, forgotten to be kind. To Millie Bratton for her insight; Sandea for permeating my home with her beautiful spirit; to Preston Bailey for being who he is and allowing me to bask in his glow; to Jack Orr for his eternal "kvelling," and of course deep gratitude to Peter Aschkenasy, mentor and friend for life.

From Laura: Thanks to my family and friends for their understanding when deadlines have eaten into the time I should — and would rather — be spending with you.

Publisher's Acknowledgments

We're proud of this book; please send us your comments through our online registration form located at www.dummies.com/register.

Some of the people who helped bring this book to market include the following:

Acquisitions, Editorial, and Media Development

Project Editors: Linda Brandon; Mary Goodwin

Acquisitions Editor: Stacy Collins

Acquisitions Coordinator: Lisa Roule

Fact Checker: Kathy Ehrich

Technical Editor: Joell Smith

Illustrator: Liz Kurtzman

Permissions Editor: Carmen Krikorian

Media Development Specialists: Megan Decraene; Brock Bigard

Editorial Manager: Christine Beck

Media Development Manager: Heather Dismore

Editorial Assistant: Alison Jefferson

Composition

Project Coordinator: Nancee Reeves

Layout and Graphics: Amy Adrian, Karl Brandt, Angela F. Hunckler, Stephanie Jumper, Clint Lahnen, Tracy K. Oliver, Jacque Schneider, Rashell Smith

Proofreaders: Rachel Garvey, Angel Perez, Carl Pierce, Nancy Reinhardt, Marianne Santy

Indexer: Sharon Hilgenberg

Special Help
Mary Fales; Shelley Lea; Rev Mengle

Publishing and Editorial for Consumer Dummies
Diane Graves Steele, Vice President and Publisher, Consumer Dummies
Joyce Pepple, Acquisitions Director, Consumer Dummies
Kristin A. Cocks, Product Development Director, Consumer Dummies
Michael Spring, Vice President and Publisher, Travel
Brice Gosnell, Associate Publisher, Travel
Suzanne Jannetta, Editorial Director, Travel

Publishing for Technology Dummies
Richard Swadley, Vice President and Executive Group Publisher
Andy Cummings, Vice President and Publisher

Composition Services
Gerry Fahey, Vice President of Production Services
Debbie Stailey, Director of Composition Services

◆

Cartoons at a Glance

By Rich Tennant

The 5th Wave By Rich Tennant

"Would you ask the men with the pink 'Simplicity' boutonnieres not to group around the 'Butterscotch' rose bush. It plays havoc with the entire color scheme of my garden."

page 313

The 5th Wave By Rich Tennant

LITTLE MISS MUFFET PLANS HER WEDDING DAY MENU

"We'll start with the curds and meatballs, curd stuffed dates and curds-in-a-blanket. Then, we'll have the sweet and sour curds over a mound of whey..."

page 133

The 5th Wave By Rich Tennant

"It's nice that you picked a professional radio DJ for the reception music, but I wish he'd quit announcing the weather and sports scores between every third song."

page 89

The 5th Wave By Rich Tennant

How many times do I have to say it – ring BEARER, ring BEARER!!

page 235

The 5th Wave By Rich Tennant

"Along with 'Invitations', 'Announcements' and 'Save the Day' cards, I'd like some 'I Told You So' cards for people who thought I'd never get married."

page 43

The 5th Wave By Rich Tennant

JONATHAN COURTS DISASTER

"Why of course I'll marry you, Jonathan! We'll have a big wedding and all the guests get to pick where, when, and how it should be held."

page 7

Fax: 978-546-7747
E-mail: richtennant@the5thwave.com
World Wide Web: www.the5thwave.com

Contents at a Glance

Table of Contents

Introduction

*W*hen we wrote *Weddings For Dummies*, we set out to cram it full of truly useful information for anyone planning a wedding. Judging from the overwhelmingly positive response we received from grateful couples (not to mention professional wedding consultants), we figured that our mission was accomplished.

But then our publisher asked us if we'd be interested in working on a wedding *kit* with specific tools that would make the wedding-planning process even easier. We brainstormed. One way to do the book, we realized, would be to include tips on tapping into the vast amount of information available on the World Wide Web. Another way would be to design some tools of our own (superior to those available on the current market) to help people keep track of expenses, sort out the guest list, comparison shop for vendors and sites, and negotiate contracts.

Just as with *Weddings For Dummies*, we decided that we could make this kit better than all the other wedding books out there. We wondered how many people really use those tedious forms in so many "planners." After all, every wedding is different, and most people must end up doing their own thing. If only we could provide a flexible template and offer couples a way to customize worksheets — now, *that* would be truly helpful.

And then we had it — use the technology available! So, as a bonus with this book, you receive a CD-ROM that contains the worksheets from the book, Excel spreadsheets, and hot links to useful Web sites. This interactive system offers you the flexibility to plan your wedding on your computer — or to print out files and take them with you as you interview vendors and scout spaces.

We wrote this book to serve as a complement to *Weddings For Dummies*. For that reason, we purposefully avoid rehashing chunks of that book; at most, we summarize key points. Our goal with *Wedding Kit For Dummies* is to enhance the information imparted in *WFD*, elaborate on certain aspects, and simplify the planning process with worksheets, checklists, and forms that are incredibly useful.

The volumes are designed to work together — for real people planning real weddings in the new century.

How to Use This Book

As we say, this book is a companion to *Weddings For Dummies* — the hands-on yang to *WFD*'s theoretical yin. Throughout this book, we cross reference text in the first volume, so keep your copy of *Weddings For Dummies* handy as you read along.

At the end of every chapter, you find a list of forms that appear on the CD-ROM. In some cases you might want to print out the forms and take them with you as you meet with vendors. Other times you might prefer to copy the forms to your computer and customize them to your own needs.

The Internet has revolutionized the way people live, including the way they plan their weddings, so we feature numerous Web sites throughout the book. One caveat: the dot-com world is changing rapidly, with sites popping up and folding in the blink of an eye. We apologize in advance for any sites that are defunct by the time you read this. (Hey, they seemed like a good idea at the time!) We suggest you utilize the powerful search engines on the Web to find new and better sites, for in the market's Darwinian ways, the survivors are bound to be vastly improved.

Another caveat concerns the contracts in this book. We adapted and edited several professional contracts as examples of what to expect when you deal with vendors. These do not appear on the CD-ROM. Most vendors have their own contracts — you don't hand them yours. For vendors who don't, we provide templates for "delivery" sheets, which you can customize and give to them as confirmations of your order.

Finally, we suggest you invest in a wheelbarrow, forklift, or snowplow to handle the reams of worksheets you'll soon be printing out from the CD-ROM. Sorry about that — we can't stand the thought of you planning your wedding without being totally prepared.

How This Book Is Organized

So many aspects of planning a wedding need to be done concurrently that it's difficult to pick a starting point. And, if you've read *Weddings For Dummies*, you know that we're not fans of dogmatic timelines. We set up this book in a way that we think makes sense — big picture stuff and budget matters up front, then guest lists and invitations, followed by the ceremony, the reception, and other miscellaneous details. However, you might find that you need to fast-forward to the reception chapters because the space you want gets booked a year in advance. No problem. This ain't a Stephen King novel — you can jump around all you want without missing any major plot twists. Just be sure you do backtrack at some point so that you don't forget to order the cake or the ring.

Part I: Getting Started

We don't waste a lot of time with chitchat in this section. Knowledge is power, so we jump right in.

Chapter 1 gives you a preview of the horror — er, joy! — to come. We help you pick a wedding date, and then provide the mother of all to-do lists of things to accomplish between the time you read that chapter and the day of your wedding. We also give you a few handy data worksheets so that you can keep track of all the little people who are helping you pull this extravaganza together. Then in Chapter 2, it's time to get real and focus on the financial picture. We try to ease the pain by providing a wedding budget spreadsheet where you can plug in the numbers and go.

Part II: Be Our Guest

Keeping track of all the people you invite, their RSVPs, and the gifts they send can be complicated. This section helps you manage the guest list, from invitations to seating charts.

In Chapter 3, we come to the rescue with a specially designed spreadsheet program for keeping track of guests. If you're not familiar with Excel, it's worth taking some time to learn the basics so that you can make your wedding planning go more smoothly. The spreadsheet is also useful for figuring out seating charts for meals. Chapter 4 is all about selecting the right invitation for your wedding style, whether you order cards from a stationer or create your own. In Chapter 5, we explore the growing trend of destination weddings and how to finesse all the hospitality details that they entail. (This chapter also serves as a honeymoon-planning field guide.)

Part III: Ceremony Survival Plan

The wedding ceremony is the emotional climax of the day, and the words, the music, and the timing need to be as close to your dream wedding as possible. In this part, we walk you through the planning of each step.

We start with choosing a site and an officiant in Chapter 6, and then move on to content, helping you determine the sequence of service, suitable vows, and meaningful readings. We also give examples of wedding programs — a lovely guide and memento for the day. Ceremony music is so important that we devote all of Chapter 7 to it, from choosing the songs you like to finding the right musicians to play them. Finally, in Chapter 8, we think it's about time that you plot out the wedding day schedule — an indispensable tool for a successful day — and we show you how.

Part IV: A Rousing Reception

Whether you plan a simple champagne toast or a five-course seated dinner, a lot of decisions need to be made, from where to hold the reception to what food to serve to which flowers to order. We tackle all that and more in this part.

Chapter 9 is essential reading. Here we explain how to compare on-premise and off-premise venues. Chapter 10 is a primer on putting together a winning playlist of favorite songs for the band or DJ. Then it's on to our favorite subject — food! — in Chapter 11, where we help you compose the perfect menu, among other tasty topics. In Chapter 12, the subject is roses and whatever else your nose and eye desire. We explain how to work with a florist to get the decorative effect you want.

Part V: Gifts, Garb, Pics, and Tips

This is the catchall section, where we dump all the other details we couldn't fit into other parts of the book.

We know that you're very concerned about all the gifts you're going to receive, and so, yes, we devote a lot of time in Chapter 13 helping you plan your registry. Please read this chapter before venturing online or into a department store to register. Chapter 14 is devoted to wedding attire — the bridal gown, the groom's garb, and the attendants' get-ups — and how to whittle down the vast array of choices out there. After you're all dressed up, you'll want to record your decked-out selves for posterity, and Chapter 15 helps you select the photographer or videographer you feel most comfortable with. Speaking of posterity, Chapter 16 helps you with other details, such as submitting newspaper announcements, changing your name, and making toasts. We realize that none of these things go together, but that's okay — it's all good stuff!

Part VI: The Part of Tens

A favorite among *...For Dummies* fans, this section rounds up a lot of information for quick reference, including innovative solutions regarding wedding planning. In Chapter 17, we explain how to use the World Wide Web as a tool for finding information and shopping for your wedding needs. Chapter 18 is also technically oriented as we help demystify the wonders of Excel so you can better use the budget and guest list spreadsheets provided on the CD-ROM. Finally, it's time for a little fun, so in Chapter 19 we explore some of our favorite locations for destination weddings. Bon voyage!

Icons Used in This Book

No matter the budget, anyone planning a wedding wants to get the most bang for the buck. This symbol means we are about to impart vital information regarding a practical money matter. While many times we tell you how to save money, we just as often explain why pinching pennies in a particular area may not be wise.

Although we don't advocate being a slave to calendars and endless to-do lists, every now and then a timely reminder or heads up is in order. When you see this symbol, adjust your personal wedding timetable accordingly.

Weddings, like life, can be unpredictable, but certain mistakes, pitfalls, and tacky traps are easily avoided. Defuse these little bombs while you can.

This quizzical fellow is a familiar face to ...*For Dummies* aficionados, and in this book he pops up to indicate when you're about to encounter an important clue to working with a spreadsheet or other digital-age dilemma.

Some aspects of creating a successful wedding are so important — and so easily overlooked — they bear repeating. We'll mark the repetitions with this symbol.

Yes, we realize that your Aunt Myrtle graduated with honors from the TJTWID (That's Just The Way It's Done) Etiquette Academy, but we're here to tell you that times have changed, and so have certain ironclad rules of decorum. There are alternative ways for handling many wedding situations.

Take it from us — you're about to read some information you can really use.

This icon indicates that you'll find one of our handy-dandy forms or worksheets on the CD-ROM.

Forms are not the only items on the CD. We use this icon to flag helpful Web sites that you can link to from our CD-ROM as well as to point out what software programs have been included. Please note that some software programs are trial versions only. See the CD Appendix for details.

Part I
Getting Started

The 5th Wave By Rich Tennant

JONATHAN COURTS DISASTER

"Why of course I'll marry you, Jonathan! We'll have a big wedding and all the guests get to pick where, when, and how it should be held."

In this part . . .

You get a look at the big-picture issues that will shape your wedding, including what has to be done between now and the big day (and by whom), and how much it's going to cost you. We introduce you to some wonderful spreadsheets and forms that help you keep all of these details in order and on track.

Chapter 1

Big Picture Stuff

*1*f you've read *Weddings For Dummies* (and for your own sake, we hope you've committed it to memory), you know that we're not huge fans of those Stalinist manuals that dictate when you must perform every last detail, down to synchronizing your watches 72 hours before the ceremony. But we do believe in being organized. After all, a wedding is a complex affair to orchestrate, and keeping track of all the details, phone calls, expenses, and decisions is a job and a half.

Before you can get down to all those details, you need to understand the big picture. That's what this chapter is all about. From choosing a date to creating a nothing-left-to-chance wedding-day schedule, we help you understand what needs to be done and give you the tools to get your wedding off to a great start.

Doing the Dates

Now that you've decided to go for it, you probably feel like there are several things you should be doing at once — making a preliminary guest list (see the sidebar "Guesstimating the guest list" in this chapter), calling all your friends, surfing online for a reception site, gazing stupefied into each other's eyes — but for now, please flip open your Palm Pilots, Filofaxes, or wall calendars, and start thinking about when you're really going to tie the knot. If you're stumped about how to zero in on a date, we suggest you review Chapter 1 in *Weddings For Dummies*. Even if you have your hearts set on a particular date, choose some back-ups to be safe.

We recommend that you go through the Every-Last-Thing Checklist (later in this chapter) with your betrothed and divvy up the duties. Look at your calendar, estimate, and write in reasonable due dates for each task; then hang the calendar on the wall in a place of honor. Take those target dates and enter them in the columns in Form 1-1. This gives each of you a one-glance cross-reference when you need ammunition for who didn't do what.

Any kind of calendar will do, but we think a year-at-a-glance format is most helpful. Form 1-1 shows a simple big-picture view, which you also find on the CD-ROM.

A Year-at-a-Glance Wedding Planner

Date	Jan.	Feb.	March	April	May	June	July	Aug.	Sept.	Oct.	Nov.	Dec.
1												
2												
3												
4												
5												
6												
7												
8												
9												
10												
11												
12												
13												
14												
15												
16												
17												
18												
19												
20												
21												
22												
23												
24												
25												
26												
27												
28												
29												
30		▓										
31		▓		▓		▓			▓		▓	

Form 1-1:
Track target dates for planning tasks.

Guesstimating the guest list

Before you get too far along in your planning, sit down with your fiance and jot down the names of everyone you think you might want to invite. Keep in mind that both sets of parents will inevitably insist on inviting some dear old family friends or relatives who never crossed your mind. Your initial list will increase or decrease depending on your budget and other variables, but it should be in the ballpark. It's essential to have some idea of the number — however rough — of people who will attend your nuptials so that you can zero in on a venue and, of course, estimate your total budget. For help in keeping track of this vital list of names, see Part II of this book, specifically Chapter 3.

Remember that the mysterious folks who calculate wedding statistics say that you can expect 10 to 20 percent of those invited not to attend. That's the national average and it could be irrelevant to your situation, so don't bank on this to plan the size of your venue or to determine your budget bottom line. You might be the lucky ones blessed with 100 percent attendance.

If you'd like to use an electronic calendar for keeping track of your dates, you can get a marvelous (and free!) one online at AnyDay.com, www.anyday.com. You can synchronize AnyDay.com's calendar with your Palm Pilot. You can also use calendars in Microsoft Outlook, in Lotus Notes, or for Palm Pilots.

You find a plethora of wedding-planning software on the market. These programs generally include calendars, as well as templates for invitation lists, seating charts, registries, and so on. Unfortunately, we've not tested one that's impressed us. For one thing, they seem to be written by people who've never planned a wedding. They assume everybody and every wedding is the same, and we have yet to see the software engineer-wedding expert who can create a program that takes into account all the unique details that actually go into creating such an event.

If, however, you feel more comfortable using a complete program in tandem with *Wedding Kit For Dummies*, one of the better ones is My Wedding Organizer ($49.95) by Reliable Source, Inc. We include a link on the CD to their Web site (www.weddingsoft.com) for a free trial version.

We've kept our templates simple, flexible, and user-friendly. On the CD-ROM you find planning worksheets created in Word, and budget and guest-list templates in Excel. We feel these are the easiest programs for you to customize and easily keep track of things.

Black-out dates

No matter which calendar system you use, make sure that all holidays and other special days are clearly marked. Some holiday or three-day weekends might seem like a perfect opportunity to have a wedding. Other times can be off limits depending on your religion or nationality.

For example, conservative and Orthodox Jews avoid getting married during the 49 days — except on the 33rd day — between Passover and Shabbat. In any case, here are some dates to take into consideration when choosing a date.

New Year's Day

Martin Luther King Jr. Day

Presidents' Day

St. Patrick's Day

Palm Sunday

Passover

Good Friday

Easter

Mother's Day

Memorial Day

Father's Day

U.S. Independence Day

Labor Day

Rosh Hashanah

Yom Kippur

Columbus Day

Veteran's Day

Thanksgiving

Christmas Eve and Day

The Every-Last-Thing Checklist

Form 1-2 (also on the CD-ROM) is the mother of all to-do lists. It contains everything that could possibly be involved in a marriage ceremony and a wedding reception. Don't get intimidated by the mass of marital minutiae — many items won't pertain to your wedding at all but we've included them just in case.

We present all these tasks in a loosely logical order and assume that you're smart enough to pick and choose as necessary. With this full-gamut checklist, it's easy to customize your planning process based on your own reality, deadlines, and desires. However, because the good venues, caterers, and bands usually get booked well in advance, we recommend that you attend to those issues early in your planning.

In Form 1-2, we refer you to the appropriate chapter in this book — as well as in *Weddings For Dummies* — for more information. We indicate appropriate chapters in *Weddings For Dummies* with the initials "*WFD*."

The Every-Last-Thing Checklist

Done	Task	See Chapter	Who's Responsible	Deadline or Target Date
	Announce your engagement.	Kit: 16; WFD: 13, 17		
	Hire a professional wedding consultant.	WFD: 1		
	Send announcement of engagement to local or hometown paper.	Kit: 16 WFD: 13, 17		
	Check with newspapers about wedding announcement requirements, especially due date required.	Kit: 16 WFD: 13, 17		
	Set a date for the wedding.	Kit: 1 WFD: 1		
	Create a budget for the wedding.	Kit: 1, 2 WFD: 1		
	Compile the guest list with addresses and phone numbers.	Kit: 1, 3 WFD: 1		
	Make a list of possible venues and caterers.	Kit: 5, 9,11 WFD: 2, 8		
	Choose reception venue and caterer.	Kit: 5, 9,11 WFD: 2, 8		
	Choose ceremony site.	Kit: 5, 6 WFD: 2, 5, 6		
	Order invitations and other stationery.	Kit: 3, 4 WFD: 13		
	Arrange accommodations for out-of-town guests.	Kit: 4, 5; WFD: 6, 13, 17		
	Send save-the-date cards and an informational letter for out-of-town guests.	Kit: 4, 5 WFD: 6, 13, 17		
	Register for gifts.	Kit: 13 WFD: 14		

Form 1-2:
Nail down
all your
tasks in a
master
checklist.
(Page 1 of 7)

Done	Task	See Chapter	Who's Responsible	Deadline or Target Date
	Locate and renew vital documents you need for marriage license or honeymoon, such as passport, driver's license, visas, and birth certificate.	Kit: 16 WFD: 16		
	Select attendants, including maid or matron of honor, best man, bridesmaids, ushers, flower girl, and ring bearer.	Kit: 1, 14 WFD: 4		
	Delegate duties to consultant, attendants, friends, and family members.	Kit: 1, 14 WFD: 1, 4		
	Reserve accommodations for wedding night.	Kit: 8, 17 WFD: 18, 19		
	Shop for a wedding dress.	Kit: 14 WFD: 3		
	Order wedding gown, headpiece, shoes, undergarments, and accessories.	Kit: 14 WFD: 3		
	Tackle any major self-maintenance goals, such as having your teeth fixed, getting in shape, or changing hair color.	Kit: 14 WFD: 3		
	Hire a calligrapher or address invitations.	Kit: 3, 4 WFD: 13		
	Stuff and stamp invitations.	Kit: 4 WFD: 13		
	Mail invitations. (For destination weddings or international guests, a three-month lead time is advised.)	Kit: 4 WFD: 13		
	Plan and book honeymoon.	Kit: 5, 17 WFD: 19		
	Visit photographers and check out their work.	Kit: 15 WFD: 12		
	Hire a photographer.	Kit: 15 WFD: 12		

Form 1-2:
Nail down all your tasks in a master checklist. (Page 2 of 7)

Done	Task	See Chapter	Who's Responsible	Deadline or Target Date
	Review reels by videographers and interview.	Kit: 15 WFD: 12		
	Hire a videographer.	Kit: 15 WFD: 12		
	Have photos taken for newspaper wedding announcement.	Kit: 15, 16 WFD: 12, 13, 17		
	Submit wedding announcement and photo to newspapers.	Kit: 15, 16 WFD: 12, 13, 17		
	Interview and hire florist.	Kit: 12 WFD: 11		
	Meet with other vendors, such as tent rental, lighting specialists, transportation, and portable restrooms. Hire those vendors.	Kit: 5, 9 WFD: 2, 11		
	Choose and reserve rentals.	Kit: 9, 11, 12 WFD: 9, 11		
	Update your spreadsheet and make sure you haven't blown your budget.	Kit: 2 WFD: 1, 20		
	Meet with officiant. (Hire if applicable.)	Kit: 5, 6 WFD: 5		
	Interview ceremony musicians or meet with music director from ceremony site. Choose musical selections.	Kit: 7 WFD: 5, 7		
	Choreograph ceremony. Choose readings and vows. Write script for officiant.	Kit: 6, 7, 8 WFD: 5, 18		
	Interview and hire band or DJ.	Kit: 10 WFD: 7		
	Schedule menu tasting. Select food and wines.	Kit: 11 WFD: 8, 9, 10		
	Choose wedding cake.	Kit: 11 WFD: 9		
	Consult with rehearsal dinner host.	Kit: 4, 5 WFD: 17		

Form 1-2: Nail down all your tasks in a master checklist. (Page 3 of 7)

Done	Task	See Chapter	Who's Responsible	Deadline or Target Date
	Plan bridesmaid luncheon.	Kit: 11 WFD: 17		
	Finalize choices for flowers, linens, and other décor details.	Kit: 11, 12 WFD: 8, 11		
	Make sure all contracts are in order and deposits are paid.	Kit: 5, 7, 9, 10, 11, 12, 15 WFD: 7, 8, 11, 12		
	Select attendants' garb.	Kit: 14 WFD: 4		
	Buy or reserve groom's attire.	Kit: 14 WFD: 4		
	Arrange transportation for you and guests. Arrange transportation to airport for honeymoon.	Kit: 5, 8, 17 WFD: 18, 19		
	Buy wedding rings.	Kit: 14 WFD: 15		
	Choose party favors.	Kit: 4 WFD: 17		
	Interview hair stylists and makeup artists.	Kit: 14 WFD: 3		
	Test-drive your hair and makeup for the big day.	Kit: 14 WFD: 3		
	Buy lingerie and other honeymoon attire.	Kit: 14, 17 WFD: 3, 19		
	Have final fitting for wedding gown.	Kit: 14 WFD: 3		
	Make arrangements for getting wedding gown delivered to where you're getting dressed and then to cleaners afterward.	Kit: 14 WFD: 3		
	Attend to details such as ring pillows, guest books, and toasting chalices. Designate someone to bring these things to the ceremony and retrieve them afterward.	Kit: 1, 4, 6, 8 WFD: 4, 5		
	Change name on credit cards, Social Security cards, bank accounts, and so on.	Kit: 16 WFD: 16		

Form 1-2:
Nail down all your tasks in a master checklist.
(Page 4 of 7)

Done	Task	See Chapter	Who's Responsible	Deadline or Target Date
	Get blood test and health certificate, if necessary.	Kit: 16 WFD: 16		
	Plan extra psychotherapy sessions.	A given in all chapters, both books		
	Get marriage license.	Kit: 16 WFD: 16		
	Get massages.	A given in all chapters, both books		
	Write thank you notes.	Kit: 13 WFD: 14		
	Buy gifts for each other.	Kit: 13 WFD: 14		
	Buy gifts for attendants and other deserving people involved in your wedding.	Kit: 13 WFD: 14		
	Create a shot list for the photographer and videographer.	Kit: 15 WFD: 12		
	Give play list of songs to band or DJ. Include first dance song and the songs you absolutely don't want to hear.	Kit: 10 WFD: 7		
	Practice first dance, taking dance lessons if necessary.	Kit: 8, 10 WFD: 7, 18		
	Have a facial (give yourself a week to recover).	Kit: 14 WFD: 3		
	Create and print wedding program.	Kit: 4, 5, 5 WFD: 5, 23		
	Assemble welcome baskets for out-of-town guests and arrange for delivery to their hotels the day before.	Kit: 3, 5, 19 WFD: 17		
	Write detailed wedding-day schedule.	Kit: 8 WFD: 18		
	Fax day-of details and wedding day schedule to all vendors. Call to reconfirm specifics.	Kit: 8, 9, 10, 11, 12 WFD: 7, 8, 9, 10, 11, 12, 18		

Form 1-2:
Nail down all your tasks in a master checklist.
(Page 5 of 7)

Done	Task	See Chapter	Who's Responsible	Deadline or Target Date
	Pick up tickets, travelers checks, and last minute necessities.	Kit: 17 WFD: 19		
	Reconfirm all reservations, from rentals to honeymoon.	Kit: 17 WFD: 19		
	Update spreadsheet — still on target moneywise?	Kit: 2 WFD: 1, 20		
	Arrange for mail and newspapers to be held while you're away and for plant watering, cat feeding, etc.	Kit: 17 WFD: 4, 19		
	Pack bridal emergency kit.	Kit: 14 WFD: 3		
	Double check arrangements for your wedding attire clothing to be picked up and cleaned. Arrange for rentals, leftover liquor, if applicable, gifts, and other paraphernalia to be picked up after the wedding (assuming you are leaving directly for your honeymoon).	Kit: 11, 14 WFD: 3, 4, 8, 10		
	Cut hair.	Kit: 14 WFD: 3, 4		
	Treat yourself to a manicure and pedicure.	Kit: 14 WFD: 3, 4		
	Write any toasts you plan to give.	Kit: 16 WFD: 17		
	Determine seating chart.	Kit: 3 WFD: 11		
	Address escort and place cards.	Kit: 3, 4 WFD: 11		
	Stuff, stamp, and address announcements.	Kit: 3, 4 WFD: 13		
	Host bridesmaids' luncheon.	Kit: 11 WFD: 17		
	Rehearse ceremony.	Kit: 5, 6, 8 WFD: 5, 18		
	Attend rehearsal dinner.	Kit: 5, 9 WFD: 17		

Form 1-2:
Nail down all your tasks in a master checklist. (Page 6 of 7)

Done	Task	See Chapter	Who's Responsible	Deadline or Target Date
	Make sure best man and maid of honor have the rings.	Kit: 8 WFD: 4, 18		
	Write all final checks and set aside cash for gratuities.	Kit: 2 WFD: 18		
	Give gratuities and officiant fee to best man or wedding consultant.	Kit: 2 WFD: 18		
	Get married.	Kit: 6 WFD: 5		
	Mail wedding announcements or have someone do it for you.	Kit: 4, 8; WFD: 4, 13		
	Chill out.	You can toss out these books now!		

Form 1-2: Nail down all your tasks in a master checklist. (Page 7 of 7)

The When, What, Where Cheat Sheet

Even if you have a memory like Proust or trust your Palm Pilot to never conk out, you (and several people near and dear to you) will be grateful for a quick-and-dirty crib sheet of key dates, locations, names, and numbers for your wedding. Form 1-3 gives you a handy place to jot all this information down. (You also find Form 1-3 on nice heavyweight paper at the front of this book. If you need to make extra copies or update this form — and we're sure you will — you find blank templates on the CD-ROM.)

Everyone's 411 at a Glance

As you plan your wedding, you'll make a lot of phone calls and send a lot of e-mails. It helps to have everyone's contact information pulled together in one place.

As you assemble your team, use Form 1-4 to record pertinent phone numbers and information. (You also find a copy of Form 1-4 on the cheat sheet of this book and on the CD-ROM.) Wrangle home and cell phone numbers when you can.

Form 1-4 also comes in handy whenever one of the vendors, mothers, or members of the wedding party needs to put out an all-points bulletin to the players — just print them out a copy from your computer.

When, What, and Where for the Wedding of
_____ & _____

Engagement Party

Date:_____ Time:_____

Host:_____

Place:_____

Address:_____

Phone:_____

Bridal Shower

Date:_____ Time:_____

Host:_____

Place:_____

Address:_____

Phone:_____

Bachelor Party

Date:_____ Time:_____

Place:_____

Address:_____

Phone:_____

Ceremony Rehearsal

Date:_____ Time:_____

Place:_____

Address:_____

Phone:_____

Other Pre-Nuptial Event _____

Date:_____ Time:_____

Place:_____

Address:_____

Phone:_____

Form 1-3:
Record
information
for all the
events
surrounding
your
wedding as
well as for
the big day
itself. (Page
1 of 2)

Rehearsal Dinner

Date:_____ Time:_____

Place:_____

Address:_____

Phone:_____

Ceremony

Date:_____ Time:_____

Place:_____

Address:_____

Phone:_____

Reception

Date:_____ Time:_____

Place:_____

Address:_____

Phone:_____

Post-Wedding Get-Together _____

Date:_____ Time:_____

Place:_____

Address:_____

Phone:_____

Honeymoon

Date:_____ Time:_____

Place:_____

Address:_____

Phone:_____ E-mail:_____

Flight info:_____

Car:_____ Other:_____

Form 1-3:
Record
information
for all the
events
surrounding
your
wedding as
well as for
the big day
itself. (Page
2 of 2)

Everyone's 411 at a Glance

Key Player	Name and Company	Contact Info	
Bride		Phone:	Cell:
		Beeper:	E-mail:
Groom		Phone:	Cell:
		Beeper:	E-mail:
Bride's Parents		Phone:	Cell:
		Beeper:	E-mail:
Groom's Parents		Phone:	Cell:
		Beeper:	E-mail:
Wedding Consultant		Phone:	Cell:
		Beeper:	E-mail:
Maid of Honor		Phone:	Cell:
		Beeper:	E-mail:
Best Man		Phone:	Cell:
		Beeper:	E-mail:
Officiant		Phone:	Cell:
		Beeper:	E-mail:
Ceremony Site		Phone:	Cell:
		Beeper:	E-mail:
Reception Site		Phone:	Cell:
		Beeper:	E-mail:
Caterer or Banquet Manager		Phone:	Cell:
		Beeper:	E-mail:
Liquor Services		Phone:	Cell:
		Beeper:	E-mail:

Form 1-4:
Enter contact info for all key players on your nuptial team for quick and easy reference. (Page 1 of 3)

Key Player	Name and Company	Contact Info	
Cake Maker		Phone:	Cell:
		Beeper:	E-mail:
Ceremony Musicians		Phone:	Cell:
		Beeper:	E-mail:
Reception Musicians		Phone:	Cell:
		Beeper:	E-mail:
Photographer		Phone:	Cell:
		Beeper:	E-mail:
Videographer		Phone:	Cell:
		Beeper:	E-mail:
Florist		Phone:	Cell:
		Beeper:	E-mail:
Decorations (balloons and so on)		Phone:	Cell:
		Beeper:	E-mail:
Lighting		Phone:	Cell:
		Beeper:	E-mail:
Rental Company		Phone:	Cell:
		Beeper:	E-mail:
Portable Toilets		Phone:	Cell:
		Beeper:	E-mail:
Transport		Phone:	Cell:
		Beeper:	E-mail:
Parking Service		Phone:	Cell:
		Beeper:	E-mail:
Jeweler		Phone:	Cell:
		Beeper:	E-mail:

Form 1-4: Enter contact info for all key players on your nuptial team for quick and easy reference. (Page 2 of 3)

Key Player	Name and Company	Contact Info	
Gown		Phone:	Cell:
		Beeper:	E-mail:
Tuxedo		Phone:	Cell:
		Beeper:	E-mail:
Attendants' Attire		Phone:	Cell:
		Beeper:	E-mail:
Travel Agent		Phone:	Cell:
		Beeper:	E-mail:
Stationer		Phone:	Cell:
		Beeper:	E-mail:
Calligrapher		Phone:	Cell:
		Beeper:	E-mail:
Other		Phone:	Cell:
		Beeper:	E-mail:

Form 1-4:
Enter contact info for all key players on your nuptial team for quick and easy reference. (Page 3 of 3)

Forms and Links on the CD-ROM

You'll find the following forms and links on the CD, as presented in this chapter:

Form 1-1	A Year-at-a-Glance Wedding Planner	Track target dates for planning tasks
Form 1-2	The Every-Last-Thing Checklist	Nail down all your tasks in a master checklist
Form 1-3	The When, What, Where Cheat Sheet	Record information for all the events surrounding your wedding as well as for the big day itself
Form 1-4	Everyone's 411 at a Glance	Enter contact info for all key players on your nuptial team for quick and easy reference
Link	My Wedding Organizer	www.weddingsoft.com

Chapter 2

Love Is a Money-Spender Thing

In This Chapter

▶ Tracking the burn rate with a spreadsheet

▶ Plugging in prices and shaving expenses

▶ Totaling the tips without tipping the total

As you start to think about what all this is going to cost, you may imagine calculator tape curling up on the floor and the number googol (1 with a hundred zeroes after it). Don't panic — budget! Monitoring a budget that tracks all the expenses associated with your wedding is the best way to keep on top of things and prevent costs from spiraling out of control. And it's not hard.

When politicians create budgets, it's often a battleground. Hopefully, your efforts won't include the posturing and rhetoric of a political standoff. When the dust settles, the money should be allocated toward the things that matter most to you.

With this Credit Card, Lottery Jackpot, or Parental Loan, I Thee Wed

Unfortunately, we can't give you a cut-and-dried formula that tells you how much to spend on any aspect of your wedding. Some experts have tried to provide such guidelines — pie chart generalizations that turn out to be utterly useless in the real world. Who's to say what percent of your budget needs to go to food, wine, or your gown?

On some Web sites, you can type in a total dollar figure and the number of guests and — presto change-o! — you have a budget telling how to spend your wedding dollars. Such exercises provide a rough sense at best, but the fact is that no two weddings are alike. Your job is to get the wedding you want for the price you can afford. If you dream of getting married on a deserted island off the coast of Maine and need to rent a boat to get your guests to the ceremony, you might have to cut back in other areas, such as the quality of the wine, to come in on budget. No cookie-cutter budget formula can accommodate the special touches that make your wedding unique.

If others are chipping in for your wedding, try to get your "donations" in a chunk rather than in dribs and drabs for every purchase and deposit that crops up.

Start Spreadsheeting the News

For tracking your wedding expenses and keeping to the bottom line, nothing beats a simple spreadsheet. To the uninitiated, spreadsheets may look intimidating with all those numbers, but they're really a breeze to use. And once you figure out how they work, you'll have an easy way to see, at a glance, what this shindig is actually costing.

We've created a wedding expense spreadsheet, Form 2-1, using Microsoft Excel, which is a fairly user-friendly program once you master a few basic moves. We explain the big picture later in this chapter, and for more advanced maneuvers, see Chapter 18. We provide the framework; all you need to do is load your own version of Excel software, plug in the numbers, and go.

You don't have to be a CPA with Deloitte & Touche to work with a spreadsheet. The wedding budget template we include on the book's CD-ROM is just slightly more complicated than playing bingo. By learning a few simple functions, you'll find that massaging the numbers is not only easy, it's addictive.

The first thing to know is that a spreadsheet is a table made up of horizontal rows and vertical columns. Each intersection of a row and column forms a little box known as a *cell*, and each cell is named for the column and row. For example, cell B14 is the fourteenth row down in the B column. (If you ever played the game Battleship as a kid, you know what we mean.)

A spreadsheet is a highly interactive environment that allows you to work with numbers and text in a large grid of cells. A cell can contain a number, text, a formula, or nothing at all. A formula is a way to tell Excel to perform a calculation using information stored in other cells.

Getting to know your spreadsheet, one category at a time

Take a moment to familiarize yourself with Form 2-1 on the following pages. As you can see, the document is divided into 16 sections detailing expenses. Aside from your target budget number, you don't have to enter anything on page 1, the summary page. The subtotals of each section are automatically transferred to the appropriate cell on page 1.

The various sections in Form 2-1 help you track the following expenses:

- ✔ **Summary page:** The first page (Sheet 1) contains the subtotals of the subsequent categories on the following pages (Sheet 2).
- ✔ **Ceremony:** Venue, officiant, music, and religious accessories.
- ✔ **Clothing:** Bride, groom, and attendants, plus makeup and hair.
- ✔ **Reception:** Rentals, drink, food, cake, labor, gratuities, and parking. Note that we have provided expense categories for on-premise receptions — hotels, catering halls — and off-premise locations, where the venue has no in-house capability to provide food and service. You can delete any unneeded expense lines as you go (see Chapter 18 for tips on how to do that).
- ✔ **Tenting:** Tent, ventilation, floor, tent lighting, and rest rooms.
- ✔ **Lighting:** All lighting needs for ceremony and reception.
- ✔ **Stationery:** Invitations, maps, ceremony, place cards, escort cards, calligraphy, postage, programs, and so on.
- ✔ **Flowers:** For reception and ceremony.
- ✔ **Music/Audio:** Band, DJ, ceremony, and equipment.
- ✔ **Photography:** Photography and videography fees and prints.
- ✔ **Gifts:** Attendants, family, friend, and each other.
- ✔ **Transportation:** Bride and groom, parents, guests, and wedding party.
- ✔ **Lodging:** Bride and groom, parents, guests, and wedding party.
- ✔ **Wedding Consultant:** Fee, expenses, and labor.
- ✔ **Rings:** Engagement and wedding.
- ✔ **Miscellaneous:** Whatever else you have.
- ✔ **Contingency:** We recommend you factor in a cushion of 10 percent of your total budget, just in case.

Input nothing in these columns. Numbers are
automatically transferred from Budget Details sheets.

Form 2-1:
Tracking
your budget
on a spread-
sheet —
Sheet 1
summarizes
details from
Sheet 2.
(Page 1
of 10)

SUMMARY BUDGET Your name and wedding date						
Last updated	**3-Jun-00**					
	Estimated Cost	**Actual Cost**	**Deposit Paid**	**Paid to Date**	**Balance Due**	**Total Paid**
Ceremony	$0	$0	$0	$0	$0	$0
Clothing	$0	$0	$0	$0	$0	$0
Reception	$0	$0	$0	$0	$0	$0
Tenting	$0	$0	$0	$0	$0	$0
Lighting	$0	$0	$0	$0	$0	$0
Stationery	$0	$0	$0	$0	$0	$0
Flowers	$0	$0	$0	$0	$0	$0
Music/Audio	$0	$0	$0	$0	$0	$0
Photography	$0	$0	$0	$0	$0	$0
Gifts	$0	$0	$0	$0	$0	$0
Transportation	$0	$0	$0	$0	$0	$0
Lodging	$0	$0	$0	$0	$0	$0
Wedding Consultant	$0	$0	$0	$0	$0	$0
Rings	$0	$0	$0	$0	$0	$0
Miscellaneous	$0	$0	$0	$0	$0	$0
Contingency @10%	$0					
Total	*$0*	*$0*	*$0*	*$0*	*$0*	*$0*
Target budget	$0	$0				
Current expenses	$0	$0				
Balance (over)/under	$0	$0				

Current expenses are
automatically transferred
from the estimated and
actual costs in the
budget detail.

The balance is calculated by subtracting
current expenses from your target. If the
number is in parenthesis, you're over budget.

In this cell, enter the target budget —
what you'd like your wedding to cost.

This cell calculates what you owe by subtracting payments from actual costs.

Input estimated and actual numbers in these columns.

Use these columns to track payments made to vendors.

Form 2-1:
Tracking your budget on a spreadsheet — page 1 of Sheet 2 covers the ceremony. (Page 2 of 10)

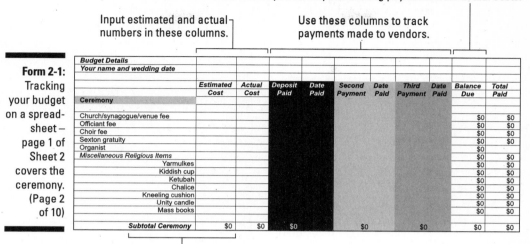

Budget Details Your name and wedding date	Estimated Cost	Actual Cost	Deposit Paid	Date Paid	Second Payment	Date Paid	Third Payment	Date Paid	Balance Due	Total Paid
Ceremony										
Church/synagogue/venue fee									$0	$0
Officiant fee									$0	$0
Choir fee									$0	$0
Sexton gratuity									$0	$0
Organist									$0	
Miscellaneous Religious Items										
Yarmulkes									$0	$0
Kiddish cup									$0	$0
Ketubah									$0	$0
Chalice									$0	$0
Kneeling cushion									$0	$0
Unity candle									$0	$0
Mass books									$0	$0
Subtotal Ceremony	$0	$0	$0		$0		$0		$0	$0

This cell automatically totals the activities in the rows above.

Form 2-1:
Tracking your budget on a spreadsheet — page 2 of Sheet 2 covers wedding attire. (Page 3 of 10)

Budget Details Your name and wedding date	Estimated Cost	Actual Cost	Deposit Paid	Date Paid	Second Payment	Date Paid	Third Payment	Date Paid	Balance Due	Total Paid
Clothing										
Bride's ensemble										
Dress or suit									$0	$0
Alterations									$0	$0
Gloves									$0	$0
Headpiece and veil									$0	$0
Jewelry									$0	$0
Shoes									$0	$0
Undergarments									$0	$0
Groom's garb									$0	
Cufflinks/studs									$0	$0
Cummerbund/braces									$0	$0
Waistcoat									$0	$0
Manicure									$0	$0
Shoes									$0	$0
Tuxedo/suit									$0	$0
Tie									$0	$0
Attendants' Attire										$0
Dresses									$0	$0
Undergarments									$0	$0
Hats									$0	$0
Flower girl's ensemble									$0	$0
Gloves									$0	$0
Ring bearer's garb									$0	$0
Shoes									$0	$0
Tuxedoes/suits									$0	$0
Waistcoats									$0	$0
Wedding Day Prep										
Hair stylist									$0	$0
Makeup artist									$0	$0
Manicure									$0	$0
Gratuity									$0	
Subtotal Clothing	$0	$0	$0		$0		$0		$0	$0

Skip off-premises details if you're having an on-premises event.

Calculate food costs by multiplying the cost per head times the number attending.

Budget Details
Your name and wedding date

		Estimated Cost	Actual Cost	Deposit Paid	Date Paid	Second Payment	Date Paid	Third Payment	Date Paid	Balance Due	Total Paid
Reception											
Off Premise											
Site rental fee										$0	
Rentals										$0	
Food										$0	
Additional meals										$0	
Beverage										$0	
	Bar set up									$0	
	Liquor costs									$0	
	Wine									$0	
	Champagne									$0	
	Beer									$0	
Cake										$0	
	Cake									$0	
	Groom's cake									$0	
	Cutting fee									$0	
Labor (excluding gratuities)										$0	
	Servers									$0	
	Bartenders									$0	
	Parking attendants/service									$0	
	Restroom attendants									$0	
	Coat check									$0	
Gratuities (optional)										$0	
Tax										$0	
On Premise										$0	
Misc. Rentals										$0	
	Chairs									$0	
	Risers									$0	
	Dance floor									$0	
	Linens									$0	$0
Beverage										$0	$0
	Bar set up fees									$0	$0
	Liquor costs									$0	$0
	wine									$0	$0
	Champagne									$0	$0

Skip on-premise details if you're having an off-premise wedding.

Form 2-1:
Tracking your budget on a spreadsheet — pages 3 and 4 of Sheet 2 covers the reception. (Page 4 of 10)

		Estimated Cost	Actual Cost	Deposit Paid	Second Payment	Third Payment	Balance Due	Total Paid
	Mixers/soft drinks						$0	$0
							$0	$0
Food							$0	$0
	Food						$0	$0
	Additional meals vendors						$0	$0
Cake							$0	$0
	Cake						$0	$0
	Groom's cake						$0	$0
	Cutting fee						$0	$0
							$0	$0
Labor (excluding gratuities)							$0	$0
	Carvers							
	Bartenders							
Valet Parking							$0	$0
Gratuities (optional)							$0	$0
Tax								
	Subtotal Reception	$0	$0	$0	$0	$0	$0	$0

Tax alert! Remember to add applicable sales tax.

Form 2-1: Tracking your budget on a spreadsheet — page 5 of Sheet 2 covers details for tenting, lighting, and stationery. (Page 5 of 10)

Budget Details / Your name and wedding date	Estimated Cost	Actual Cost	Deposit Paid	Date Paid	Second Payment	Date Paid	Third Payment	Date Paid	Balance Due	Total Paid
Tenting										
Tent									$0	$0
Tent air conditioning/heat									$0	$0
Tent floor									$0	$0
Tent lighting									$0	$0
Portable rest rooms									$0	$0
Generator										
Tax										
Subtotal Tenting	$0	$0	$0		$0		$0		$0	$0
Lighting										
Lighting Company									$0	$0
Tax										
Subtotal Lighting	$0	$0	$0		$0		$0		$0	$0
Stationery										
Invitations & envelopes									$0	$0
Reception/ceremony cards									$0	$0
Reply cards & envelopes									$0	$0
Thank you notes									$0	$0
Menus										
Save-the-date cards										
Place cards									$0	$0
Escort cards									$0	$0
At-home cards									$0	$0
Maps									$0	$0
Calligraphy									$0	$0
Announcements									$0	$0
Programs									$0	$0
Postage									$0	$0
Tax										
Subtotal Stationery	$0	$0	$0		$0		$0		$0	$0

Form 2-1:
Tracking your budget on a spreadsheet — page 6 of Sheet 2 covers flowers for the ceremony and reception. (Page 6 of 10)

Budget Details Your name and wedding date	Estimated Cost	Actual Cost	Deposit Paid	Date Paid	Second Payment	Date Paid	Third Payment	Date Paid	Balance Due	Total Paid
Flowers										
Ceremony Flowers										
Altar flowers									$0	$0
Bride's bouquet									$0	$0
Attendants' bouquets									$0	$0
Tossing bouquet									$0	$0
Corsages									$0	$0
Boutonniers									$0	$0
Flower girl basket									$0	$0
Ring pillow flower									$0	$0
Hair flowers									$0	$0
Pew bows or flowers									$0	$0
Chuppah									$0	$0
Ring pillow									$0	$0
Aisle Runner									$0	$0
Reception										
Centerpieces									$0	$0
Room pieces									$0	$0
Escort tables									$0	$0
Cake flowers									$0	$0
Hors d'oeuvre trays									$0	$0
Additional décor									$0	$0
Bathroom baskets									$0	$0
Linens										
Set-up and break down costs									$0	$0
Tax										
Subtotal Flowers	$0	$0	$0		$0		$0		$0	$0

Form 2-1:
Tracking your budget on a spreadsheet — page 7 of Sheet 2 is for music and photography. (Page 7 of 10)

Budget Details Your name and wedding date	Estimated Cost	Actual Cost	Deposit Paid	Date Paid	Second Payment	Date Paid	Third Payment	Date Paid	Balance Due	Total Paid
Music/Audio										
Ceremony musicians									$0	$0
Cartage fees									$0	$0
Cocktail music									$0	$0
Band(s) reception									$0	$0
Costuming (tails or dinner jacket)									$0	$0
Disc jockey									$0	$0
Wireless microphone (for toasts)									$0	$0
Piano rental									$0	$0
Sound system									$0	$0
Gratuity (optional)										
Overtime									$0	$0
Tax										
Subtotal Music	$0	$0	$0		$0		$0		$0	$0
Photography									$0	$0
Photographer's fee									$0	$0
Pre-wedding portraits									$0	$0
Estimated additional albums										
Videography									$0	$0
Video copies									$0	$0
Tax										
Subtotal Photography	$0	$0	$0		$0		$0		$0	$0

Form 2-1:
Tracking your budget on a spread-sheet — page 8 of Sheet 2 covers gifts for attendants, transportation, and lodging. (Page 8 of 10)

Budget Details Your name and wedding date	Estimated Cost	Actual Cost	Deposit Paid	Date Paid	Second Payment	Date Paid	Third Payment	Date Paid	Balance Due	Total Paid
Gifts										
Bridesmaids' gifts									$0	$0
Ushers gifts									$0	$0
Bride and groom (to each other)									$0	$0
Parents									$0	$0
Party favors									$0	$0
Welcome baskets									$0	$0
Tax									$0	$0
Subtotal Gifts	$0	$0	$0		$0		$0		$0	$0
Transportation									$0	$0
									$0	$0
Bride and groom									$0	$0
Parents									$0	$0
Guests									$0	$0
Wedding party									$0	$0
Gratuity (optional)										
Tax										
Subtotal Transportation	$0	$0	$0		$0		$0		$0	$0
Lodging									$0	$0
Bride and groom									$0	$0
Parents									$0	$0
Guests									$0	$0
Wedding party									$0	$0
Tax										
Subtotal Lodging	$0	$0	$0		$0		$0		$0	$0

Form 2-1:
Tracking your budget on a spread-sheet — page 9 of Sheet 2 covers the wedding consultant and rings. (Page 9 of 10)

Budget Details Your name and wedding date	Estimated Cost	Actual Cost	Deposit Paid	Date Paid	Second Payment	Date Paid	Third Payment	Date Paid	Balance Due	Total Paid
Wedding Consultant										
Fee									$0	$0
Expenses (include travel)									$0	$0
Additional labor									$0	$0
Tax										
Subtotal Wedding Consultant	$0	$0	$0		$0		$0		$0	$0
Rings										
Engagement									$0	$0
Wedding									$0	$0
Tax										
Subtotal Rings	$0	$0	$0		$0		$0		$0	$0

The contingency is automatically calculated at
10% of the entire estimated cost of your wedding.

Form 2-1:
Tracking
your budget
on a spread-
sheet —
page 10 of
Sheet 2
covers the
miscellane-
ous items
and
contingency
costs. (Page
10 of 10)

Budget Details Your name and wedding date	Estimated Cost	Actual Cost	Deposit Paid	Date Paid	Second Payment	Date Paid	Third Payment	Date Paid	Balance Due	Total Paid
Miscellaneous									$0	$0
Babysitter									$0	$0
Guest book									$0	$0
Marriage license fees									$0	$0
Subtotal Miscellaneous	$0	$0	$0		$0		$0		$0	$0
Contingency @10%	0								$0	$0
TOTAL ALL EXPENSES	$0	$0	$0		$0		$0		$0	$0
Target budget	$0	$0								
Current expenses	$0	$0								
Balance (under)/over	$0	$0								

The bottom line — the total cost of your wedding appears on this row.

Running down the left-hand side of Form 2-1, you see a long list of things (line items) you might have to purchase or rent for your wedding. While we have included just about every possible item that might go into producing a wedding, not everything will pertain to every couple. Plug in numbers only for the line items that relate to your wedding and ignore the others. (If you want to delete an item, see Chapter 18 for tips on working in Excel.)

Using the columns from left to right across the top of the page — Estimated Cost, Actual Cost, Deposit Paid, Balance Due, Total Paid, and so on — you can track what each item costs, payments made to date, and how much you owe on the balance. (The spreadsheet automatically calculates the balance due by subtracting payments from actual costs.) This format allows you not only to project the total cost of your wedding but also to keep a running tally of how much you have paid to date.

There are formulas embedded in some cells that automatically calculate subtotals and totals. Every time you change the data in a cell, all corresponding numbers change throughout the entire budget. For example, suppose you estimated that the band's fee was going to be $1,200 but it's actually $975. When you enter $975 in the Actual Cost cell, the subtotal for the Music/Audio category decreases as does the Total Cost of your wedding.

Plugging in the numbers

Our spreadsheet is not cast in stone, and you can modify Form 2-1 as much as you need to. Making changes isn't complicated, and we encourage you to tailor the spreadsheet to your wedding. We tell you how to do that in the following steps, and we show you how to start using your spreadsheet to track your expenses:

1. **Personalize it.**

   Enter your name and wedding date under the line that says Summary. To do this, move the cursor (which looks like a fat plus sign) to that cell (the intersection of a row and column) and click. Then type in your name ("Billy Badger and Ella Fant's Wedding 9/23/2001"). Your name will automatically appear on the top of each page.

2. **Type in the date.**

   Directly below and to the right of your name is a cell for keeping track of when you last updated the spreadsheet. Type in today's date. It's a good idea to change this every time you work on the spreadsheet. If you press Ctrl and the semicolon keys while the cursor is in the date cell, the current date appears automatically.

3. **Enter the target budget.**

   This is the all-important number that will keep you on track. It's what you'd like the total cost of your wedding to be — not a moving target, but a goal.

   Go to the bottom of page 1, which summarizes details from the rest of the spreadsheet, and type in an amount for your target budget. Using this figure, the spreadsheet will automatically calculate how much you're over or under (fat chance) the amount you've decided to spend on your wedding.

4. **Go to Sheet 2.**

   Now you're ready to hit the budget running! At the bottom of the screen, you see a tab for Sheet 2. Click on it and you'll open the first of several pages containing the detailed expenses for each category.

   Note the set up of Sheet 2. The sheet comprises ten columns that allow you to keep track of various activities, including estimates of costs, actual costs, deposits and payments that you make (and the date you make them), the balances you owe, and the total you have paid.

5. **Estimate your costs.**

   Start plugging in some guesses of what things will cost. Strict accuracy doesn't matter at this point — you're trying to get a rough idea of what categories apply to your wedding and thus how much you think you may be spending in each category.

As you enter numbers in the Estimated Cost column, subtotals in those categories appear at the bottom of each section and automatically on the summary page. (Once you get spreadsheet savvy, you can delete any rows or columns you don't need — see Chapter 18.) Keep refining your estimates as you gather new information.

6. Update your estimated costs with actual costs.

At some point, your estimates become actual figures. Suppose that after you select your venue and have a preliminary discussion with the banquet manager, you estimate that the food would cost around $40 per person (which is the amount you put into the estimated column). By the time you finished your menu tasting, that cost had gone up to $44 because you selected a wider assortment of passed hors d'oeuvres. Now you enter that new figure in the actual cost column. In this case it would be the number of people (125) multiplied by the cost per head (125 x $44), which means you'd put $5500 in the Actual Cost column for Food in the Reception section of the spreadsheet.

7. Record payments.

Where you stand with your vendors — what you've paid and what you owe — is an important part of managing your wedding. The spreadsheet allows you to see at a glance the record of deposits and subsequent payments along with dates those payments were made. In cases when you pay in full in one payment, enter the amount in either the Deposit Paid or Second Payment column. This amount will update the Total Paid column and the balance due will be $0.

In cases where you make more than two payments after a deposit (a rare occurrence), combine payments in one of the columns. Total the payments and enter that number in one of the columns, or see Chapter 18 for tips on creating formulas in Excel.

The spreadsheet on the CD-ROM is a template. Once you open it and work on it, use the "save as" function under the *File* menu to name and save the document on your hard drive or floppy disk. The version you save onto your hard drive or disk should be the actual file you work on. And don't forget to back up your work on a regular basis.

Buffer zone

The spreadsheet automatically adds a 10 percent contingency fee to all your estimates. This expense appears on the contingency line near the bottom of the spreadsheet. Why? Because you need a little cushion to help you absorb the inevitable overages and emergencies that occur — like when your brother from Alaska forgot to bring his special smoked salmon and now it has to be shipped overnight. A contingency allows you to overcome those costs without going back to the well.

Keep your budget as up to date as possible. Making changes every time you get new information saves you from a depressing "face the music" session the week before your nuptials. Tracking your expenses also gives you the powerful sense of having something under control at a time when everything else seems hopelessly at sixes and sevens.

Include sales tax in all your budgeting, where appropriate. Many vendors give bids that just say "plus sales tax." Or they might say "plus plus," meaning plus tax and gratuity. Take a moment to calculate the amount and add it to your costs.

Take a Tip: Calculating Gratuities

You will want to reward the people who make your wedding day run smoothly. When it comes to weddings, the rules for gratuities are a lot more subjective than the 15 to 20 percent you're used to leaving on the table after a meal. Form 2-2 should help you estimate any gratuities you want to pay.

The amount you tip varies according to local customs, the size of your wedding (the more people, the larger the tip), and not least of all, the quality of service. If you're unsure of local practices, check with your catering manager. Depending on the venue and the vendor, gratuities might be calculated as part of your contract. Even with this kind of arrangement, you might want to reward some people who go above and beyond the call of duty.

Gratuities paid at hotels and other on-premise locations differ from those paid to catering staff brought in to work at a site. (For an explanation of on-premise versus off-premises facilities, see Chapter 9.) It's also important to realize there are no absolute formulas for party gratuities. Ask the banquet manager or party-account executive you've been working with for suggested amounts.

Usually, catering staff are paid by the hour (delineated on your bill) and in-house staff is paid by a percentage of the bill, about 18 to 22 percent.

Before giving a gratuity, double check that it isn't already included in your contract or on your invoice. You might wish to give something additional, but not as large an amount.

No matter where you live, guests should not be expected to tip restroom attendants or parking valets. You may wish to post a discreet sign in appropriate places saying: "Gratuities have been paid by your host."

The Gratuity Worksheet

Recipient	Tipping Guideline	Gratuity Estimate
Banquet manager or Catering party manager	$200 and up or a personal gift, depending on the size and complexity of wedding	$
Bartender, Head	$50 and up	$
Bartender	$25 and up	$
Bathroom attendants	$1-$2 per guest or a flat fee arranged with venue	$
Bride's dresser	15-20 percent of fee	$
Chef	$100 and up	$
Civil ceremony officiant	$15-$25 if appropriate	$
Clergyperson	$25 and up, depending on the size of the wedding. Often a donation to the house of worship	$
Coatroom attendants	$1-$2 per guest or a flat fee arranged with venue management	$
Cooks	$25 each	$
Hairdresser	10-20 percent of fee depending on number of heads	$
Head captain or Maitre d'	1 – 3 percent of food and beverage, depending on number of guests and amount of bill $150-$300 for off-premises, depending on number of guests	$
Room captain	$50 and up	$
Hotel chambermaid	$1-2 per day	$

Form 2-2: Tracking gratuities for all the players. (Page 1 of 2)

Recipient	Tipping Guideline	Gratuity Estimate
Makeup person	10-20 percent of fee depending on number of faces	$
Musicians (ceremony)	15 percent of fee	$
Musicians (reception)	$25-$50 per band member, especially if guests make numerous requests	$
Parking attendants	$1-$2 per car; or 15 percent of bill for valet parking-usually included on bill	$
Photographer	$100 for extraordinary service if service is on flat rate with no overtime fee	$
Porters	$15 each	$
Tailor	10 percent of fee	$
Transportation driver	$25 additional for bus or van driver 18-20 percent for limo will be on bill; $25 in addition for exceptional service	$
Wait staff	$10-$20 for off-premises waiters $25 and up for waiters who wait on head table, off or on premises	$
Wedding consultant	15 percent of fee; 15-20 percent if charged hourly just for the day of the wedding; or a personal gift	$
	TOTAL	$

Form 2-2: Tracking gratuities for all the players. (Page 2 of 2)

After you tally the gratuities, enter the amounts on your budget spreadsheet.

Controlling Costs: Till Debt Do Us Part?

Now that you've had a chance to digest the budget game and you've plugged in a few numbers, you might be staring off into space muttering or running out to pick up a truck load of lottery tickets. Don't despair — keeping a handle on your wedding expenditures actually eases enormous amounts of your pre-aisle angst. Follow these tips for additional help in capping your money fears:

✔ Keep checking the bottom line. It's the best way to avoid magical thinking. If you've gone over budget precipitously in one category, look at the other categories for a place to make up the difference. Remember — something's got to give!

✔ Look for liquor on sale. If you're holding your reception where you can bring in the liquor, watch for special sales on cases of wine and champagne in the months before your wedding.

✔ See if the venue has its own sound system that you can use in lieu of cocktail musicians or renting a stereo and speakers.

✔ Serve only passed hors d'oeuvres as guests arrive and get their drinks. Buffet stations are lovely during the cocktail hour, but they add considerably to the per-person price.

✔ Elope. (Just kidding!)

✔ Alternate floral table arrangements with some composed solely of groups of candles, which are less expensive.

✔ Have your wedding earlier in the day. The later in the day you have your wedding, the more you have to feed and fete your guests. At a breakfast, brunch, or tea reception, you can get away with serving less food and liquor.

✔ Think about having your wedding on an off-night, such as Thursday, or during a less-popular month. Remember that off-season can vary according to where you live or where your wedding is being held.

✔ Stay organized and stick to your wedding-day schedule so you can avoid overtime charges.

✔ Examine contracts and costs carefully and ask questions. Are tax, gratuity, and overtime included? These are the hidden costs that can throw your budget off completely.

✔ Have a small fancy wedding cake for presentation, and a plain sheet cake (that is sliced in the kitchen) for serving. (See Chapter 9 of *Weddings For Dummies* for details.)

✔ Negotiate with vendors where possible (without being obnoxious), especially when it comes to frivolous charges such as cake-cutting fees and corkage fees.

✔ Cut the head count by inviting fewer people, or have a two-tier reception such as a cocktail party for a large group followed by a sit-down dinner elsewhere for 20 close friends and family.

✔ Offer just wine, sparkling wine, and beer or pre-mixed drinks such as pitchers of margaritas or mimosas. These can be much less expensive than having an open bar.

Forms on the CD-ROM

Form 2-1	The Wedding Kit Budget Tracker	Tracking your budget on a spreadsheet.
Form 2-2	The Gratuity Worksheet	Tracking gratuities for all the players.

Part II
Be Our Guest

The 5th Wave   By Rich Tennant

"Along with 'Invitations', 'Announcements', and 'Save the Day' cards, I'd like some 'I Told You So' cards for people who thought I'd never get married."

In this part . . .

Your guests are an integral part of your wedding day. You need to treat them right every step of the way, from sending them a handsome invitation in a timely manner to tracking their responses to thanking them for gifts. We also delve into the increasingly popular world of destination weddings and explain how to pull off one of these memorable events. In this part, we tell you how to give all of your guests the royal treatment — and yourself a break.

Chapter 3

Naming Names

· ·

In This Chapter

▶ Creating a master guest list

▶ Keeping tabs on who's coming and who's not

▶ Mapping out seated receptions

▶ Recording gifts received and thank-yous

· ·

*Y*our ceremony is over and you have started to breathe again. You float into your reception blissfully arm in arm with your new spouse and, as you are deluged with hugs and kisses, out of the corner of your eye you, notice your cousins, the Harsabeebees. Standing with them grinning ear to ear, are the freshly scrubbed Harsabeebee kids — all seven of them. You can't recall seeing their names on any of your cocktail-napkin-scrawled invitation lists, and you certainly haven't included them in the guest count, let alone given them places to sit. The ensuing panic could have been avoided if you had worked with a comprehensive master guest list.

Here we are to the rescue! We give you the Master Tracker spreadsheet in Excel for you. In this chapter, we explain how to use it and all the ways it will save you time and aggravation.

Guest Quest: The Master Tracker

An integral part of hosting any event is managing the guest list. Whether you are hosting a destination wedding for ten couples or an elaborate seated dinner for 500, without a decent estimate of the guest count, you can't start shopping for spaces, determine a budget, or even begin talking with caterers.

Form 3-1, the Master Tracker, guides you through this process. (It's on the CD-ROM.) With Form 3-1 you can

✔ Make a full wish list of invitees, incorporating the lists from everyone who has a say in whom to invite.

✔ Compile the final list of those to be invited, including accurate contact information.

✔ Track RSVPs for up to three events (helpful for those having brunches and other activities during a wedding weekend).

✔ Compile a "B" list of people to send invitations to when others can't make it.

✔ Track gifts received and thank-you notes sent.

✔ If you are hosting a seated meal, assign tables.

✔ Reformat the information for convenience in addressing envelopes and calligraphing escort cards and place cards.

After you assemble your list of people you are actually going to send invitations to, compile their accurate addresses, correct spelling of their names, and titles. This task should be started as early as possible; otherwise, you will be hunting down people long after they're wondering why they weren't invited to your wedding. Pulling this information together can be a big project, which makes it a perfect opportunity to enlist the help of parents and attendants.

Open up Form 3-1 on the CD-ROM. This database consists of three *sheets*, which you get to by clicking on the tabs Sheet 1, Sheet 2, and so on at the bottom of the screen. Sheet 1 is the Master Guest List, Sheet 2 is for recording RSVPs and figuring out the seating chart, and Sheet 3 is for keeping track of gifts received and thank-you notes sent. The names you enter on Sheet 1 are automatically transferred to the other two sheets.

Creating the master guest list

So, who's going to receive a coveted invitation to this special event? You might start out wanting each and every person you've known in your lifetime to witness your recitation of vows — until the caterer starts using the phrase "Enough food to feed an army." Or you might be thinking of an intimate party for 30 good friends, but then your future in-laws threaten to jump if certain people aren't invited. Either way, you'll probably want to make some big changes to your guest list over time. We've designed the spreadsheet to make it easy to play the numbers game, adding or subtracting potential invitees, before you place your invitation order.

We suggest that you start by entering on the list everybody you might possibly want to invite. This is a rough cut; there's no need to fill in their address and other data at this point unless you want to. From this list you can cull the actual invitees. The rest might get announcements (if you decide to send them) or be relegated to a "B" list of invitees, those whom you'd like to invite but don't have room for unless others can't attend.

If you are "wait-listing" some guests, remember these two very important considerations for the B list:

✔ Make sure that the "kindly RSVP by" date on your A list is early enough so that you can send out a second mailing without it seeming ludicrously late.

✔ Print a second set of RSVP cards solely for your B list that don't specify an RSVP date. (You don't want your B-list guests to receive an invitation with an RSVP date that's already past!)

Sheet 1 of Form 3-1, the Master Guest List spreadsheet, helps you put together information used in addressing invitations by a calligrapher or anyone else handwriting envelopes for you. Some calligraphers will work only with a list of names in "label" format, not listed in one horizontal line. If that's the case, you might have to create a special calligraphy list in a word-processing program. Make sure to ask about format preferences when speaking to your calligrapher.

On Sheet 1 you can record all the necessary data about your invitees, such as the name, salutation (Mr., Ms., Dr., and so on), address, and any other names to appear on the inner envelope. (For details on the art of the invitation, see Chapter 13 of *Weddings For Dummies.*)

The Master Guest List is not only for wedding invitations. Because there is a trend toward large rehearsal dinners (especially with destination weddings), the guest list has a column to designate invitees to that event. You probably won't be the one doing the actual inviting to such a dinner, but the spreadsheet makes it easy for you to print out a list for the generous hosts. You can also designate which guests are members of the wedding party, which is helpful for seating.

The invitation process is a numbers game. You use the #Invited and the A/B List columns on the Master Guest List to manage these numbers. Your goal is to track only those people who are currently invited; that is, you want to record people only from your A list in the #Invited column. You can enter the names of people on your B list; just don't record anything in the #Invited column and make sure to designated them as B-listers in the A/B List column.

When you switch people from the B list to the A list, change their designation in the A/B list column and then add the number of people invited. For those getting downgraded, do the opposite.

Enter the actual number of people to be invited for each invitation in the #Invited column. That way, you are ensured of counting invitees, not just envelopes. For example, if one invitation is sent to a family of four, make sure to put *4* in the #Invited column.

The current tally of all those invited appears at the top of the page. The spreadsheet is designed with this flexibility so that you can focus first on getting all the potential names together in one place and then manipulating the list to reach a final count.

Sheets 1 and 2 of Form 3-1 use Excel's powerful *AutoFilter* function. AutoFilter allows you to create lists within lists for various purposes. For example, on the Master Guest List spreadsheet, you may need to use AutoFilter to hide the B list when you want a list of people currently being invited or to create a list of invitees to the rehearsal dinner. The AutoFilter function is activated via the pull-down menu (the little down-facing arrow) in column headings with that function. On the A/B list, for example, you'd click on the menu and then select A. The AutoFilter then shifts all the B's to the background. To revert to the full list, select "all" from the pull-down list. On Sheet 2, the RSVPS/Table Assignments sheet, by selecting Y on the pull-down menu in the *RSVP Y/N* column, you can create an instant list of those attending.

Designate your "A" and "B" list.
Remember "B" list should not have a number in the # Invited column.

This cell automatically tallies the numbers in the #Invited column.

Form 3-1:
On Sheet 1, you can create various guest lists. AutoFilter allows you to create lists within lists.

Badger/Beaver Wedding June 21, 2000
Master Guest List

		Total Number Invited	17							
First Name	*Last Name and outer envelope extras*	*# invited*	*A/B List*	*Rehearsal Dinner*	*Wed Party*	*Street Address*	*City*	*State*	*Zip*
Mr. and Mrs. Harry	Badger	2	A	Y	Y	2324 Forest Lane	Pleasant Glen	WI	76543
Mr. John and Ms. Jane	Doe	2	A	N		4747 Bland Street	Easy View	CA	95213
Ms. Starr	Fishman	2	A	N		9087 Beach Edge Road	Tidal Pool	GA	79876
Ms. Organza	Kerfuffle and Guest	2	A	N		1859 Whirlwind Drive, NW Apt. 7C	East Haven	NY	10086
Mr. Sylvester and Ms. Kanga	Rue	2	A	N		3303 Outback Lane	West Grassland	CO	98765
Master Wally	Russ III	1	A	Y	Y	2704 Sea Breeze Drive	Salt Spray	FI	84326
Mr. and Mrs. King	Salmon		B	N		8976 Headwaters Drive	Forest Glen	OR	90876
Dr. Howard and Ms. Gloria	Smith and Family	4	A	N		175 Apple Blossom Way	Macintosh	WA	97654
Ms. Mara	Supial and Guest	2	A	Y	Y	22 Pocket Lane, Apt. 17B	Austin	TX	67543
Mr. and Mrs. Spotsford	Trout		B	N		3701 Eddy Lane	Clearwater	VT	5679

Be sure to get all proper names of guests and family members invited.

If you have addressed invitations to a friend and guest, find out the guest's name when it's time to write his or her table assignment card. Such attention to detail shows you are happy to have the person at your wedding. The last name column on the Master Guest List Sheet is also intended to allow for the addition of "and Guest" or "and Family" so your envelope addressers have the proper information.

Recording RSVPs

If you are mailing several invitations addressed "and Family" or "and Guest," the only way to keep an accurate guest count is to include a "number attending" line on your RSVP card. You must include this line no matter how inelegant it might look on your pristine cards. Otherwise, if someone has decided to come sans guest, or Mr. and Mrs. Pacman who were invited with all the little Pacsters decide to leave them at home, you'll never know for sure until the moment of truth.

The RSVP/Table Assignments sheet (Sheet 2 of Form 3-1) kicks in after the invitations are mailed and the responses start coming in. The names on the Master Guest List spreadsheet automatically appear on this worksheet, which facilitates keeping track of RSVPs. As responses come in, put a Y (for those attending) or an N (for those missing the occasion) in the RSVP column.

Also — and this is crucial for an accurate guest count — enter the number attending, *not* the number that were invited, in the appropriate column. The total guest count automatically tallies at the top of the page. You can either leave the column blank or input a zero for those not attending.

The spreadsheet is designed to record RSVPs and head counts for up to three events (the reception plus two other events). If you are having additional events that are being catered or hosted, keeping track of who and how many are attending various events is important. We call these additional get-togethers Event two and Event three; you, of course, can change the names of these events as you like (such as Brunch or BBQ) by changing the names in cells (see Chapter 18 on Excel tips).

Accommodating special dietary needs shows your guests that you are committed to their having a good time. The spreadsheet has a column for tracking such needs so that you have this information handy for the caterer or restaurant. You designate the codes you need — for example kosher, vegetarian, vegetarian non-dairy, or diabetic — by inputting either the word or abbreviation of your choosing in the column.

Hiding columns

If you are overwhelmed when you see all these columns on the various spreadsheets, we have a solution. Hiding columns is a way to get the data in the form you need for various tasks and reports. To hide a column, select its letter at the top of the spreadsheet, click on Format, select Column, and then Hide. To make the column reappear, follow the same path (of course you can't click on the column that's hidden so go directly to format) and select Unhide. (If there are columns you don't use at all, delete them. See Chapter 18 for the details.)

Here's an example of how you can use the Hide function to create a special meals list for your banquet captain or maitre d'. While holding down the Control key (which allows you to select non-adjoining columns), select all those columns *except* the following: First Name, Last Name, Table Number, and Special Needs. Then click Format, Column, Hide, and you've got a slick little report to print out.

If the response cards are being sent to your parents, you need to work out a plan for updating this worksheet. One person controlling this list makes for fewer mistakes.

If you are hosting a seated meal with table assignments, save yourself an enormous amount of planning time by completing the name information in the *Escort Card* and *Place Card* columns as you record your RSVPs. Keep an eye out for husbands and wives who use different last names, incorrect familiar names, and corrected spellings if there were changes from the initial mailing list.

Seating for Meals

Once you have decided on the approximate size of your reception, ask the caterer or banquet manager for a floor plan with numbered tables, including how many guests should be seated at each table. (See *Weddings For Dummies*, Chapter 11, for more information on composing a seating chart.) This information allows you to assign tables with real numbers, rather than having to "re-name" them later. You can also visualize who should be seated where in the room.

While you can't finish a viable seating chart until all your responses are in, you can go down the list in Form 3-1 and start creating tables with obvious groupings such as the wedding party, cousins, or high school friends.

After you make some assignments, _sort_ the list in ascending order (see Chapter 18 for more information on sorting). People not yet seated (with no number in the Table # column) will be pushed to the bottom of the list. Then you have a quick view of who still needs a seat.

You don't have to seat people together that you invited together. For example, you might want to split kids and parents in one family, with all the tykes sitting at a separate table. You can easily designate such splits by inserting rows for each person to be seated at a different table and inputting the names. See Chapter 18 for instructions on how to do this.

Make sure that you adjust the head count in the _Attending reception_ column so that the parents are listed as two people (excluding the kids) and the children are listed as one each. This is necessary only when you have inserted rows to indicate couples or families seated at different tables.

When doing seating charts, here are some ideas for sorting data to make sure noone is left out:

- ✔ Create an alphabetized list of attendees with their table number beside their name. You'll need such a list to address the escort cards. Also, have the list handy at the reception for people who can't find their seats. Functions used: Hide all columns except First Name, Last Name, and Table #. Sort by last name column in ascending order.

- ✔ Make a list of names grouped by table. Again this is a check on your numbers, and it ensures you have counted the correct number of tables, which is essential for centerpieces, linens, or other rentals, and for the caterers' service plan. This sort enables you to notice any glaring mistakes, such as feuding relatives seated at the same table, early enough to redo your seating. Functions used: Hide all columns except First Name, Last Name, and Table #, and sort in ascending order by table number column.

- ✔ Generate a list for a second or third event: Useful for getting a count for a caterer or creating guest list for a host. Functions: Hide all rows except First Name, Last Name, RSVP for that event, and numbers attending that event. AutoFilter by RSVP column and select Y.

Remember this is the actual number attending — not everyone invited.

This is the tally from the Reception Attending column.

Form 3-1: The RSVP column in Sheet 2 works in conjunction with the table assignment function.

Badger/Beaver Wedding June 21, 2000
RSVPs, Table Assignments, Escort Cards, and Place Cards

			Reception			Event Two		Event Three	
Total Attending			16				14		10
First Name	Last Name	RSVP	Reception Attending	Table #	Special needs	Event two	Number Attend	Event three	Number Attend
Mr. and Mrs. Harry	Badger	Y	2	6	K	Y	2	N	
Mr. John and Ms. Jane	Doe	Y	1	8	V	Y	2	Y	1
Ms. Starr	Fishman	Y	2	11		Y	2	Y	2
Ms. Organza	Kerfuffle and Guest	Y	1	16		N		Y	1
Mr. Sylvester and Ms. Kanga	Rue								
Master Wally	Russ III	Y	2	13	K	Y	2	Y	2
Mr. and Mrs. King	Salmon	Y	2	16	V	Y	2	Y	2
Buffy	Smith	Y	1	12	F	Y	1	N	
Jack	Smith	Y	1	15		Y	1	N	
Dr. Howard and Ms. Gloria	Smith and Family	Y	2	2		Y	2	Y	2
Ms. Mara	Supial and Guest	Y	2	9		N		N	
Mr. and Mrs. Spotsford	Trout								

Note: Family members can be broken up and assigned to different tables by adding rows.

You can make up as many special needs codes as you like.

Tracking Gifts

A list of your wedding gifts, including who gave what, when it was received, and when you sent your thank-you notes, will give you great peace of mind. In emergencies, you can use the list to appease your mother who is bound to call and ask why Aunt Penny hasn't received a thank-you yet. "Not true!" you can reply, pointing to the notation on your spreadsheet that you mailed a thank-you four days ago.

Sheet 3 of Form 3-1, the Gift Tracker, allows you to track all this information regarding your guests and their gifts. Names are automatically transferred from the Master Guest List (Sheet 1), so all you need to do is input the gift, the date it was received, and the date a thank-you was sent. Sheet 3 also has columns to track the same information for engagement and shower gifts, should friends and family bestow those on you as well.

In some cases — smaller weddings and destination weddings, for example — you may receive gifts from people who weren't invited to the wedding. You can add as many people as you like to the Gift Tracker spread sheet. The added names appear only on the Gift Tracker and not either of the other spreadsheets.

Input rows for names of gift givers who do not appear on your master list.

Input rows for names of gift givers who do not appear on your master list.

This is the date you received the gift.

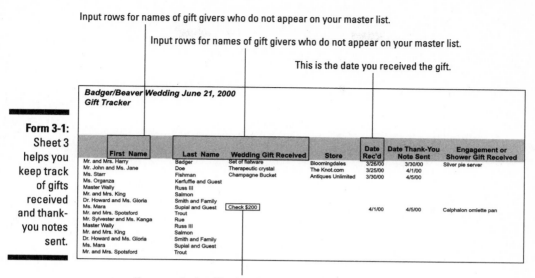

Form 3-1:
Sheet 3
helps you
keep track
of gifts
received
and thank-
you notes
sent.

If you are sharing this with other people — parents,
for example — consider not including dollar amounts.

Forms on the CD-ROM

Form 3-1   The Master Tracker   Keep track of the important facts and figures
in the Master Guest List, RSVP/Table
Assignments sheet, and Gift Tracker.

Chapter 4

Invitations and Other Stops Along the Paper Trail

In This Chapter

▶ Planning your stationery wardrobe

▶ Steering yourself toward a stationer

▶ Titling tips and proper forms of address

*I*n this chapter we provide tools for helping you figure out what to order in terms of invitations and other stationery. We give you tips on selecting a stationer and placing an impeccable order. The wording and spelling used on invitations is an esoteric artform, which we explain in excruciating but necessary detail in Chapter 13 of *Weddings for Dummies*. One bonus in the following pages is a section that was cut from *WFD* for space — a chart delineating the proper forms of address for religious, political, and professional personages. (It's trickier than you might think!)

Pinning Down Your Paper Needs

Although we find the term "stationery wardrobe" hokey, it's useful in describing the variety of paper goods you might consider for your wedding. And you thought it was just invitations! No, not even close. Possibilities range from save-the-date mailings to destination wedding itinerary letters, from cocktail napkins to place cards and menus (see Figure 4-1).

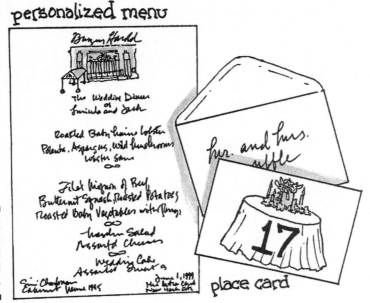

personalized menu

place card

Figure 4-1:
A sample
personalized
menu and
place card.

Ordering your personal stationery and thank-you notes at the same time you order your invitations can save you money because the same address plates can be used.

Form 4-1, the Stationery Wardrobe Worksheet, which can be found on the CD-ROM, lists the printed items you may wish to order for your wedding. While most stationery sources carry everything listed in Form 4-1, you may decide to order your invitations from one vendor, and have other items offset or create them on your own laser printer.

Couples who are married or live together receive one invitation not two. The same goes for families with children under 13. Count the number of invitations needed (not invitees) when you order invitations.

"Informal" notes are a quick way to let people know that you've received their gift and will send them a thoughtful, hand-written thank-you note later — presumably when you're back from your extended three-month honeymoon. These notes are usually printed and say that the bride (who uses her married name) "has received your very kind gift and will write you later of her appreciation." We find this formality a bit stodgy, especially since traditionally just the bride sends them. If you're going to the trouble of addressing and mailing something, why not just write the real note and be done with it? Or send an e-mail indicating receipt of the gift and promising a real note to follow. Your money would be better spent on nice personal stationery (particularly note cards) that you can use for a variety of correspondence for a long time after the wedding.

At-home cards, which inform friends and relatives of your new address, are another anachronism but one that still has some utilitarian value, even in this day of pre-marital cohabitation. If you're setting up house at a new address after the wedding, you may want to send these out. List your names on the at-home cards as you would like to be addressed after you're married. For example, if you dislike being referred to as Mrs. Bill So-and-so, don't write it that way, even though that's the traditional wording for at-home cards.

Stationery Wardrobe Worksheet

Item	Quantity	Unit Price	Style	Printed Envelopes (Y/N)	Paper Stock, Color	Font Style
Save–the–dates						
Other mailings (hotel info)						
Invitations						
Envelopes (single or double)						
Response cards and envelopes						
Ceremony cards						
Reception cards						
Pew cards						
Map/direction cards						
Welcome basket notes and itinerary cards						

Form 4-1: Create your wedding stationery wish list. (Page 1 of 2)

Item	Quantity	Unit Price	Style	Printed Envelopes (Y/N)	Paper Stock, Color	Font Style
Ceremony programs						
Escort cards						
Place cards						
Menus						
Cocktail napkins						
Hand towels						
Matchbooks						
Favors						
Announcements and envelopes						
At-home cards						
Thank you notes						
Personal stationery						
Rehearsal dinner invitations						
Other party invitations						
Next day brunch invitations						
Other						

Form 4-1:
Create your wedding stationery wish list.
(Page 2 of 2)

Selecting a Stellar Stationer

After you have an idea of the kind and style of stationery products you want to order, use Form 4-2, the Stationer Interview Checklist, which you find on the CD-ROM, to help you shop for a stationer.

The kind of paper goods you're in the market for will dictate where you go to shop. For more expensive, engraved, or custom products, you should work with a professional who specializes in stationery. If your tastes are less extravagant, many party or business supply shops carry invitation books to order from. If you have something unusual in mind, but don't have the budget to go with it, many suppliers sell wonderful papers as well as all the trimmings and tools for you to create your own masterpieces. All you need is a laser printer, some artistic talent, and lots and lots of time.

Stationer Interview Checklist

☐ Is there someone on staff to help with the wording?

☐ How soon will a proof be ready?

☐ What are the proof charges?

☐ After the proofs are approved, when will the order be ready?

☐ Can we get the envelopes in advance?

☐ How many extra envelopes are included with each order?

☐ Are double envelopes included? Tissue?

☐ Does the invitation come in different papers or colors?

☐ What are the choices of envelope linings?

☐ How much extra does it cost to have lined envelopes?

☐ Is there an extra charge for printing a return address on the back flaps?

☐ Does the vendor ship or (if local) deliver? What is the charge?

☐ What ink colors are possible? Can you do a custom color? What is the cost?

☐ What fonts are available? Does the vendor have sample invitations in the various fonts?

☐ Is the printing method thermographed, offset, engraved, or letterpress?

☐ Are logos or monograms possible? What styles?

☐ In what increments are the invitations available? Is there a charge for re-ordering?

☐ Are there rush charges? What are they?

☐ What calligraphy service is available for addressing the envelopes? Is computerized calligraphy offered? What is the cost per line?

☐ Do the invitations come completely finished? In other words, scored or ribboned, if that's necessary?

☐ How much of a deposit is required? When is the final payment due?

Form 4-2:
Know what to ask the stationer before you call.

If you have decided on a specific invitation or stationery product, or a specific design, you might wish to compare vendors. Some companies discount the major invitation brands.

After you have interviewed prospective stationers, jot down their information and estimates and compare them on Form 4-3, which you find on the CD-ROM. Just be sure to compare identical products. The addition of a ribbon or a change in ink color can change the price considerably.

The Bid Picture: Stationers Comparison Worksheet

Stationer and Contact Info	Items Included	Cost Estimate	Notes
Name: Phone: Address: E-mail:			
Name: Phone: Address: E-mail:			
Name: Phone: Address: E-mail:			
Name: Phone: Address: E-mail:			

Form 4-3: Compare stationery suppliers to get the best deal.

Placing the Order

If you are sending in your own stationery order (as opposed to using a stationer), the stationery company should supply an order form that you fill out according to their specifications.

If a store, wedding consultant, or stationer is putting together your order, they should handle the paper work. However, take a few minutes to go through Form 4-4 before your appointment to save time. Form 4-4 appears on the CD-ROM.

Invitation Information Worksheet

Components

☐ If all guests are invited to both the ceremony and reception, do you want all the information on one card or do you want separate cards for the ceremony and reception? (If not everyone is invited to ceremony, the invitation should be to the reception with an enclosed ceremony card.)

☐ Do you want an insert card listing directions and a map? Who provides the artwork?

☐ Do you want tissue?

☐ How many invitations do you need? How many envelopes?

☐ How many response cards do you need? How many envelopes?

☐ Do you want to order other stationery such as informals, at-home cards, or personal note cards?

☐ Do you want to include escort cards and envelopes, place cards, or pew cards?

☐ What are your plans for programs, menus, and other mementos?

Names

☐ Who is hosting and how should their names appear? Mr. and Mrs.? First names? Separate lines with "and" in between?

☐ If the bride is not a host, how should her name appear? Use her title?

☐ If the groom is not a host, how should his name appear? Use his title?

Dates and location

☐ Do you want the date written out or as a numeral?

☐ How should the street address appear?

☐ Do you want just the city or the city and state?

☐ By what date do you want response cards sent back?

☐ What address should go on the at-home cards? Do you want other information, such as phone number and e-mail address?

Form 4-4:
Assemble all of your invitation information for quick reference.
(Page 1 of 2)

Wording

❑ What is the exact wording you prefer?

❑ Do you want to use traditional English spellings ("honour" not "honor")?

❑ What type of dress are you going to specify (such as black tie)?

Style

❑ What kind of paper do you prefer? What color, stock, and weight?

❑ Which typeface style do you prefer?

❑ Do you want the copy to be all upper case, all lower case, or upper and lower case?

❑ Which color ink do you prefer? Do you want more than one color of ink? What extra charge, if any, is there for more than one color of ink?

❑ Do you want to incorporate a monogram, logo, family crest, or other motif?

❑ Do you want a bow or ribbon on each invitation? Will you tie these yourself or have the printer do it for a fee?

❑ Do you want the invitations engraved, thermographed, offset, or laser printed?

❑ Do you want any part of your invitations or envelopes calligraphed? Who will do this?

❑ Is the invitation printed horizontally or vertically?

❑ Do you want the copy flush left, centered, or flush right?

❑ What size invitation do you want? What extra cost, if any, is there for oversized invitations?

Envelopes

❑ Whose address goes on the back flap? How should it appear?

❑ Whose address goes on the front of the RSVP envelope? How should it appear?

❑ Do you want the envelopes sent ahead for addressing?

Form 4-4:
Assemble
all of your
invitation
information
for quick
reference.
(Page 2 of 2)

Be sure to use the precise spellings and wordings you would like to appear on the invitation, including full street and location names. Don't assume the stationer is psychic and already knows what you want to say and how to say it. If you want to use "Mr." for the groom, for example, indicate so on Form 4-4. Specify full names (first, middle, and last) and titles (Mr., doctor, military, and so on). Print or enter your information in both upper and lower case letters where you would like each.

No matter how tight you are on time or money, always insist on seeing a proof of each piece to be printed. Errors are still fixable at the proof stage. Even if there's a fee for changes, it sure beats trying to erase a line on 200 invitations.

The announcement may use the same wording as the invitation, such as "Jane and Harold wish to announce their marriage . . ." Or one or both sets of parents may want to send announcements themselves, even if they are not "hosting" the wedding.

Creating Your Own Invitations

If you're ambitious, creative, and eager to save money, try making your own invitations. For something really down-home and whimsical, you can throw out all those uptight etiquette books and invent your own style (see the sidebar "A wedding original" in this chapter).

With the software packages available today, you can produce an invitation that's nearly professional quality. However, unless you invest in your own printing press, you can't produce an engraved product or even a thermographed one. But if you seek a casual style, then the do-it-yourself kits work fine.

Printing your own wedding invitations doesn't always save you money. Although you're eliminating the middleman — the printer — you may, depending on the company you work with, still have to buy the paper and the software. And you should also take into account your own time, experience, and anxiety level. How many sheets of gilt-edged vellum will you mess up before you get the process down pat?

The software program The Complete Wedding Publisher, for wedding invitations and other items, is extremely thorough. The program allows you to design your invitations and other stationery. You can then order paper stock from a list of vendors specified by the company. You find a trial version on the CD-ROM, or you can order the full package at www.ed-it.com/p_wedsoc.htm.

A wedding original

One of the wittiest invitations we've seen was for a friend's wedding in Texas. He and his bride-to-be are not the fussy types and had waited several years before deciding to tie the knot. They chose to set a casual, fun tone for the day by sending out an invitation they created on their computer and photocopied. It consisted of a single sheet folded into thirds. "The Plot Thickens . . ." was the opening line. When you lifted the flap, the text read:

> When we last visited our heroes, they were slogging their way through the vicissitudes of urban living.
>
> Suddenly, as if struck by a thunderbolt (or perhaps the sound of a cargo jet flying over at 3:45 a.m. – @$*&%^!!), they decided to get married.
>
> Their analyst thought it might be the first sign of an impending midlife crises. She was fired.
>
> Their friends thought, "Those rowdies, they'll use any excuse to throw a big blowout. They're such party animals, you know... always up past the 10 o'clock news – and on a school night!"

When you opened the invitation, there was a computer graphic of two entwined wedding bands and the details of the wedding, which they didn't get from Emily Post:

> *So, don't miss the next exciting episode...*
>
> Will their dogs insist on a prenuptial agreement?
>
> Will the cats look good in pink?
>
> And just what is the cats' signature color, anyway?
>
> Is there conversation after marriage, or just a lot of head-nodding?
>
> You won't know unless you attend the premiere gala on
>
> **Saturday, May 8**
>
> (sorry, no sequels)

The invitation concluded with addresses and maps to the ceremony and reception and the warning, "No shirt, no shoes, no service." The response card continued the theme of the serial novel:

Sue and David:

We're as stunned as everybody else that you're finally getting married. We never would have guessed that plot twist.

❑ Yes, we'll be there! We'll have a total of _____ people in attendance.

Children are welcome as long as they don't act too much like grown-ups.

❑ Sorry, we can't make it. Please try to have fun anyway.

M_____

You can also order invitations over the Internet. If you search for "imprintable papers" on your favorite search engine, you will find paper and invitation companies where you can laser print your own invitations. Here are a few that might turn up in your search:

✔ **C&J Papers:** cjpaper.com
✔ **Sand Scripts:** sandscripts.com/catalog/social/imprintable.html
✔ **Papermania:** papermania.com
✔ **Discount Invitations:** discount-invitations.com

As you design your invitations, you may want to incorporate a personal logo for your wedding. Software programs such as Microsoft Paint and Quark Illustrator are useful for creating graphic designs for this purpose. However, you must have a good laser printer that can produce camera-ready art for your professional printer. Once you create this art, you can have it imprinted on party favors, cocktail napkins, guest towels, yarmulkes, and other goodies for your guests.

Tips for Titles

Unless you hobnob in diplomatic circles or work as an executive assistant to some corporate titan or socialite, you probably don't have to worry very often about addressing personages with fancy professional, political, or religious titles. But now that you're getting married, here's your chance. As you can read in Chapter 13 in *Weddings For Dummies*, you can use just first names on place cards, but if you want to use professional titles, Table 4-1 explains how.

Table 4-1:	Titles of Address		
Official	*Envelopes*	*Introduction*	*Place Card*
Protestant clergy with degree (male)	The Reverend Doctor Peter Pickle and Mrs. Pickle	Dr. Peter Pickle	Dr. Pickle or Dr. Peter Pickle
Protestant clergy with degree (female)	The Reverend Doctor Jane Cash and Mr. Cash	Dr. Jane Cash	Dr. Jane Cash
Protestant clergy without degree (male)	The Reverend Peter Pickle and Mrs. Pickle	Mr. Pickle	Mr. Pickle or Mr. Peter Pickle
Protestant clergy without degree (female)	The Reverend and Mr. Cash	Ms. Cash or Mrs. Cash	Ms. Cash or Mrs. Cash or Mrs. Buck Cash or Ms. Jane Cash
Bishop of the Episcopal Church (male)	The Right Reverend Peter Pickle and Mrs. Pickle	Bishop Pickle	Bishop Pickle or Bishop Peter Pickle
Bishop of the Episcopal Church (female)	The Right Reverend Jane Cash and Mr. Cash	Bishop Cash	Bishop Cash or Bishop Jane Cash

Official	Envelopes	Introduction	Place Card
Bishop of the Methodist Church (male)	The Reverend Peter Pickle and Mrs. Pickle	Bishop Pickle	Bishop Pickle or Bishop Peter Pickle
Bishop of the Methodist Church (female)	The Reverend Jane Cash and Mr. Cash	Bishop Cash	Bishop Cash or Bishop Jane Cash
Mormon Bishop	Bishop and Mrs. Peter Pickle	Mr. Pickle	Mr. Pickle or Mr. Peter Pickle
Roman Catholic Bishop and Archbishop	The Most Reverend Peter Pickle	His Excellency	His Excellency Bishop Pickle
Monsignor	The Right Reverend Monsignor Peter Pickle	Monsignor Pickle	Monsignor Pickle or Monsignor Peter Pickle
Priest	The Reverend Father Peter Pickle	Father Pickle	Father Pickle or Father Peter Pickle
Nun	Sister Mary Margaret	Sister Mary Margaret	Sister Mary Margaret or Sister Cash
Eastern Orthodox Communion Bishop	The Right Reverend Peter Pickle	His Excellency	His Excellency Bishop Pickle
Easter Orthodox Communion Priest	The Reverend Father Peter Pickle	Father Pickle	Father Pickle or Father Peter Pickle
Rabbi (male)	Rabbi and Mrs. Isaac Pickle	Rabbi Pickle Rabbi Isaac Pickle	Rabbi Pickle or
Rabbi (female)	Rabbi Rachel Cash and Mr. Cash	Rabbi Cash	Rabbi Rachel Cash
U.S. Senator (male)	Senator and Mrs. Pete Pickle	Senator or Senator Pickle	Senator Pickle or Senator Peter Pickle
U.S. Senator (female)	Senator Jane Cash and Mr. Cash	Senator Cash	Senator Cash or Senator Jane Cash
U.S. Representative (male)	The Honorable and Mrs. Peter Pickle	Mr. Pickle	The Honorable Peter Pickle or Mr. Pickle or Mr. Peter Pickle

(continued)

Table 4-1: *(continued)*

Official	Envelopes	Introduction	Place Card
U.S. Representative (female)	The Honorable Jane Cash and Mr. Cash	Ms. Cash or Mrs. Cash	Ms. Cash or Mrs. Cash or Ms. Jane Cash
Mayor (male)	Mayor and Mrs. Peter Pickle	Mayor Pickle	The Mayor of Wigglebury
Mayor (female)	Mayor Jane and Mr. Buck Cash or The Honorable Jane Cash and Mr. Buck Limestone (if his name is different from hers)	Mayor Cash	The Mayor of Wigglebury
Judge (male)	Judge and Mrs. Peter Pickle	Judge Pickle	Judge Pickle or Judge Peter Pickle
Judge (female)	The Honorable Jane Cash and Mr. Cash	Judge Cash	Judge Cash or Judge Jane Cash
Ambassador (male)	The Honorable Peter Pickle, Ambassador of the United States	Mr. Ambassador	Ambassador Pickle or Ambassador Peter Pickle
Ambassador (female)	The Honorable Jane Cash, Ambassador of the United States	Madam Ambassador	Ambassador Cash or Ambassador Jane Cash
Doctor (male)	Dr. and Mrs. Peter Pickle	Dr. Pickle	Dr. Pickle or Dr. Peter Pickle
Doctor (female)	Mr. Buck and Dr. Jane Cash	Dr. Cash	Dr. Cash or Dr. Jane Cash
Doctors	The Drs. Billy and Betty Bopper	Dr. Bopper	Dr. Bopper or Dr. Billy Bopper, Dr. Betty Bopper

Although people in the South sometimes refer to a Ph.D. as Doctor, usually the title is reserved for a medical doctor.

A word from some distinguished guests

In the your-tax-dollars-hard-at-work department, if you send an invitation to the President and First Lady, you'll get a lovely note back on White House stationery expressing their regrets that they can't make it (unless, of course, you're a personal friend or a head of state.) The address is The Honorable [first, middle, and last name of sitting president] William Jefferson Clinton, 1600 Pennsylvania Avenue NW, Washington, D.C., 20500. You can also send an invitation to the Pope by addressing it to His Holiness John Paul II, Prefettura della Casa, 00120 Citta del Vaticano, Italia, and he will send you a papal blessing.

Forms on the CD-ROM

Form 4-1	Stationery Wardrobe Worksheet	Create your wedding stationery wish list.
Form 4-2	Stationer Interview Checklist	Know what to ask the stationer before you call.
Form 4-3	The Bid Picture: Stationers Comparison Worksheet	Compare stationery suppliers to get the best deal.
Form 4-4	Invitation Information Checklist	Assemble all of your invitation information for quick reference.

Chapter 5

Traveling On: Destination Weddings

In This Chapter

▶ Picking a destination for a wedding away

▶ Presenting coming attractions

▶ Welcoming your guests

*1*f you're newly engaged, and in the first throes of wedding planning, you're probably coming upon the term "destination wedding," "far-away wedding," or "weekend wedding" in everything you read.

What is all this buzz about destination weddings? Is this yet another gimmick the wedding loonies made up to vex hapless couples? No, in fact, this idea makes sense. While the term sounds, admittedly, like "wed-speak," the realities of contemporary couples, who are well-traveled or whose friends and family are separated by great distances, have made these weddings increasingly popular.

In general, there are three types of destination weddings:

✔ You and your beloved have relocated far from your roots, have many good friends where you have landed, and want to stay put for your wedding.

✔ You and your fiancé drag your friends and business associates to where one or both of you are from.

✔ You pick an entirely new, different, and fascinating location to hold your celebration and invite guests to join you there (and where you will be honeymooning afterward). For our purposes, we will dub this type of destination wedding "a wedding away."

All three scenarios have lots in common. Whenever you're expecting gobs of people from "elsewhere" — and most likely for at least a three-day weekend wedding — your wedding plans entail a special level of research, logistics, and hospitality. Proper planning can make a destination wedding memorable and unique.

Even if you're not planning a destination wedding, you may find many useful tips in this chapter for planning your honeymoon and accommodating your guests.

Finding a Far-Away Destination

So you want to have your wedding away. Get ready for mucho research, because there are many factors involved in choosing a successful destination. Determining whether to get married in Katmandu, Kansas, or the Caribbean is not just a matter of where you think you'll get the best wedding photos. If you're traveling overseas, for example, there are legal and logistical requirements to consider. If you're hosting guests who are traveling to attend your ceremony and festivities and who might be there for several days, you need to take their comfort and expenditures into account.

Form 5-1, the Destination Location Checklist, which you also find on the CD-ROM, helps you sort out all the factors so that you can decide on a destination venue that works for you and your guests. (For location ideas, see Chapter 19.)

Only the very bravest souls, those inviting fewer than ten guests or those with an enormous amount of time and energy, should consider planning a far-away destination wedding without at least *some* professional help (and we don't mean psychotherapy, although it can't hurt). This doesn't mean that it's necessary to use a full-service wedding planner — unless your wedding is large or complicated — but planners who specialize in weddings away (often located at the destination itself) are helpful with legal logistics as well as site surveys and vendor recommendations. Travel agents will often act as the "point-person" for your guests to book with, saving you a lot of work.

For questions to ask when interviewing travel agents see Chapter 19 of *Weddings For Dummies*.

Finding destination help on the Web

The Web offers many sites to help you come up with some possible venues for your wedding and honeymoon. You can also use the Web to find an experienced destinations wedding coordinator or travel agent.

Go to your favorite search engine and enter *destination weddings* or the name of the country or state that interests you. (For example: *weddings in Scotland.*) This search should pull up several options of both planners and other vendors. Travel sites such as *Expedia.com, Travelocity.com,* and *Orbitz.com* are also helpful for getting an idea of prices.

Other sites that may be helpful include:

- **Thehoneymoonspecialist.com:** This is a full-service travel agency that specializes in honeymoon travel. They have a large, varied roster of suppliers in the travel industry that they work with including cruise lines and adventure travel companies (www.honeymoonspecialist.com).

- **Modernbride.com:** Lots of interesting information on destination weddings and honeymoons, such as travel agent surveys and articles. Local resources nationwide through Modern Bride's local magazines (www.modernbride.com).

- **Bestfares.com magazine:** You can log onto this site and peruse the travel news headlines for free. There are umpteen articles filled with ways to save money on travel. The subscription price of $60, which enrolls

you as a member in Best Fare's travel club, is well worth it for the discounts and information provided (www.bestfares.com).

- **Tncweddings.com:** This very elegant site from *Town & Country* magazine has a "destination finder." You select either the U.S. or international and, aside from some salient facts, the site recommends upscale accommodations worldwide (www.tncweddings.com).

- **Weddinglocation.com:** Businesses pay to be listed on this Web site. Couples can search locations by region, city, or country based on a long list of criteria. The site is under the auspisces of respected wedding planner Beverly Clark (www.weddinglocation.com).

- **Weddingtrips.com** (phone 877-Wed-Away): The site is owned by *Destination Weddings* and *Honeymoon* magazine. One can book either full service travel or destination wedding planning services through this site (www.dwhmagazine.com or www.weddingtrips.com).

- **Worldbridal.com:** Here you can get planning help as well as legal requirements for destinations worldwide (www.worldbridal.com).

- **Heartofeurope.com:** This travel agency offers wedding planning and a link to their full legal requirement page (heartofeurope.com/legal.htm).

Destination Location Checklist

❑ What are the legal and religious requirements for getting married there?

❑ What are the residency requirements?

❑ How difficult is it for your guests to get to? Is a change of planes necessary?

❑ Are airfare and lodging affordable for guests?

❑ Are blood tests or immunizations required for marriage licenses?

❑ Will guests require vaccinations? Can the certifying doctor be in the U.S.?

❑ What are the necessary documents to get married in this destination?

❑ Must proof of divorce or proof of being a widow(er) be certified?

❑ Do documents need to be translated into the native language?
   Are the original documents necessary?

❑ Do these documents need to be sent in advance?

❑ How long do you have to wait after your arrival to obtain a marriage license?

❑ After getting the license, how long is the waiting period?

❑ Are witnesses necessary? Must they be citizens of that country?

❑ Are civil ceremonies allowed? Which religious ceremonies are permitted?

❑ What is the name of a reputable wedding coordinator and/or a travel agent
   specializing in destination weddings who can help with bookings for your
   guests and with hiring vendors?

❑ Can you make at least one site–inspection trip?

❑ Would you like to spend your honeymoon there?

❑ What's the weather like in the season you're planning to get married?

❑ How long before your wedding is it suggested you arrive?

Form 5-1:
Research
the perfect
destination
for your
wedding.

It Takes a Village

After you settle on the venue, it's time to get down to the specifics, like where to put all the people who are coming for your festivities. You are, for all practical purposes, assembling a small community for the weekend, and you need to think through all the details for a smooth sojourn.

Depending on the location, you may have several choices about where to put your guests up for the night whether it's a villa, a bed-and-breakfast, a hotel, a resort, or other suitable accommodations.

Form 5-2, the Lodging Checklist, which we've also put on the CD-ROM, can help you select a hotel, motel, lodge, or teepee that will make your guests feel comfortable.

Lodging Checklist

❑ Is the facility suitable for your ceremony and/or reception?

❑ If you are selecting a few different places for your guests to stay, are they all convenient to the ceremony and reception sites and other planned activities?

❑ Are group rates available for several rooms? Must you guarantee a certain number of guests to obtain a group rate? Is there a special phone number for your guests to call to reserve their rooms?

❑ How far in advance must rooms be reserved?

❑ Will your guests be given priority for suites and upgrades?

❑ How convenient is the destination to the airport? What kind of transportation is available?

❑ Are there activities or places of interest for your guests?

❑ If you are inviting families, is child care available? Are there activities for children?

❑ Is the venue used to catering to groups? Do the proprietors seem wedding friendly?

❑ Are there perks such as a complimentary bridal suite, changing rooms, hospitality suite, or spa services?

❑ Is there an all-inclusive package option?

❑ Is the venue handicapped accessible?

❑ Is it possible to host a rehearsal dinner or next-day brunch in a separate space at or near the location?

❑ Is there a wedding coordinator on site, or someone who is experienced with weddings? Is there a charge for this service?

❑ If it's a resort, is a wedding-honeymoon package offered?

Form 5-2:
Decide where your guests will lay their weary heads.

Attention Guests: Mark Your Calendars Now!

Pre-invitation missives have become an accepted part of many types of weddings. However, they are particularly important for destination weddings because such events require more than the usual commitment of time and money.

Asking guests to save the date

To ensure that some of your favorite people are not off skiing in St. Moritz, hosting their own nuptials (with the same guest list), or scheduling elective surgery for the week of your wedding, it's a good idea to give them a written heads-up four to six months in advance of the wedding date.

A save-the-date card can be a short and sweet postcard or a chatty letter. Figures 5-1 and 5-2a show two different styles for asking guests to save the date. Figure 5-2b shows what a longer save-the-date letter might look like.

The easiest and least expensive way to create a save-the-date letter is to type it on your computer, and then print it on a good quality laser printer using one of the many beautiful papers available for laser printing. For postcards, you might hand write your note on one and have them photocopied on a quality machine. If you want something more formal, perhaps with a logo that carries through on all the items sent out, see Chapter 4 on printing invitations.

Figure 5-1:
A short-and-sweet save-the-date card.

Please Save the Date
for the wedding of

Molly Fox
and
Joseph Hall

To be held on Saturday, April 6, 2002
On the Island of Jamaica

Please plan on joining us for a wondrous weekend
of Red Stripe, Reggae, and Rejoicing!

Details and Invitations to follow

Dearest friends and family,

Well, it's really happening. We're actually going to make it legal. Of course, you wouldn't expect us, with our odd predilections, to get married here in Chicago, would you? That would be too easy! Sooo:

Please Save The Dates

The weekend of Friday April 5-Sunday April 7
to join us as we formalize our bond, on the island of Jamaica.

We would be truly delighted to have you there!

Further details to follow shortly . . .

With love,

Molly and Joe

Figure 5-2a:
A chattier save-the-date letter.

Although you've given guests fair warning, you still need to send out regular invitations at least six weeks before the wedding. See Chapter 4 for details.

If your wedding weekend has an air of formality, or if various parties each have different hosts (such as the rehearsal dinner or next-day brunch), you may send out individual invitations for each event, as well.

A peek at coming attractions

Your guests need to know as much as you can tell them about your destination in order to facilitate their travel planning. You can include this information along with your save-the-date notice (see the previous section), or you can send it out in a separate mailing. Just be sure to give your guests enough time with the information.

Figure 5-2b:
A save-the-date letter and information package.

Your missive should include the following vital data, if appropriate to your wedding:

✔ Reservations phone number for site(s), general price variables, and how your group is listed.

✔ An overview of the destination including a map (see the sidebar "Mapping the Way" for more information).

✔ Typical weather for that time of year.

✔ A rundown of the festivities, a preliminary schedule of events, general dress codes, and suggestions of things to bring, such as golf clubs or tennis racquets.

✔ Travel agent information or recommendations on booking air travel.

✔ The name of a contact person at the hotel.

✔ Information on transportation to and from the venue.

✔ Travel requirements such as vaccinations, passports, and visas.

✔ Child-care information.

✔ Phone numbers and the names of contacts for services that need to be booked in advance, such as spa treatments, scuba diving, or skiing lessons.

Some resorts and hotels provide pre-printed room reservation cards to be mailed back by your invitees. If yours does, include these with your mailing. Figure 5-3 shows a sample wedding-preview letter that tells guests everything they need to know.

Molly and Joe are getting married!!!

By now you've heard the fantastic news that we are getting married on April 6, 2002, in Jamaica. We are tickled pink that you are planning to join us for our wedding and a weekend of festivities to celebrate.

Why Jamaica?

There were many trips to Jamaica as single souls, where we both fell head over heels in love with this magical island, never knowing that each other existed. And then — one trip together that cemented our relationship and sealed our futures together. It seemed like the only place for us to commit to each other surrounded by our dear friends and family.

Air reservations

Due to the popularity of trips to the islands at this time, we urge you to call early to make your airline reservations. We have contracted with "Fly By Night" travel agents, at 1-800-233-4272 or www.flybynight.com, for a discounted rate for our guests on both Delta and Air Jamaica. If you wish to ask specific questions, please contact Celeste at extension 23 and tell her you are with the Fox-Hall wedding.

Accommodations

We have blocked rooms at a discounted rate at the Island Heaven resort and spa. The rates vary from rooms in the Lodge ($) and the Poolside Cottages ($$) to the Fantasy Suites ($$$$). The rest of your stay is included in your room rate, or as our guests.

Please be certain to say you are a member of the Fox-Hall wedding party when booking. The rooms are reserved for us until February 15, after which they will be released. Please call early so as not to be disappointed (and disappoint us, of course).

Transportation

A shuttle bus from Island Heaven will meet every flight that has our guests arriving on it. There will be representatives from the resort directly outside the customs area, with signage. If you prefer to rent a car, (which we don't recommend as driving is on the "other side" of the road, and the roads aren't exactly state of the art), there is a rental agency at the airport, and our travel agent will reserve one for you in advance. Just ask her when you make your other reservations.

Figure 5-3:
Give your
guests the
pertinent
information.

Activities

There will be a beach barbecue on Friday evening, the Main Event on Saturday at 5 p.m., followed by dinner and dancing under the stars, and a farewell brunch on Sunday at 10 a.m. (for those of you who can tear yourselves away from paradise). We will be going into honeymoon seclusion after that, so be sure to get your fill of us beforehand as we will be definitely incommunicado!

Golfing, tennis, scuba, snorkeling, coladas, daiquiris, rum punch, naps, sun, naps, sun. . . . If you wish to book any spa services, such as a massage or hair styling, it is best to book these early as well. Call the spa directly at 1-800-234-5678.

Weather

The average temperature is a perfect 85 degrees — balmy, not humid. A light sweater or jacket may be necessary at night. The rest of the time, wear plenty of sun block and something to keep it in place.

Dress

With the exception of our wedding ceremony and the celebration that follows on Saturday — which is island-dress-up (you interpret) — all other activities are strictly casual. Penalties for overdressing will be administered.

Babysitting

We are aware that many of you may be bringing your kids and making this a family vacation. They are welcome to all events — WITH THE EXCEPTION of the ceremony and the party following. We have contracted with a bonded child care service that was recommended by our wedding consultant. They can be reached at We Be Kid-Care, 1-800-231-6789.

Questions

If there is anything we haven't covered here please call or e-mail either of us:

Molly: 212-555-9878 or Mfox@baddabing.com
Joe: 212-555-7865 or Jhall@baddabing.com

Watch for more mailings and information as April approaches. (You know we can't help ourselves!)

We are really looking forward to seeing you in Jamaica, mon.

Love,
Molly and Joe

Mapping the way

An accurate and attractive map is a key part of any destination preview package (and often a good idea as an insert with the invitation).

If the directions are simple and you have some artistic ability, you may want to draw a map freehand, complete with cute landmarks and street signs. Or you can take a ready-made map and star favorite sites — "the world's best hot dogs!" — and write a lexicon.

The Web also offers resources for creating maps. A search for *custom invitation maps* on the Web turns up several companies that create customized maps with your wedding date and specified information. A few of these include `sigmamaps.com`, `themapsmith.com`, and `pwi.netcom.~animated/wedding`. Also, many Web sites offer maps of just about any destination, complete with driving directions, that you can print out. Some are zoomable, others include shopping, lodging, and other businesses near your targeted destination. Check out these sites for such maps: MapQuest (`mapquest.com`), Expedia.com (`maps.expedia.com`), Rand McNally (`randmcnally.com`), and Excite (`maps.excite.com`).

Handling the Happenings

Destination weddings often last up to four days — you need more time with these events to fit everything in without exhausting your guests. Usually they run from Thursday (for parents, siblings, and key wedding party members) through Sunday.

As most Jewish ceremonies cannot be performed before sundown on Saturday, a spring or summer "wedding weekend" would most likely run from Saturday to Monday with the pre-nuptial dinner after sundown on Saturday, and the wedding itself on Sunday afternoon or evening. Other circumstances might have a daytime ceremony or a different schedule completely.

Working out the weekend: A typical timeline

Here's a typical breakdown of events (don't forget to include this information in your preview letter; see the previous section):

- **First evening (Thursday):** Bride, groom, and parents, perhaps siblings have dinner. Might be anything from casual at home to elegant restaurant. Early arrival guests are on their own, although it's great if you can have their welcome package in their room when they arrive (see the next section in this chapter for more information).

- **Second day (Friday):** Guests start arriving and checking in. (You might need to meet some people at the airport. Be sure to provide transportation for all guests who won't be met personally by you.) The hospitality suite or gathering area is opened to guests. This is part of the fun of a weekend wedding with 20 or more guests, a gathering place for them to congregate and get to know each other.

✔ **Second evening (Friday):** If people are traveling any distance to attend your wedding, it's hospitable to entertain them while they are there. If you are hosting a wedding-away, you should include everyone at this pre-nuptial event. (See the sidebar "Rehearsal dinner details" in this chapter for more information.) If you are traveling to one of your hometowns, or guests are coming to your area, you are not obligated to entertain guests who live near your destination. Provide transportation to and from the event.

✔ **Third day — Wedding Day (Saturday):** Schedule some optional group activities during the day — a softball game, antiquing, or diving, or just give recommendations of museums or landmarks to see. You could also schedule spa or salon appointments, or get gym passes for guests.

✔ **Third evening — Wedding Night (Saturday):** Tonight's the big shebang! Provide transportation to and from the ceremony, and to and from the reception. Possibly offer a late-night bar or "coffee and" option, depending on timing of reception.

✔ **Fourth day (Sunday):** Brunch, usually hosted by a relative or friend. Very casual. Make sure to provide assistance with transportation to airport. If you are leaving for your honeymoon on Sunday, don't feel obligated to attend the brunch. If you are honeymooning at the resort where your wedding took place, or staying overnight, drop in and say your good-byes at the brunch.

Don't over-plan your wedding weekend. Leave your guests enough downtime to enjoy the place you've chosen so that both you and they can have a vacation.

Putting guests in the right mood

After you've plotted out the days before, during, and after the wedding, you should apprise guests of the flow of events. Prepare an itinerary letter and leave it with the front desk of the hotel to be given to them upon check-in. Better yet, slip it into a welcome package, which we discuss in "Winning Welcomes" later in this chapter. Even if you've sent the information before, send it again — doing so will save you from answering thousands of the same questions. The letter should contain the following tidbits:

✔ A heartfelt welcome, and immediate directions to the hospitality suite.

✔ A day-by-day synopsis of the trip, although don't stress them out with too many must-attend events.

✔ A reminder of when and where exactly the wedding will take place.

✔ Transportation details.

✔ Phone numbers of doctors, babysitters, and other troubleshooters.

Figure 5-4 shows you a typical itinerary letter.

Welcome!

You made it! We are sooooo appreciative that you made the trip, and so excited to have you here with us, that we had to have another Red Stripe just to calm down! So, because we know all of you, and realize you haven't really read anything we've sent you, we're going to go through this weekend step by step. Please read this letter entirely and thoroughly. There will be a quiz!

There is a Hospitality Suite set up for our guests on the second floor terrace (off the elevator to the right), starting Thursday at 4 p.m. In the suite you will find lots of munchies, a stocked fridge, games for the kiddies, and more. Meet and greet the other Fox-Hallers there whenever — it's open 24 hours. (What did you expect from us?)

If it's Thursday when you read this, come say hello to us — PLEASE. We are the ones lying like lumps on the beach with lots of little umbrella drinks around us. (Oh, that doesn't really distinguish us, does it?) Well, you'll recognize us. Anyway, Thursday is free time. Enjoy yourselves — we won't bother you.

Friday evening

Joe's parents, Eunice and Lester, are very graciously hosting: 6 p.m. cocktails by the main pool followed by a barbecue on the beach — VERY CASUAL (we're serious) The kids are welcome!

Late-night gathering (although not for us — we need our beauty sleep). The bar at the far end of the Cottages. Livingston (our world's-most-favorite bartender) will be eagerly awaiting you.

Saturday

Breakfast is served till noon (for those of you who closed the bar with Livingston). Your options for the day are the following.

We have reserved spa services for our guests, our treat — massages, wraps, isolation tanks (just kidding) — from 8 a.m. to 5 p.m. There are approximately 20 appointments available, so book early and don't fight.

Deep sea fishing — our treat. The kids 6 and up will love this. Leaves at 12:30 p.m., returns at 3:30 p.m. Lunch is served on board. Tickets and sign-up are in our hospitality suite. You must sign up by Friday at 8 p.m.

Beach volleyball — men against women (wedding theme), organized by our (very competitive) Maid of Honor, Cheryl, and our (very laid back) Best Man, Russ. Promises to be very interesting. . . . Betting starts at 9:30 a.m., and the games begin at 10 a.m. on the main beach (it's too hot after that).

Figure 5-4:
Apprise
your guests
of the flow
of events
during their
stay.

For those truly energetic folks who can't go anywhere without sightseeing, there is a shuttle into town for the Saturday morning Farmers and Flea market. Just remember that customs is very strict about fruits and vegetables, and so on.

Sun and sand, sun, sand, sand, sun, lunch, swim, sun, sand, sand, sun, swim.

Saturday evening: The Main Event

Well, this is, of course, what we've asked you here for, as witnesses, so the people back home will believe we really did it!

Dress: We have received many queries on this subject. Let's put it this way — nothing is considered inappropriate. Just dress to celebrate with us. We've left the fashion police back in Chicago.

6 p.m.: Guests gather at main lobby.

6:15: Ceremony begins at the Gazebo at the far end of property. If you miss the lobby gathering, take a left at the door facing the ocean and just keep walking.

Approximately 7: We're married!!!!

The celebration: Dinner and Dancing under the Jamaican sky, till???

You don't need directions; you won't be able to miss it.

For the kids: There will be three sitters in the hospitality suite (all bonded), from 5 p.m. on. Dinner will be served there. There will also be a clown, games, and videos. What more could you ask for?

Sunday, 10:30 a.m. to 1:30 p.m.

Molly's mom, Anna, the consummate hostess, is throwing a farewell-gossip-about-the-wedding brunch, on the south terrace. Drop in whenever you can get it together. It's very informal. As check out time is 11:30 a.m., pack and leave your bags at the front desk, and they will get loaded into the shuttle when it's time to depart.

We, as promised, are disappearing . . .

For those of you who are staying, the hospitality suite will remain open until 3 p.m. on Sunday, so please partake.

So, how do we know there are still going to be questions? Well, we know you.

The 411's:

The concierge: Mindy, across from front desk. She is an encyclopedia about the island and can make reservations for any special services. She's also great to chat with.

Our wedding coordinator: The formidable and efficient Thelma Rule. She can tell you about logistics, kid care, and general party info. Reach her onsite at 80, offsite 45-36-7890.

The Maid of Honor: Cheryl (she knew what she was getting into with this job) in room 345.

The Best Man: Russ (he didn't) in room 368.

The Director of Services: Steven Ziadie. Ask to be connected to the front office. He's good for hotel-specific questions and room problems.

That's all for now! We are looking forward to a wonderful weekend together, and, once again, thank you so much for coming. It really means a lot to us.

Love,
Molly and Joe

Rehearsal dinner details

Even if you are holding your rehearsal the day of the wedding (although if you have several people in your wedding party, we strongly suggest that you have your rehearsal before that), you will usually have a pre-nuptial dinner or "rehearsal" dinner.

If you wish to have an intimate (just your wedding party), rehearsal dinner, and you have some out of town guests, you have options:

- ✔ Ask a friend or relative to host a separate party (finances to be decided upon) for your other guests, which could include a barbecue, boat ride and picnic, or cross country ski outing followed by dinner by the fireplace.

- ✔ Have your rehearsal and dinner the day before your guests arrive, or consider having it as a luncheon the day before if your attendants can arrive earlier.

- ✔ Invite everyone for dessert, coffee, and liqueurs at another venue after your dinner and join them.

Rather than print two different letters, enclose an additional note in rooms for your attendants. Depending on how elaborate your ceremony, you might include a ceremony schedule (See Chapter 8 of this book), times of rehearsal, and any other pertinent specifics that don't pertain to the rest of your guests.

Winning Welcomes

A great way to show appreciation for those who have decided they could not miss your wedding, even if it is on the other side of the equator, is a welcome package that says, "We're glad you're here."

This gift can be anything from a beribboned basket to a backpack with your wedding logo on it. The contents don't need to be elaborate or expensive; just try to make them as personal as you can. A creative welcome package could include the following:

- An itinerary of the wedding weekend: when and where as well as transportation details.

- A customized map of the area that pinpoints your personal favorite places. In a city, you might add art galleries, flea markets, shops, and restaurants. At a resort, you might highlight snorkeling spots or the best bartender. (See the sidebar "Mapping the way" in this chapter for tips on creating maps.)

- A snack and beverage. Try to find things that are truly indigenous and hard to get elsewhere. For example, in New York City, you could include Zabar's bagel chips, New York State apple cider, and a Metro card. In the Caribbean, the brand of rum the island is noted for (Cocksbur in Barbados, for example) and tropical fruits. In Italy, a local red wine and artisan-made cheese. Include something different for the kids, such as candy or giant cookies.

- Inexpensive, kitschy souvenirs such as postcards, key chains, or magnets.

- Some printed information on the destination, salient or humorous factoids, ("Did you know the Ferris Wheel was invented in Pittsburgh?"), or a good travel-guide book.

- Where and when to find the hospitality suite.

Who pays for what?

Unfortunately, we can't give you any firm rules here. Everything is dependent on the size of the wedding and the couple's (and their invitees') finances. But here's what seems to be generally accepted for a destination wedding: Guests pay for their airfare and hotel rooms; the couple or their parents (usually the groom's parents) host the rehearsal dinner, or a friend pays for the meals listed above, and another goody such as a massage or gym pass or a sightseeing tour.

Hosts are also responsible for transportation to and from the ceremony and reception, and usually transportation from the airport. All other expenses, such as other transportation, other meals, or room service are the guest's responsibility. For wedding attendants, often the couple will pick up their entire tab, or at least the hotel bill (minus extras), and beauty services for the women for the wedding.

While we're at it, we might as well give you a few travel tips:

- ✔ Pack your honeymoon clothing and accoutrements separately from your wedding weekend outfits. That way, you will feel like you are getting a fresh start on your honeymoon.

- ✔ Arrange for someone to take your wedding clothing back home and drop it off at the cleaners or rental place. Ditto the guest book and other mementos. (For info on getting your gown there in the first place see Chapter 19 of *Weddings For Dummies*.)

- ✔ Use ATM machines for your travels rather than exchanging money at the hotels or using traveler's checks. The exchange rate is much better this way.

- ✔ For a list of some helpful items to throw in your suitcase see *WFD* Chapter 19.

Forms and Links on the CD-ROM

Form 5-1	Destination Location Checklist	Research the perfect destination for your wedding.
Form 5-2	Lodging Worksheet	Decide where your guests will lay their weary heads.
Link	Thehoneymoonspecialist.com	www.thehoneymoonspecialist.com
Link	Modernbride.com	www.modernbride.com

Link	Bestfares.com	www.bestfares.com
Link	Tncweddings.com	www.tncweddings.com
Link	Weddinglocation.com	www.weddinglocation.com
Link	weddingtrips.com	www.weddingtrips.com
Link	Worldbridal.com	www.worldbridal.com
Link	Heartofeurope.com	heartofeurope.com/legal.html

Part III
Ceremony Survival Plan

The 5th Wave   By Rich Tennant

"It's nice that you picked a professional radio DJ for the reception music, but I wish he'd quit announcing the weather and sports scores between every third song."

In this part . . .

Here's the part of the book that's guaranteed to take the knock out of your knees during the ceremony. After reading this section, which we pack full of information about planning your ceremony — from writing your vows to creating a program and a wedding-day schedule — you'll be prepared to take care of every detail of your ceremony.

Chapter 6

Sensational Ceremonies:
All Together, Vow!

Many books and Web sites treat the content of ceremonies in depth; rather than provide "chapter and verse" for vows and readings, our intent in this chapter is to help you visualize the kind of wedding you want and to steer you in the right direction for creating that ceremony. Music, of course, is a key component, and we explore that fully in Chapter 7. (We also cover the broad strokes of major religious ceremonies, as well as rehearsal logistics, in Chapter 5 of *Weddings For Dummies*.)

In addition to formulating the ceremony script, we also go over the other components — choosing the ceremony site and the person who's going to pronounce you husband and wife, choreographing the processional, and seeing to last-minute details.

Choosing a Venue and an Officiant

The first step is to find the right location and the right person to marry you. If you belong to a particular church or synagogue, proceed directly to booking a date and following whatever protocol the institution has for marriage preparation.

If you need to look around for a location and officiant, Form 6-1, the Ceremony Site and Officiant Worksheet, which you also find on the CD-ROM, helps you evaluate both officiants and ceremony sites.

Ceremony Site and Officiant Checklist

❑ If you're interested in a particular house of worship, do you have to join the congregation and use their officiant? Or is it B.Y.O.O. — bring your own officiant?

❑ Are video cameras and flash photography allowed on site?

❑ What are the lighting conditions? Can you set up special lights or have candles on the premises?

❑ Is the sound adequate or will you need to supply a sound system?

❑ What floral arrangements or other decorations are available or allowed? When can the florist get in to set up?

❑ What is the parking situation? How many spaces can be reserved for your wedding party?

❑ Can you have the reception at the same venue? If not, how far is the site from your reception venue?

❑ Would the officiant perform the ceremony in a venue other than a house of worship, if that's your preference?

❑ What marital preparation programs are required?

❑ How many times can or must you meet with the officiant?

❑ Do you have a good rapport or connection with the officiant? Does he or she seem interested in you personally? How long is the extended interview with you? How much does the officiant want you to divulge about yourself?

❑ Would it be permitted to have a ceremony in the round? Or with the bride and groom facing their guests?

❑ Are there certain traditions such as who escorts the bride down the aisle that must be adhered to?

❑ Does the officiant have a set script? Are you allowed to edit it or create your own script and vows?

❑ Will the officiant be present at the rehearsal? Is there an extra fee for this?

❑ How long will the ceremony take?

❑ Will the venue have other weddings that day? If so, at what time?

❑ Will the officiant have any other weddings that day? If so, at what time?

❑ What are the rules and recommendations regarding music for the ceremony?

❑ Are there any rules or restrictions regarding dress at the site?

❑ Are there any restrictions against throwing rice, birdseed, or flower petals?

❑ What is the officiant's fee and when do you pay it? Do you pay the officiant directly or make a donation to a house of worship?

❑ Is the officiant legally certified to marry you in the state or country where the wedding is taking place?

❑ Can you speak to other couples the officiant has married?

❑ Can you attend another ceremony where the officiant is presiding?

❑ May you sign the marriage certificate before the ceremony for convenience?

Form 6-1:
Locate
the right
officiant
and venue
for you.

What to Do to Say "I Do"

Creating your ceremony can be broken down into three steps:

1. **Consider the tone, religious nature, or other statement you wish to express.**

2. **Decide the "order of worship" — that is, the sequence of the service, which we explain later in this chapter.**

3. **Choose or create the content, including words, music, prayers, and readings.**

Chances are that you've chosen to marry someone who shares your values and with whom you're simpatico on matters of religion. If not, you may need to spend considerable time on Step 1, hashing out the major themes of your wedding ceremony. You both need to feel comfortable with the type of ceremony you choose and the level of compromise it takes to reach that decision. After those issues are figured out, you can get on with the fun part — choosing how the ceremony will proceed and what will be said.

Deciding the sequence of the service

The order of events in a ceremony determines its spirit and flow. At different points you may have music for drama or scriptural readings for contemplation. You want to keep things moving apace without rushing, and you want each moment to reflect both the seriousness and joy of the occasion.

You may opt to follow the ceremony order verbatim as prescribed by your house of worship. However, if you're crafting your own script or having an interfaith wedding, you may want to ad lib or edit the steps.

Most ceremonies incorporate some or all of the following elements:

✔ **Opening words:** Or what David Glusker and Peter Misner call "gathering words" in their excellent book, *Words For Your Wedding* (HarperCollins). These are usually spoken by the officiant to welcome the participants, introduce the couple, and state the purpose of the gathering. These words set the tone of the ceremony and are formal, yet cordial.

✔ **Opening prayers:** Also known as the invocation, these words further establish the tone and religious nature of the rites to follow.

✔ **Charge to the couple:** A reminder to the couple that they are taking a solemn vow before God.

✔ **Declaration of consent:** These are the words spoken before the vows are taken, and they ensure that the bride and groom are entering freely into the marriage contract.

✔ **Presentation of the bride:** The ritual of the father "giving" the bride to her betrothed. Because many people now object to the image of the bride being treated as property, the rite is sometimes modified to express support and affirmation of the union by family and friends.

✔ **Bible readings:** Scripture lessons are a significant part of the Judeo-Christian tradition. In Christian ceremonies, there are typically three readings, one of the Old Testament, Epistle, and Gospel.

✔ **Exchange of vows:** The most crucial part of the ceremony, these words express the covenant between two people.

✔ **Blessing and presentation of rings:** The ring is a physical reminder of the commitment between the bride and groom, and there are usually special words chosen to express this sentiment.

✔ **Pronouncement or declaration:** The climax of the ceremony — the moment when the officiant announces that the couple is now officially married.

✔ **Wedding prayers:** After the couple exchanges vows, they ask for God's blessing in celebrating their marriage.

✔ **Affirmation of the community:** In Christian ceremonies, this part of the script affords the guests a chance to affirm that they will help the couple uphold their vows. In a Jewish ceremony, this takes the form of the guests shouting "Mazel tov!" after the couple stamps on the wineglass.

In the following sections, we outline the sequence of basic ceremonies for a few major religions in the United States.

Protestant ceremony sequence

Most Protestant ceremonies are based on the *Book of Common Prayer*. The traditional Protestant ceremony can be completed in about 15 minutes, although it usually takes longer depending on the readings and musical selections. The vows may vary depending on the sect. The basics of the ceremony are as follows:

✔ Music and Processional

✔ Welcome or Opening Statement

✔ Charge to the Couple

✔ Questions of Willingness/Statements of Intentions

✔ Presentation of the Bride

✔ Exchange of Vows

✔ Blessing and Presentation of Ring or Rings

✔ Declaration of Marriage

✔ Wedding Prayer

- The Lord's Prayer
- Benediction
- Recessional

A few denominations have enriched the service with other steps. The United Church of Christ, for example, includes a scripture lesson and sermon after the presentation of the bride. The United Methodist Church includes a Thanksgiving portion of the ceremony in which the couple offers a special prayer (in addition to the Lord's Prayer), and they have the option of taking Holy Communion or an Agape Meal.

Episcopal ceremony sequence

Weddings in the Episcopal Church usually follow this order:

- Entrance
- Address to the Congregation
- Charge to the Couple
- Declaration of Consent
- Affirmation of the Community
- Hymn, Psalm, or Anthem
- Ministry of the Word
    - Opening Prayer
    - Holy Scripture
    - Homily or Other Response
- The Marriage
    - Exchange of Vows
    - Blessing and Presentation of Ring or Rings
    - Pronouncement
- The Prayers
    - The Lord's Prayer
    - Intercessory Prayers
- The Blessing of the Marriage
    - Prayer of Thanksgiving
    - Benediction
    - The Peace

- Holy Communion (Optional)
- Recession or Hymn

Roman Catholic ceremony sequence

If you're Roman Catholic, you must get married in the Church, and your parish probably requires you to participate in a pre-Cana program and other steps. You must also decide whether or not to celebrate your ceremony within the context of Nuptial Mass.

The Roman Catholic Church publishes ample material on the marriage ceremony, so we won't attempt to duplicate it here, except to give the basic format for the rite of marriage during mass:

✔ Entrance (Procession)

✔ Entrance Rite or Penitential Rite

✔ Liturgy of the Word

✔ Old Testament

✔ Responsorial Psalm

✔ Epistle

✔ Gospel

✔ Homily (Sermon)

✔ Rite of Marriage

- Statement of Purpose
- Questions of Willingness and Consent
- Exchange of Vows
- Blessing and Exchange of Rings

✔ Liturgy of the Eucharist

- The Lord's Prayer
- Nuptial Blessing
- Blessing at the End of Mass

✔ Breaking of the Bread

✔ Communion

✔ Prayer After Communion

✔ Final Prayer and Blessing

✔ Dismissal

✔ Recessional

In the Liturgy of the Eucharist, the order of the mass is followed with modifications suited to the wedding rite.

Jewish ceremony sequence

These are the elements that may be included in a Jewish ceremony:

- Processional
- Circling the Groom, or The Bride and Groom Circling Each other three to seven times
- Opening Scriptural Sentences
- A Prayer Invoking God's Presence
- An Address by the Rabbi
- Blessing of the First Cup of Wine
- The Statement of the Marriage Covenant
- The Seven Benedictions
- The Blessing (Shevah Berachot) and Sharing of Wine
- The Ring Ceremony
- The Wedding Declaration or Pronouncement (the rabbi reads the *ketubah* or marriage contract)
- Silent Prayer
- The Seven Benedictions Over the Second Cup of Wine
- Drinking from the Second Cup of Wine
- The Breaking of the Glass
- Recessional
- Yichud

Word for word: Scripting your vows

When it comes to your wedding vows, there's a lot to be said for the power of history. Many religious services are thousands of years old. Reciting the words that have bound together countless generations before you can give you a feeling of strength and connectivity. You might feel that altering those words will diminish their meaning or insult your forebears. If so, stick with your religious protocol and you'll be happy.

However, it is increasingly popular for couples to personalize standard ceremony rituals, cobble together elements from various religious, ethnic, and cultural traditions, and not only write their vows but also script the entire ceremony.

If you've ever been to a wedding where the officiant digressed onto some weird, inappropriate tangent or didn't seem to know the couple's names, you might see the wisdom of taking matters into your own hands. But loose-cannon officiants aren't the only reason behind the trend. Times have changed, and people are getting married under different circumstances — second marriages are commonplace, couples often live together beforehand, women are breadwinners in their own right, and people have a wide range of experience that affects their views of religion, marriage, and themselves. Many couples feel that their wedding should reflect their personal vision and commitment as much as it reflects their contract with the community.

Before you get too creative, keep in mind that while it's fine to acknowledge the folly of life or the human comedy, this is still a solemn moment. Having the officiant say, "Congratulations, dude — you may now play tonsil hockey with the bride" is too flip.

When in doubt, crib from the standard vows uttered by countless couples through the ages:

- ✔ *The Book of Common Prayer:* I, [name] take thee, [name] to be my wedded [husband/wife], to have and to hold from this day forward, for better, for worse, for richer, for poorer, in sickness and in health, to love and to cherish, till death do us part, according to God's holy ordinance; and thereto I plight thee my faith.

- ✔ **Roman Catholic:** I, [name], take you, [name], to be my [husband/wife]. I promise to be true to you in good times and in bad, in sickness and in health. I will love you and honor you all the days of my life.

- ✔ **Civil:** I, [name], take you, [name], to be my lawfully wedded [husband/wife]. Before these witnesses, I promise to love you and care for you as long as we both shall live. I accept you with your faults and strengths, even as I offer myself to you with my faults and strengths. I will support you when you need support, and turn to you when I need support. I choose you as the person with whom I will spend my life.

- ✔ **Muslim:** I pledge, in honesty and sincerity, to be for you an obedient and faithful [husband/wife].

Technically, there are no wedding vows in Jewish wedding liturgy. However, in deference to the American tradition of saying "I do," many rabbis have added commitment vows after the ring ceremony.

For contemporary vows, there are as many variations on the theme as there are married couples. The language ranges from the prosaic to the mystical.

You can find many sources for vows in a number of books and Internet sites devoted to the subject. Here are a few examples to get your inspirational juices flowing:

- Our miracle lies in the path we have chosen together. I, [name], enter into this marriage with our knowing that the true magic of love is not to avoid changes, but to navigate them successfully. Let us commit to the miracle of making each day work, together.

- I, [name], covenant with you to be your (husband/wife). I offer you my love and my support throughout our lives. I commit myself to years of growth and sharing as I encourage you to move in new directions. I will strive to achieve my potential as God's creature and will celebrate your progress toward the same goal. I give myself as I am and as I will be, and I do so for all of our lives.

- Respecting each other, we commit to live our lives together for all the days to come. I, [name], ask you to share this world with me, for good and ill. Be my partner, and I will be yours.

- Today we move from "I" to "we." [Name], take this ring as a symbol of my decision to join my life with yours until death should part us. I walked to this place to meet you today; we shall walk from it together.

- Today, I, [name], join my life to yours, not merely as your (husband/wife), but as your friend, your lover, and your confidant. Let me be the shoulder you lean on, the rock on which you rest, the companion of your life. With you I will walk my path from this day forward.

- I, [name], came here today to join my life to yours before this company. In their presence I pledge to be true to you, to respect you, and to grow with you through the years. Time may pass, fortune may smile, trials may come. No matter what we may encounter together, I vow here that this love will be my only love. I will make my home in your heart from this day forward.

Ideas for readings

As you script your ceremony, you may want to incorporate poems, scriptures, lyrics, quotations, or other readings that are personally meaningful. We could overfill hundreds of tomes and CDs if we were to reprint actual possibilities here. Instead, let us give you some general directions to explore:

- **Scriptural:** Genesis, Song of Solomon, The Talmud; 1 Corinthians; Romans; John; Matthew; Ephesians; Psalms; Confucius; I Ching.

- **Literature:** *The Little Prince* by Antoine de Saint-Exupéry; *The Velveteen Rabbit* by Margery Williams; Kahlil Gibran; *Soul Mates* by Thomas Moore; *The Art of Loving* by Erich Fromm.

✔ **Poetry:** Elizabeth Barrett Browning; Shakespeare; Shelley; Marge Piercy; Walt Whitman; Carl Sandburg; e e cummings; T.S.Eliot, John Donne.

Other personal touches

Besides music, which we cover in Chapter 7, you may want to include a few other flourishes such as:

✔ Light a unity candle symbolizing that you have become as one and your families have been united. This ritual actually involves three candles — the bride's parents light one, the groom's parents light the other, and the bride and groom light the center taper from the light of those two.

✔ Incorporate the Rose Ceremony, which is an increasingly popular addendum where the bride and groom give a rose to their parents.

✔ Have church bells peal immediately after you say your vows.

✔ Release butterflies, birds, or bubbles as you walk up the aisle or down the church steps.

✔ Have your dog walk down the aisle, perhaps serving as ring bearer if the pet is extremely well trained.

Depending on your religion or the style of ceremony, you may need to purchase specific props and decorations, such as flowers, pew bows, chalices, kneeling pillows, ring pillows, prayer books, and so on. Be sure to include these expenses in your budget, as we explain in Chapter 2.

Who Walks with Whom

Choreographing your ceremony is largely a matter of lining up the wedding party in the right order and sending them down the aisle at the right moment. That moment is usually signaled by a musical movement, or when the previous party reaches a certain point, such as the second row.

It's not a bad idea to have your wedding consultant or other astute volunteer cue each person to begin walking; sometimes it's difficult for someone at the back of the church or off to the side to see or hear what's going on.

For a Christian or secular ceremony

For a Christian ceremony, and most secular ceremonies, the priest or minister usually arrives at the altar from a side entrance, followed by the groom and best man, who take their places next to the officiant.

Before the processional begins, the VIPs are seated, the last being the mother of the bride, who is seated on the aisle in the front row. Then the officiant comes out, followed by the groom. Sometimes ushers and bridesmaids are paired together; other times they walk down the aisle singly. After everyone is in place around the altar, they turn and gaze expectantly up the aisle to greet the bride, who, after a dramatic pause, begins her stroll. They then turn and face inward toward the bride and groom.

To make sure that everyone knows when they're supposed to commence walking, fill out Form 6-2, the Processional Worksheet for a Christian Ceremony (also on the CD-ROM) and give all the wedding party members a copy. Indicate in the third column whether each person should walk in singly or coupled with another member of the wedding party. Also, if they're to walk in a different order than is listed in Form 6-2, you can edit the worksheet in Microsoft Word. The couples should "match" in the correct pairing on the way out when they leave.

Processional Worksheet for a Christian Ceremony

Wedding Party Member	Name	Walks With...	Musical or Visual Cue
Ushers			
Bridesmaids			
Flower girl			
Ring bearer			
Maid of honor			
Bride and her father (or both parents)			

Form 6-2: How to cue your wedding party for a Christian ceremony.

The recessional for a Christian or civil ceremony is usually the opposite of the processional. Once the bride and groom make their getaway up the aisle, everyone follows in the opposite order that they came in, starting with the maid of honor and best man, and followed by coupled attendants, the bride's parents, and then the groom's parents.

For a Jewish ceremony

In a traditional Jewish ceremony, the rabbi and/or cantor are the first to walk down the aisle and take their places under the chuppah. The grandparents begin the processional and take their seats in the first rows. The right side is the bride's; the left the groom's.

Form 6-3, the Processional Worksheet for a Jewish Ceremony, should help with the pacing of the participants. You also find Form 6-3 on the CD-ROM.

Processional Worksheet for a Christian Ceremony

Wedding Party Member	Name	Walks With...	Musical or Visual Cue
Bride's grandparents			
Groom's grandparents			
Ushers			
Best man			
Groom and his parents			
Bridesmaids			
Maid of honor			
Bride and her parents			

Form 6-3: How to cue the wedding party in a Jewish ceremony.

For a Jewish recessional, the bride and groom go back up the aisle, followed by the parents, rabbi, grandparents, and then coupled attendants.

Getting with the Program

A wedding program serves many purposes — as a lovely memento of the day, a way to honor the participants, and a "playbook" that guides everyone through the steps of the ceremony.

Some houses of worship create programs for couples getting married, or you can design your own. Programs can be simple or elaborate, photocopied on plain paper or engraved on card stock, calligraphed or typeset, unadorned or embellished with artwork, ribbons, and color. And they may contain many (or all) of the following elements:

- Date, time, and place of the wedding
- Family crest or a special logo or artwork designed for the occasion
- Names of the bride and groom
- Names of the attendants and their relationships to the bride and groom
- Name(s) of the officiant(s)
- Names of the soloists, musicians, and the pieces performed
- Parents' names
- The order of service
- Words to the readings, songs, prayers, and blessings — with sources
- Foreign language translations
- Explanations of religious or ethnic rituals, customs, or military traditions
- Thank-yous to parents
- Tributes to deceased parents, relatives, or friends
- Reception site information

Figure 6-1 shows you a typical example of how a program can be put together for a Protestant ceremony. Figure 6-2 gives you a structure you can build off of for planning a program for a reform Jewish wedding ceremony.

Sample Program for a Protestant Wedding

The Marriage

of

Harriet Henshow and Randolph Roosterhaus

Sacred Sea Foam Chapel

Crashing Rocks Bay

Saturday, July 19, 2003

Figure 6-1:
An example
of a simple
program for
a Protestant
wedding.

~ Officiating ~

The Rev. Philip Phetherfrend

The Wedding Party

Matron of Honor	Claudia Cuckold
Bridesmaids	Phyllis Flatface Jessica Jacquelope Val Liam
Best Man	Peter Porcini
Groomsmen	Stanley Snout August Antspantz Kevin Kibbutz
Readings	Charlotte Webb Ima Biggsow
Organist	Wallace Tuttle

Order of Service

Prelude
       Cannon in D   Johann Pachelbel
       Air (Orchestral Suite No. III in D Major, S. 1068)   Johann Sebastian Bach

Processional
       Trumpet Voluntary   Jeremiah Clarke
       Grand Triumphal Chorus   Alexandre Guilmant

Call to Worship

Prayer

Presentation of the Bride

Parzival   Wolfram Von Eschenbach

Scripture Reading   Romans 12:1-2, 9-18

Meditation

The Marriage Vows

Exchange of the Rings

Sonnet 116   William Shakespeare

Pastoral Prayer & The Lord's Prayer

Declaration of Marriage

Apache Wedding Poem

Benediction

Recessional
       Wedding March   Felix Mendelssohn
       (From A Midsummer Night's Dream)

Sample Program for a Reform Jewish Wedding

Wedding of

Bebe Rebecca Kerfuffleberg

and

Isaac Ezra Blandstein

Saturday
October 30, 2001

Temple Israel
Sea Mist, Florida

Figure 6-2:
A sample
program for
a reform
Jewish
wedding.

Both of us are very happy we are able to spend this special day surrounded by so many of our family and friends. We have decided to include many beautiful traditions in our wedding ceremony. It is our hope that this brief explanation, which we incorporated partly from a booklet written by Rabbi Katzenberg, will help all of our guests to fully understand and participate in our celebration.

~ Bebe and Isaac

The Wedding Processional

Rabbi Philip Katzenberg

Cantor Mark Tonalman

Sally Kerfuffleberg	Bebe's grandmother
Adam Kerfuffleberg	Bebe's cousin
Betty Greenberg	Isaac's grandmother
Samuel Greenberg	Isaac's grandfather

Bridesmaids and Ushers

Elaine Kerfuffleberg	Bebe's cousin
Jonathan Schwartz	Isaac's high school friend
Sarah Levine	Bebe's friend from college
Andrew Silverstein	Isaac's friend from college
Tess Hyams	Bebe's cousin
Abraham Silk	Isaac's cousin

Best Man

Michael Blandstein	Isaac's brother

Isaac will walk to the Chupa with his parents, Mark and Tammy.

Matron of Honor

Mimi Kerfuffleberg	Bebe's sister

Bebe will walk to the Chupa with her parents, Theodore and Roberta.

Wedding Ceremony

A Jewish wedding is not merely between two individuals, or their family and circle of friends; it is a cause of celebration for the entire Jewish people. A wedding is not just about two people finding happiness; it's more about the potential of this couple to make the world a better place by the virtue of being together as one.

The upcoming marriage of Bebe and Isaac was at an Aufruf at a Shabbat service at Temple Israel on September 15, 2001. Bebe and Isaac were called to the bimah and given honors before the Torah.

Prior to the ceremony, the civil marriage license was witnessed and signed by James Kerfuffleberg (Bebe's brother) and Harry Blandstein (Isaac's uncle). The Ketubah (Jewish marriage document) was witnessed and signed by Fred Solomon (Bebe's uncle) and Kirk Blandstein (Isaac's cousin). The Ketubah was a revolutionary concept, protecting the bride's right and obligating the husband to look out for her welfare.

The wedding takes place under the Chupa, symbolic of the home Bebe and Isaac will build together. The Chupa has no walls; the marriage begins with just a roof, and Bebe and Isaac will build the walls with love and friendship. The Chupa is open on all sides so that family and friends will always feel welcome.

A blessing of birkat erusin, or betrothal, is recited over the wine, followed by another in praise of God, who brought Bebe and Isaac together. Bebe and Isaac drink from the same cup of wine to represent the life that they will share from this day forth.

Next comes the giving and accepting of rings. Jewish custom requires that wedding bands be made of a single piece metal with no adornments breaking the circle, representing the wholeness achieved through marriage and the hope for an unbroken union. Bebe is using the wedding band of her great-great grandmother when she was married 96 years ago. Isaac will place the ring on Bebe's right index finger and recite the formula of betrothal: "Behold you are betrothed to me with this ring according to the laws of Moses and Israel." Bebe will then present Isaac with a ring and recite, "I am my beloved's, and my beloved is mine."

The Ketubah is then read and presented to Bebe. After the chanting of the seven marriage blessings — sheva b'rachot — the couple drinks from a second cup of wine.

At the conclusion of the ceremony, Isaac will step on and break a glass. This ancient practice has many interpretations. One of the most traditional is that it reminds us of the destruction of the holy temple in Jerusalem and the many losses that have been suffered by the Jewish people. Another explanation is that love, like glass, is very fragile and must be protected because, once broken, it is hard to put back together again. (A special thanks to artist Linda Fishbein for the beautiful colored glass used in the ceremony, which will be made into a mezuza.)

Yichud (seclusion): Immediately following the ceremony, Bebe and Isaac will leave the Chupa and spend their first few minutes as husband and wife alone together in a private place.

Dear Family and Friends,

We are thrilled and thankful that all of you are able to be here with us today. We are lucky to have such wonderful family and friends. Thank you for being such a special part of our lives.

Dear Parents,

Thank you for your love and never-ending support throughout our lives. We love and appreciate all of you very much.

Dear Siblings,

Thank you for all of your love and guidance through the years. We realize that we are fortunate to have all of you not only as family but also as our best friends.

Dear Bridal Party,

You represent a very special part of our lives. Thank you all for being such good friends through the years and for being a part of this special day.

At this time, we lovingly remember our grandparents, Jerome Keffuffleberg and Babe Blandstein.

Accomplishing a Snag-Free Ceremony

After the ceremony rehearsal, review Form 6-4, the Last-Minute Ceremony Checklist, to make sure that last-minute details have been attended to. A version of Form 6-4 appears on the CD-ROM so that you can subtract, add, or amend any of the items on this checklist.

Last-Minute Ceremony Checklist

❑ Does everyone have the transportation schedule?

❑ Who has the rings?

❑ Have you switched your engagement ring to your right hand?

❑ Are the programs at the church?

❑ Does everyone have his or her bouquet, corsage, or boutonnière?

❑ If you're having a Jewish ceremony, is the wine, kiddish cup, and glass to be broken set up?

❑ It you're having a Christian ceremony, are the unity candle, chalices, and prayer books in place?

❑ Is the aisle runner in place?

❑ Who has the marriage license?

❑ Does the officiant have your script?

❑ Is the lighting set up?

❑ Are the special mikes, speakers, or other sound equipment set up?

Form 6-4: Conquer all last-minute details.

Forms on the CD-ROM

Chapter 7

Cue the Music: Ceremonial High Notes

. . . .

In This Chapter

▶ Setting your ceremony's musical tone

▶ Deciding who plays what and when

▶ Choosing musicians who hit the right notes

. . . .

The music at a wedding sets the tone for the entire event. From the moment guests start arriving, the air is filled with a sense of joy and anticipation — complemented by a mix of moderate-tempo melodies. As the music shifts to a slower, more-contemplative tempo, signaling the wedding party's processional, the excitement builds. Then there's a momentary interlude of silence followed by a dramatic burst of music — and the bride appears. She walks with a sense of purpose and exhilaration, as if guided by every note of music. Everyone sits (or stands) up and takes notice. A few burst into tears.

As the ceremony unfolds, a carefully chosen song or two may be played, conveying the couple's sentiments or celebrating their religious beliefs. Then the ceremony is over, and the newlyweds march up the aisle to a triumphant musical number. Upbeat music buoys the rest of the wedding party and the guests along and puts them in the mood to celebrate further at the reception.

The musical pieces you choose and the way they're played are highly personal decisions, and ones you should consider carefully. We provide suggestions for various types of ceremonies and guidelines for creating your own musical menu.

They're Playing Our Song

Certain songs, such as Mendelssohn's *Wedding March* and Wagner's *Bridal Chorus from Lohengrin* ("Here Comes the Bride"), have become wedding clichés. But that doesn't mean you should be afraid to use such chestnuts. The key is to have them played by musicians who know how to make the music sound as if the pieces are perfect for *your* wedding. But first, you need to peruse your musical options and decide how to incorporate them into your service so that they convey the moods you have in mind.

Use the Internet to get a sense of possible music for your ceremony. Sites such as cdnow.com allow you to download songs using MP3 technology. However, at this writing, the technology is still slow and complicated, and the selections are extremely limited. On the CD-ROM you can also find a free version of Music Match Jukebox 5.0, a program that allows you to "rip" (record) your own CD of songs.

We also suggest that you buy a few CDs or tapes to listen to in order to choose your ceremony music. Two popular ones usually found in the classical music section of record shops are: *The Wedding Album* on RCA and *Music for Weddings*, EMI Records, LTD

Music in five parts

In general, you need to choose music for five parts of the ceremony:

- ✔ **Prelude:** Played for 15 minutes to a half an hour before the ceremony, this music sets the mood for your event. Keep that in mind when you make your selections — whether you prefer a festive, elegant, or religious spirit.

- ✔ **Procession:** This music sets the pace for attendants walking down the aisle. The music should be loud enough for them to keep time to (in a natural fashion), yet not as loud as the music for the bride. For drama, the musicians may play a fanfare as the bride enters and then switch to a more nuanced piece. Or they may stick with one piece and play a little louder (forte!) as the bride appears.

- ✔ **Ceremony:** Couples may designate music to be played or a choir or soloist to sing at a point in the ceremony, perhaps before a reading or during the lighting of a unity candle.

- **Recession:** At the end of the ceremony, this music should be powerful and joyous. In any case, it's usually louder and quicker than the processional music.

- **Postlude:** A continuation of music, upbeat and celebratory, that keeps the guests feeling they're a part of the wedding until they leave the ceremony space.

A soloist, a choir, or something in between?

Planning the music for your ceremony is a mix and match process. You choose the musical pieces, the times they are played, and the artist(s) to perform them. While some scenarios won't work (a solo guitarist performing Clarke's *Trumpet Voluntary* just doesn't cut it), many musical works can be scored for a variety of ensembles.

When selecting which pieces to play, think about the number of musicians you can afford to hire and the equipment they'll need. The following are possible musical configurations:

- **A capella group:** Generally three or four vocalists who sing without instrumental accompaniment. Can be very upbeat and fun.

- **Soloist:** One singer with either instrumental accompaniment or a capella.

- **Choir:** At least six singers with instrumental accompaniment.

- **Piano:** Either solo or as part of an ensemble, this instrument can be an electric keyboard, a baby grand, or an upright.

- **Organ:** This instrument is an integral part of the ceremony at many churches and temples. Some very grand ones sound like a full orchestra.

- **Classical ensembles:** An almost infinite range of possibilities using various instruments (see Table 7-1).

- **Small orchestras:** Six or more pieces, such as a double string quartet or a string quartet, organ, and flute.

- **Jazz ensemble:** A trio or quartet consisting of guitar(s), bass, and drums.

- **Recorded music:** A tape or CD played on a sound system.

Classical ensembles are the most popular for weddings because of their versatility. If you want to save money, ask if some band members from the reception can play for the ceremony for an additional hourly fee.

Classical ensembles come in a variety of configurations. Table 7-1 shows some of the possibilities.

Table 7-1	Classical Ensemble Configurations
Type	**Instruments**
Duos	Flute and violin; violin and cello; two violins; harp and flute; flute and guitar
Trios	Harp, flute, and cello; violin, flute, and keyboard; two violins and a flute
String quartets	Four violins; two violins and two violas; two violins, one viola, and one cello
Woodwind quartet	Flute, clarinet, oboe, and bassoon
Brass quartet	Two trumpets, trombone, and French horn or tuba
Quintets	String quartet and piano; string quartet and harp

Composing musical menus a la carte

Depending on the type of ceremony you have, different kinds of music may be suitable at various times.

In the following sections, we provide you with some sample musical menus for different types of religious ceremonies.

Protestant

Table 7-2 shows a possible classic line up of music using the church organ and a string quartet for a ceremony in a Protestant church.

Table 7-2	Examples of Musical Selections for a Protestant Ceremony
Action	**Music**
Prelude	Quartet: *Concerto for Violin in G Minor, OP. 8* (Vivaldi); *Water Music* (Handel); *Concerto for Violin in E Major, OP.8/No. 1 "Primavera"* (Vivaldi); *Brandenburg Concerto* (Bach); *Rondeau* (Mouret)
Mothers being seated	Quartet: *Jesu, Joy of Man's Desiring* (Bach)
Groom, best man, and officiant take their places	Quartet continue with *Jesu*

Action	Music
Music stops once groom, best man, and officiant are situated then begins again	Organ and quartet: *Trumpet Voluntary*, Jeremiah Clarke
Ushers, bridesmaids, flower girl, ring bearer, and maid of honor process	Continue with *Trumpet Voluntary*
Doors open	Organ fanfare
Bride and her father process	Organ: *Bridal Chorus, Lohengrin* (Wagner)
Ceremony	No music
Recessional	Quartet and organ: *Wedding March* (Mendelssohn)
Postlude until guests have left church	Quartet: *New World Symphony* (Dvorak); *Canon in D* (Pachelbel); *La Rejouissance,* from Music for the Royal Fireworks (Handel)
Outside church as bridal party exits and guests exit (approximately 20 minutes)	Two bagpipers: Scottish folk music

Catholic

Table 7-3 shows a program planned for a church organ and a soloist.

Table 7-3	Examples of Musical Selections for a Catholic Ceremony
Action	**Music**
Prelude	Organ: *Jesu, Joy of Man's Desiring* (Bach); *Ode to Joy* (Beethoven)
Bride's mother and groom's parents are seated; groom, best man, and priest take their places at the altar	Organ: *Preludes and Fugues for Organ* (Bach, Johann Sebastian)
Processional begins; ushers process; bridesmaids process	Organ: *The Prince of Denmark's March* (Clarke)

(continued)

Table 7-3 *(continued)*

Action	*Music*
Bride and her father process	Continue with *The Prince;* music gets louder
Communion	Congregation with organist: *The Lord's Prayer.* Organist: *Lord of All Hopefulness* (Struther); *Panis Angelicus* (Franck)
Lighting of the unity candle	Organist: *When Thou Art Near (Bist Du Bei Mir)* (Bach)
Visit to Mary Shrine	Soloist: *Ave Maria* (Schubert)
Recession	Organ: *Trumpet Tune* (Purcell)
Postlude	Organ: *La Rejouissance* (Handel); *Rondeau* (Mouret); *Aria* (Peeters)

Jewish

In Table 7-4, we show musical selections for all the components that might be included in a Jewish wedding ceremony; many ceremonies will not have all these components.

Table 7-4 **Examples of Musical Selections for a Jewish Ceremony**

Action	*Music*
Prelude	Organ or piano: *Yedid Nefesh (The Love of My Soul)*
Cantor	Cantor: *Dodi Li (I am My Beloved's)*
Procession	Organ or piano: *Hanava Babanot (Beautiful One)*
Under the chuppah	Cantor: *Eshet Chayil (Woman of Valor).* Congregation: *Niggun* (wordless melody)
Recession	Organ or piano: *Siman Tov u'Mazel Tov (A Good Sign and Good Luck)*
Postlude	*Klezmer* selections

Non-denominational

A ceremony in a non-religious venue, with officiant(s) who are open to your designing all the musical elements of your wedding, may take on a completely different flavor. We show you how this can be done in Table 7-5, where the ensemble comprises a keyboard, guitar, and violin.

Table 7-5	Examples of Musical Selections for a Non-Denominational Ceremony
Action	**Music**
Prelude (mother of bride and parents of groom are seated as last piece of music ends)	*Camelot; Night and Day* (Porter); *Smoke Gets in Your Eyes* (Kern); *Here, There and Everywhere* (Lennon and McCartney); *Theme from Chariots of Fire* (Vangelis)
Groom, best man, and officiant take their places; best man and maid of honor walk down aisle	Soloist accompanied by keyboard and guitar: *In My Life* (Lennon and McCartney)
Rest of wedding party, consisting entirely of children — two sets of ringbearers and flower girls — processes	Trio: *Waltz of the Snowflakes, Nutcracker Suite,* (Tchaikovsky)
Bride and her father process	Trio: Fanfare — *Romeo and Juliet Love Theme* (Tchaikovsky)
After introduction and readings	Soloist accompanied by keyboard and guitar: *Wedding Song* (Bob Dylan)
Recession	CD recording: *Brown-Eyed Girl* (Van Morrison)
Postlude	Trio: *Embraceable You; S'Wonderful,* George and Ira Gershwin; *I've Got My Love to Keep Me Warm,* Irving Berlin

Choosing Ceremony Musicians

The music directors in churches and temples are well versed in both the possibilities of ensembles for your ceremony as well as choices the officiant deems appropriate. Most likely, if you are conducting your ceremony at a site other than a house of worship, you will have far more freedom in creating your musical program. Either way, when interviewing musicians for your ceremony, be sure to ask the following list of questions, and take notes.

Form 7-1, the Ceremony Musician Interviewing Checklist, can be found on the CD-ROM.

Ceremony Musician Interviewing Checklist

Date of Interview:

Musician:

Contact Person:

Phone Number:

E-mail:

❑ Do you have a sample tape you can send to us?

❑ Will the musicians on the tape be the ones playing at the ceremony?

❑ Can you send us a photograph of the musicians?

❑ Have the musicians worked at this venue before? If not, will the leader have a short meeting with the person in charge?

❑ Can the musicians give us some direction on musical choices for various parts of the ceremony?

❑ If we want a particular piece of music, can the musicians configure it for our ensemble? How long will that take and for what fee?

❑ If we hire a soloist or other group for the ceremony, will the musicians have a rehearsal with them?

❑ How many hours are included? If the ceremony goes long, is overtime available?

❑ What will the musicians wear?

❑ Do the musicians have any special requests — armless chairs, music lights, or tenting for outdoor ceremonies?

❑ Can the musicians be available for a rehearsal?

❑ If you are having an elaborate ceremony with complicated cues, can you negotiate a price to have the group (or at least the leader) be present at the rehearsal?

Notes:

Form 7-1:
Know what questions to ask when shopping for musicians for your ceremony.

Putting It in Writing

If you're using musicians from the church or synagogue, you won't need a contract for their services. If you're hiring an outside soloist, quartet, or other musical entity for your ceremony, you'll want to get the particulars in writing. Chances are, even independent musicians will provide some form of contract. But in case they don't, use the following contract, Form 7-2, which you'll find on the CD-ROM, to give you an idea of what you should include in your letter of agreement. (For a contract that covers musicians for both the ceremony and reception, see Chapter 11.)

Music Contract

This contract is for the musical services of singer(s) and musician(s), on the engagement described below, between the undersigned purchaser of music (herein called "PURCHASER") and the undersigned artist(s) (herein called "UNIT"), on the terms and conditions stated below.

Name of Unit/Group:_____

Unit Leader:_____ Phone:_____

Number of Vocalists:_____ Number of Musicians:_____

Place of Engagement:_____ Room:_____

Address:_____

Type of Engagement:_____

Exact day(s), hours, duration and options of employment:_____
_____

Compensation agreed upon for services: $_____ Overtime charge $_____
This contract is void if not signed and returned, along with a deposit of $_____
to the submitting party by_____ 20_____.

This contract cannot be cancelled except with the mutual consent of all parties. Upon such cancellation the deposit shall nevertheless remain non-refundable. In witness whereof, the parties hereto have hereunto set their names on the day and year appearing opposite their respective names.

Purchaser:	Unit Leader:
Signature_____	Signature_____
Full name (printed):_____	Full name (printed):_____
Street address:_____	Street address:_____
City, state, zip:_____	City, state, zip:_____
Telephone(s):_____	Telephone(s):_____

Form 7-2:
A sample contract for hiring "outside" musicians.

Forms on the CD-ROM

Form 7-1	Ceremony Musician Interviewing Checklist	Know what questions to ask when shopping for musicians for your ceremony.
Form 7-2	Music Contract	A sample contract for hiring "outside" musicians.

Chapter 8

Creating a Foolproof
Wedding-Day Schedule

*E*ven before you have an idea of the specifics for each portion of your wedding day, it will help you to block out the chronology of events. Then, as the day gets closer, you can get a grip on the details by mapping out the day minute-by-minute. True, you're not master-minding D-Day, but a little organizational wizardry never hurt any wedding.

In this chapter, we provide the tools for creating a schedule and handling all the last-minute details.

Making Sure Everyone's on the Same Page

Every wedding is unique, which makes creating a one-size-fits-all wedding-day schedule impossible. However, we figure that some prototype is more helpful than none. We explain the wedding-day schedule in detail in Chapter 18 of *Weddings For Dummies*, and although the templates we provide here are in a different format, the idea is the same.

Blank templates of the following forms appear on the CD-ROM so they can be customized by you. Besides the schedule itself, you'll need to give the players several forms including:

- A roster of all the players, including home, office, and cell phone numbers as well as beeper numbers. (See Chapter 1.)

- Transportation logistics, including names and times of arrival for everyone involved.

- Directions and addresses for ceremony and reception sites.

- Delineation of steps before, during, and after the ceremony.

- Guestimated timing for each activity, including toasts.

- Specific notes or addendums for each vendor.

Develop the schedule in tandem with your vendors and with your wedding consultant if you have one. The banquet manager can tell you how long it takes to serve and clear each course; the band leader can give you the timing for a dance set; and so on. Send the first draft of your schedule to all of your vendors, as well as anybody else (parents perhaps) who should have input. Let them make notes on it and return it to you. Hand the finished product out at the rehearsal.

The forms are created in Microsoft Word by using the Table tool. To add a row, point your cursor arrow to the far left border where you want to insert the row. Double-click so that you highlight the row (not just the first cell). Press the right button of your mouse, and you'll see a pop-up menu. Click on up to Insert Rows. To delete a row, follow the same steps, except click on Delete Rows.

The master Wedding-Day Schedule runs from a few hours before the ceremony to the last song. It gives a minute-by-minute breakdown of each activity and explains who needs to be where when and what they need to do at any given moment. Give this schedule to everyone on the team that is involved in making your day happen — all the professionals, the vendors, wedding party members, family, and anyone else who needs to know all the players and how they interconnect. Throughout this book we also provide worksheets for giving specific vendors *abridged* versions of the schedule. You may feel it's not necessary to give the long version to people who need to know only particular parts of the day — when their presence is required.

In addition to sending vendors your schedule ahead of time, remember to fax them the vendor sheets featured in other chapters. Request that they initial these sheets and fax them back to you. These initialed documents then serve as a kind of letter of agreement.

Figuring out transportation logistics

After the Who's Who worksheet, which we show you in Chapter 1, the next page of the wedding-day schedule is Form 8-1, the Wedding Transportation Worksheet, which delineates where members of the wedding party are during the day and how they're getting there. Give Form 8-1 to anyone whose name appears on it, as well as to the drivers. A blank version, which you can print out and fill in with your specifics, is on the CD-ROM.

Wedding Transportation Worksheet

Pick-Up Time and Location	Drop-Off Time and Location	Driver Wait?	Passenger(s)	Car Number and Type
10 a.m. Groom's parents' house	10:20 a.m. Hotel Fabulosity	No	Mrs. Harry Badger (Madge, groom's mother) and Buffy Badger (groom's sister)	#1, Lincoln Town Car
3 p.m. Hotel Fabulosity	3:20 p.m. Pelican Memorial Church	Yes	(Bridesmaids) Mimi Marmot, Kitty Lidder, and Poppy Porpoise	#2, Limo
4:30 p.m. Pelican Memorial Church	4:50 p.m. Hotel Fabulosity	No	(Bridesmaids and ushers) Marmot, Lidder, Porpoise, Rod Weiler, Bob Boar, and Jay Seegawl	#2, Limo

Form 8-1: Coordinate the transportation for everyone in your party.

Getting there from here

You also need to provide another addendum just in case anyone isn't familiar with the town or venues. Form 8-2, the Wedding Day Directions Worksheet, to which you may attach a map, includes addresses and directions for key stops along the way. Here's a typical set up, and you'll find a blank template on the CD-ROM.

Wedding Day Directions Worksheet

Activity	Address	Directions
Groom's parents' house	333 Seaview Drive	From airport: Take 45 South to exit 14 and turn right on Homecoming Lane. Turn left at second stop sign. Badger house is second on right. From downtown: Follow Main Street north 9 blocks toward bay. Turn left on Homecoming Lane, then left at second stop sign.
Bridal party dressing location	Hotel Fabulosity 19999 Dillydally Lane at corner of Wink Avenue	From airport: Take 45 South to exit 18 and turn right on Dillydally Lane.
Ceremony	Pelican Memorial Church 12 Breezeway at the corner of Conch Street	From airport: Take 45 South to exit 18 and turn left on Conch Street. Breezeway is three lights later. From Hotel Fabulosity: Go east (turn right out of parking lot) on Dillydally until you reach Conch Street. Turn right and go three stop signs until you reach Breezeway.
Reception	Butternut Country Club, Palisade Parkway	From church: Head north on Conch Street. Turn left at Hotdog Heaven and follow Bay Street all the way to Palisade Parkway. Turn left on Palisade Parkway. Club is 1.25 miles on the right. Valet parking.

Form 8-2:
Give people any directions they might need.

One last transportation tip: In order to schlep around all the worksheets from this book, we suggest renting a truck and perhaps booking an extra hotel suite.

Creating the Master Schedule of Events

Your master schedule begins with the pre-ceremony rituals of getting dressed and — if you're not waiting until after the ceremony — taking photographs. The timing of things to be done before the ceremony is crucial. Even seemingly little things, such as remembering to eat a little something so that you don't faint at the altar, need to be taken into account, or you may throw the whole day off track.

Then there's the ceremony itself. In chapters 6 and 7, we cover the elements of major religious ceremonies, chapter and verse, so to speak. That's where we help you create a specific schedule and script, complete with music cues, readings, and other details. For the master schedule, you're interested in the broad strokes.

Finally, the master schedule segues into the reception, where you want your caterer, band, bartender, and other vendors to know exactly when you want to eat, dance, and toast. Again, it's a good idea to send the vendors the details of their duties a week before in the succinct format we have supplied throughout the book.

We base the following example master schedule on the increasingly popular choice of taking photos before the ceremony. Many couples still prefer not to see each other before the ceremony. If you prefer to slip away and have formal portraits taken while the guests are having cocktails, configure your schedule that way.

A blank version of Form 8-3, the Sample Wedding-Day Schedule, can be found on the CD-ROM. Take a few minutes to fill it out to suit your needs.

Sample Wedding–Day Schedule

Pre-ceremony Schedule		
Time	*Events*	*Notes*
1:00-2:30	Hair and makeup.	Makeup artist and hair stylist to arrive at bride's hotel suite at 1.
2:30-3:30	Bride and attendants dress.	
2:30	Have snack.	Order from room service day before.
3:30	Dressing room photos.	Photographer to arrive at suite at 2:45.
4:00	Ushers arrive for pre-ceremony photos.	Location: Hotel Fabulosity garden.
4:00	Florist distributes boutonnières, corsages, and bouquets.	
4:10	Tête-à-tête between bride and groom before photo session.	
4:30	Family and other members of wedding party arrive for photos.	Attach shot list to this schedule. Designate someone to help pose subjects.
5:20	After photos, leave for ceremony.	

Form 8-3:
Create a broad-stroke schedule of the day to keep everyone on track. (Page 1 of 3)

Ceremony Schedule		
Time	*Events*	*Notes*
5:45	Church doors open. Prelude begins.	Invitation is for 6.
6:00	Ushers hand out programs and seat guests. Bride and bridesmaids wait in side room at church.	Aunt Ella Fant bringing programs from printer.
6:15	Processional music begins.	
Till 6:25	Processional.	See attached sheet of who walks with whom.
6:25-7:00	Ceremony.	Approx. 35 minutes. Cue recessional music after officiant says, "I now pronounce you . . ."
7:00	Recessional music begins.	
7:00-7:05	Recessional.	See attached sheet of who walks with whom.
7:05	Bride and groom, wedding party, family, and so on leave for reception in assigned cars.	See attached transportation sheet.
7:15-7:30	Postlude music plays until all the guests have left the church.	

Form 8-3: Create a broad-stroke schedule of the day to keep everyone on track. (Page 2 of 3)

Reception Schedule		
Time	*Events*	*Notes*
7:15-8:30	Cocktail hour begins on Turtle Terrace at Hotel Fabulosity. Guests start arriving.	Waiters ready with trays of wine; bars open. Background music: Barry Badger trio CD.
7:15	Weather permitting, bride and groom take outdoor portraits.	
8:15	Banquet manager adjusts lighting in dining room. Final sound check.	
8:20	Bride, groom, and parents look at room before guests are escorted in.	Banquet manager or wedding consultant to arrange.
8:25	Band starts.	
8:30	Guests escorted in and take seats.	
8:45	Wine poured. First toast by best man Barry Cuda.	
8:50-9:15	Appetizer served and cleared.	
9:15	First dance. Cut ins. Dance set (20 minutes).	See attached choreography list for cut ins.
9:35-10:20	Main course served. Three toasts during main course by Bunny Hopper, Mara Supial, and Sally Mander. Places cleared.	
10:20-10:45	Dance set.	
10:45	Champagne poured, cake cutting, bride and groom toast, cake served.	
11:10	Coffee and sweets served.	
11:10-12:30	Band plays. Bandleader announces last dance at 12:25.	

Form 8-3: Create a broad-stroke schedule of the day to keep everyone on track. (Page 3 of 3)

Dealing with Day-of Jitters

We know it's not easy getting married. And no matter how carefully you plan — or how many worksheets you print out from our CD-ROM — you may still get a case of nerves at some point in the process. To avoid feeling overwhelmed, allow yourself a little decompression time and do the following:

- Listen to relaxing music, whether that means Windham Hill or Marilyn Manson to you.

- Practice yoga, but only if you've done it before. It's no fun arriving at the altar on a stretcher.

- Breathe deeply (but don't hyperventilate).

- Indulge in aromatherapy — lavender is particularly soothing.

- Give yourself some alone time. Don't feel you have to entertain your attendants every minute of the day.

- Don't lock your knees at the altar, which can lead to fainting.

- Remember to smile — if you act like you're having fun, you just might.

- Stay in the moment. Remember where you are and stop thinking about things you forgot to do or how the photos will turn out.

- Don't think you have to close down the joint at your rehearsal dinner — leave early and get a good night's sleep.

Forms on the CD-ROM

Form 8-1	Wedding Transportation Worksheet	Coordinate the transportation of all your players.
Form 8-2	Wedding-Day Directions Worksheet	Give people any directions they may need.
Form 8-3	Sample Wedding-Day Schedule	Create a broad-stroke schedule of the day to keep everyone on track.

Part IV

A Rousing Reception

The 5th Wave   By Rich Tennant

LITTLE MISS MUFFET PLANS
HER WEDDING DAY MENU

"We'll start with the curds and meatballs,
curd stuffed dates and curds-in-a-blanket.
Then, we'll have the sweet and sour curds
over a mound of whey..."

In this part . . .

*L*et's face it — your reception is almost as important to the success of your wedding day as the actual ceremony. The chapters in this part help you plan and organize every facet of your reception such as picking out the site, hiring the caterer, and planning the music. If it has to do with the reception, you'll find it in this part.

Chapter 9

Ready to Where

*1*f something in the wedding-planning process (besides your future in-laws) is giving you sleepless nights, it's probably the task of finding a space to hold your wedding. The venue you choose ranks at the top of important planning decisions. Unfortunately, for many couples, picking the right site is akin to being sent to the Marines without being able to do a single pushup.

This chapter gives you basic training in the art of space selection. First exercise: You need to figure out the difference between *on-premise* and *off-premise* spaces. After you get a handle on these distinctions, we make it possible for you to compare costs between sites that fall into one category or the other. We also include some sample contracts so you have an idea of what may be included in the agreement when you book a venue for your wedding. Also included is a full-service lighting contract. Finally, we provide a way for you to estimate whether a space will fit the bill for the sort of ceremony or reception you want to have.

Love at First Site

The two of you are off to look at prospective spaces. Have you done your homework? (Two good places to start: reviewing Chapter 2 of *Weddings For Dummies* and Chapter 5 in this book on destination weddings.) Finding a site that visually appeals to you is only the first step. There are many questions to answer before you can decide whether the space (and the cost) can work for your wedding.

On or off?

The first thing you need to know about your reception venue is whether it's an *on-premise* or *off-premise* site. In general, *on-premise* refers to hotels, restaurants, banquet facilities, and any other place that has a full service, in-house food and beverage operation. When a venue is *off-premise,* you have to contract separately for the site and an outside caterer. Examples of off-premise venues range from a tent in your backyard to a museum to a private mansion.

After you find a place you want to investigate, whom should you ask to see? If you're looking at an on-premise catering location, you deal with someone from the banquet or the food and beverage department. For off-premise locales, you talk to a site coordinator, although this person may not be able to answer your food and beverage queries. Save those questions (which we provide later in this chapter) for the caterer.

Scoping out possible wedding venues

As you scout various options, you need to ask different questions depending on whether the space is on-premise or off-premise, and whether you intend to use the site for both the ceremony and reception or the reception alone. Forms 9-1, 9-2, 9-3, and 9-4 help you target your inquiries. Start with Form 9-1, the Evaluating Reception Sites Checklist, which is useful for any space you may consider. All these forms are available on the CD-ROM.

Evaluating Reception Sites Checklist

❑ What rooms are available?

❑ How many people does each hold? For a cocktail reception? For a seated meal with dancing?

❑ What are the air conditioning and heating systems like?

❑ When are the rooms available on the day you are interested in?

❑ If your date is flexible, are there possible discounts for certain days or months?

❑ Will there be more than one wedding or party taking place on that day?

❑ How many hours are included? What are the costs for overtime?

❑ Is there a music curfew?

❑ What time would your vendors (florists and so on) be able to get in to set up?

❑ Is there a floor plan available with square footage on it?

❑ How many restrooms are there, and what do they look like?

❑ If anything is visibly chipped, broken or out of order, will they state in writing that it will be repaired before your wedding?

❑ What is the lighting like?

❑ Are candles allowed? Do they supply them?

❑ What is the parking situation? Is valet parking available?

❑ Does the site have an arrangement with a nearby garage? Is the site handicapped accessible?

❑ Are there *any* extra costs such as security or porters?

❑ Must one use only approved florists, musicians, or other vendors?

❑ Are there photos of different kinds of weddings at the space that you can see?

❑ Where would group photos be taken? What do they recommend in terms of lighting, glare, and weather conditions?

❑ How much of a deposit is required? Is the deposit refundable?

❑ When are the other payments due? How long will they hold the date for you?

❑ Can you have right of first refusal?

Form 9-1:
Evaluate
reception
sites.

Evaluating Combination Ceremony-Reception Sites Checklist

❑ Are there separate rooms that could be used for the ceremony, a cocktail reception (if you're having one), and meal? If not, how are the rooms usually changed over — is there a place to store set tables, for example?

❑ Are there any additional fees for using extra rooms?

❑ Are there restrooms near the ceremony space?

❑ How many people will the space seat with an altar and a wide aisle?

❑ Is there a separate entrance into that area for guests? For the wedding party?

❑ Are there dressing rooms for the bride, groom, and attendants?

❑ Are chairs available for a ceremony? Who sets them up?

❑ If the ceremony site is outside, what is the rain plan?

❑ Is there a piano on-site?

Form 9-2:
Some sites
are suitable
for both the
ceremony
and
reception.

Evaluating an On-Premise Reception Site Checklist

❑ Does the pricing include food, beverages, and staff?

❑ Are tax and gratuity included? If not, what are the additional percentages?

❑ How is the bar price tallied — by consumption, hourly, or all–inclusive? What is available on the bar?

❑ What exactly is included in the menu price?

❑ Can you peruse sample menus from other weddings?

❑ How will they price meals for vendors such as the band and photographer?

❑ Is there a special price for children's meals? If so, what is it?

❑ With whom will you be working?

❑ Will you be able to have a menu tasting?

❑ Are there extra costs for such things as cake cutting, carvers, or bartenders? If so, what are they?

❑ If the site is in a hotel, is the honeymoon suite complimentary? Are changing rooms complimentary?

❑ What wines and champagnes are available? What are the charges for upgrading them?

❑ What choices are offered for linens, china, glass, and silverware?

❑ Are there additional rental charges, such as a dance floor or bandstand?

❑ Is a wedding cake included? May you supply your own?

❑ How many waiters are included in the price for a party of your size?

❑ How many bartenders?

❑ Is the menu flexible? What is the surcharge for offering a choice of entrees?

❑ What is the minimum number of guests you must guarantee?

❑ Given all the variables, what is their closest estimate on what your entire bill would be?

Form 9-3:
Check out the pros and cons of on-premise reception sites.

Evaluating an Off-Premise Reception Site Checklist

❏ What is the site rental fee? What are the additional fees for additional spaces?

❏ How many hours are included in the site rental including set-up and break down? Are additional hours possible?

❏ Do they have a list of approved caterers or may you bring in your own?

❏ Is there a list of other approved vendors?

❏ What are the smoking rules?

❏ What exactly is included in the rental (does the space own any chairs or tables, for example)? Must you use a specific rental company?

❏ May you provide your own liquor, or does the site hold a liquor license?

❏ Must you have everything picked up that evening or can you arrange for next day pick-ups? (Note: Late night pick-ups may result in additional fees from vendors and rental companies.)

❏ Does the site have a kitchen on site or must one be "built"? (Note: The latter requires extra rentals.)

❏ What is the total bottomline estimate of the site rental?

❏ Is any part of the cost tax deductible?

Form 9-4:
Figure out what an off-premise reception site has to offer.

Talking to caterers

In order to compare the total *real* costs for your food and beverage service at an off-premise site to those at an on-premise site, you must get estimates from outside caterers for the off-premise site. Comparing sites based on rental fees alone doesn't give you enough financial information to make a decision.

For this reason, we include the questions to ask in preliminary interviews with caterers here, in Form 9-5, the Caterer Interview Checklist. For more information about planning the menu and negotiating catering contracts, see Chapter 11 of this book (and Chapter 8 of *Weddings For Dummies*). You can also find Form 9-5 on the CD-ROM.

Caterer Interview Checklist

❑ What ideas, if any, does the caterer have regarding appropriate spaces for your wedding?

❑ If you have found your space already, has the caterer worked there before? If not, will the caterer make a site visit before writing a proposal?

❑ What specific menus can the caterer recommend that will work in that facility's kitchen?

❑ Does the caterer have sample menus? Are there photographs of the work?

❑ What references can the caterer provide?

❑ What are the caterer's specialties?

❑ How flexible is the caterer in planning a menu?

❑ Can you have a tasting? At what cost?

❑ How does the caterer price the menus?

❑ Is a wedding cake included? If not, what are the charges? Can you supply one? Is there a cake-cutting fee?

❑ What are the specific hourly charges for all staff such as waiters, captains, and kitchen staff? What additional gratuities are suggested? What are the overtime charges?

❑ How many staff people would they suggest for your event, and how many hours would each staff member work?

❑ How do they handle the rentals? Must you use a specific company? What choices do you have for rentals, such as glass, silver, china, and linens?

❑ What does the caterer own that will be included, such as props, platters, or kitchen equipment?

❑ Will you receive separate food, service, and rental bills?

❑ How do they handle the liquor?

❑ Assuming that you are allowed to supply your own liquor, what suppliers does the caterer suggest? Ordering suggestions?

❑ What do they charge for setups (soda, ice, fruit)?

❑ How involved will the caterer be in your wedding — just supplying food or helping with the ceremony and other facets?

❑ What is the caterer's educated estimate on *total* costs for food, liquor, rentals, and staff for your party?

Form 9-5:
Ask the right questions when interviewing prospective caterers.

Comparison shopping for a venue

Form 9-6, The Bid Picture: Reception Venues, is arranged so you can compare *total* numbers for on-premise catering establishments, total numbers for off-premise catering sites, and each of these totals to one another.

For an on-premise site, tally the cost of food, beverage, tax, and gratuities. For an off-premise site, combine the site fee with the caterer's estimates on food, liquor, rentals, and service (which you can figure out using Form 9-7). If you interview several caterers for one site, use an average of their estimated costs as the catering charge for that site.

On Form 9-6, please note that because a venue is either on-premise or off-premise — never both — you must choose either one column or the other to fill in per site.

The Bid Picture: Reception Venues

Venue Contact Information	On-Premise Cost Estimate	Off-Premise Cost Estimate	Notes
Name: Phone: Address: E-mail:	Food: $ Beverage: $ Tax: $ Gratuity: $ **Total**: $	Site rental: $ Catering: $ **Total**: $	
Name: Phone: Address: E-mail:	Food: $ Beverage: $ Tax: $ Gratuity: $ **Total**: $	Site rental: $ Catering: $ **Total**: $	
Name: Phone: Address: E-mail:	Food: $ Beverage: $ Tax: $ Gratuity: $ **Total**: $	Site rental: $ Catering: $ **Total**: $	
Name: Phone: Address: E-mail:	Food: $ Beverage: $ Tax: $ Gratuity: $ **Total**: $	Site rental: $ Catering: $ **Total**: $	

Form 9-6:
Compare
on- and off-
premise
reception
venues.

Use Form 9-7 to tally estimates from caterers and plug in those totals under "catering" in the off-premise column on Form 9-6. You can then compare *true*, total, bottom-line costs between venues, be they on- or off-premise sites.

The Bid Picture: Off-Premise Caterers

Caterer Contact Info	Cost Estimate		Notes
Name: Phone: Address: E-mail:	Food: Beverage: Staff: Rentals: **Total**:	$ $ $ $ $	
Name: Phone: Address: E-mail:	Food: Beverage: Staff: Rentals: **Total**:	$ $ $ $ $	
Name: Phone: Address: E-mail:	Food: Beverage: Staff: Rentals: **Total**:	$ $ $ $ $	
Name: Phone: Address: E-mail:	Food: Beverage: Staff: Rentals: **Total**:	$ $ $ $ $	

Form 9-7:
Compare
cost
estimates
from
caterers.

Floor Planning

We include a chart for square footage requirements for various scenarios to use in determining whether a place is suitable for the kind of event and number of guests you intend to have. This list is a guideline; the room shape, sight line obstructions such as columns, and the amount of unusable space must be taken into account as well. Hint: Whenever you make a site visit, bring a tape measure.

Table 9-1 gives you some parameters when considering whether a space is appropriate for the number of guests you anticipate.

Table 9-1	Square Footage Recommendations
Space	*Square Feet Per Person*
Ceremony	8
Cocktails without seating (pre-meal)	6-8
Cocktails with dance floor and partial seating	8
Cocktails with hors d'oeuvre stations and partial seating	12-13
Seated and served meal with dancing	13-15
Dance floor	3

For places such as hotels or catering halls that have been built for the main purpose of hosting banquets, mapping out the room is easy because these spaces lend themselves to parties. Banquet managers are usually well versed in the possible scenarios of a particular room. Other locations, such as schools and museums, however, are designed for other uses and may require ingenuity in creating a room arrangement conducive to a wedding reception. Consider creative ways to arrange tables — such as varying sizes — to utilize the space rather than sticking to a traditional banquet setup.

Here are some tips for laying out your reception/ceremony space:

- ✔ For a ceremony with chairs arranged in rows chapel style, allow 3 feet from the edge of one chair to the back of the next.

- ✔ Allow a center aisle wide enough for double the number of people walking down it. (Make sure that the aisle is of equal width from front to back.) For long rows of chairs, allow a few other aisles so people can get in and out.

- ✔ To help traffic flow, place bars and food stations around the room, not all together.

- ✔ Bars should be visible to guests, but not near the entranceway, which can cause bottlenecks.

- ✔ Don't set bars or buffets near the dance floor or music.

- ✔ For the dance floor area, take into account the space needed for the band. (Musicians should be allotted approximately 10 square feet each, with twice this space for a drummer.)

- ✔ In a tight space, don't use one-sided head tables; they take up too much room.

- ✔ Consider mixing both round and oval or rectangular tables for diverse and more-interesting seating possibilities.

Going to Contract

Forms 9-8 and 9-9 are examples of a contract for a full-service hotel, an off-premise private venue (in this case a mansion), and a contract for a historical site, such as a museum. In Form 9-10 we give you an example of a lighting company contract, which in this case, is for an elaborate tented wedding and lists numerous special effects. While minimal lighting, such as pinspots, is often built into ballrooms, anything more dramatic requires a professional lighting company. See chapter 11 in *Weddings For Dummies* for information about creative lighting effects.

A Sample Contract for a Private Venue or Catering Hall

PRIVATE VENUE, INC.

As this space functions as a retreat for various groups, there are in-house services available such as massages and sleeping accommodations.

Rental Fee: _____

    Security Deposit: _____

    Additional Hours: _____

    Membership Contribution: _____

    Additional Rentals (china, glasses, etc.): _____

    _____

    Grand Piano: _____

    Bride's Changing Room: _____

    Overnight Accommodations for Bride & Groom: _____

    _____

    Fireplaces: _____

    Seminars/Workshops: _____

    Rehearsal Dinner: _____

    Massage Therapist: _____

    Bed & Breakfast: _____

    Other: _____

    Total: $ _____

Please note that some options may be included up to one week prior to the wedding*

[Private Venue, Inc.] requires the host to rent the house's tableware and catering equipment for parties of 100 or less.

Form 9-8:
A sample contract for a private venue or catering hall. (Page 1 of 5)

[PRIVATE VENUE, INC.]

The client's rental fee provides use of the house for nine hours. This includes three hours of setup, a five-hour function and one hour for cleanup. If additional time is required, client may purchase up to two hours. The florist may come as early as 8:00 am on day of wedding to put flowers in house. Flowers may be put onto tent as soon as tent is erected. If flowers cannot be removed night of event, please arrange time with Event Director. The tent company will arrange directly with [Private Venue] acceptable times for setup and removal of tent.

Failure to leave at the agreed upon time will result in the retention of some or all of the security deposit.

No decorations may be used that are likely to cause damage to venue, contents of venue, or property. Extensive decorating to be discussed with event coordinator. No rice or confetti may be thrown in the building or on the property. No birdseed may be thrown inside the venue.

Only candles that are enclosed in glass (i.e. hurricane or votives) may be used.

No works of art may be moved without permission from event coordinator.

[Private Venue] takes no responsibility for items left after a function.

Caterers must put all rentals neatly under tents.

Garbage must be bagged and put into Dumpster. Glass and plastic to be sorted and put into containers and placed next to Dumpster.

[Private Venue] is a non-smoking facility. Guests smoking outside the buildings must use outdoor ash urns, located at entrances. Host must provide additional urns. The host will be responsible for ensuring that the guests do not drop cigarettes, cigars, or tobacco, on property. Smoking is permitted in tent; option to allow or not subject to discretion of bride and groom.

Chairs owned by [Private Venue] may be used only inside building.

Security deposit is refundable, provided all contract specifications are met.

All services, including caterers, florists, bands, and photographers, must have workman's compensation and full liability coverage as described under "referral."

Such restrictions typically appear on venue contracts.

Form 9-8: A sample contract for a private venue or catering hall. (Page 2 of 5)

[PRIVATE VENUE, INC.]

During your event, [Private Venue] will arrange for the rental of china, silver, glassware, and other rental for 100 or fewer guests. For larger parties, you will make arrangements through your caterer. Or you may use [Private Venue]'s tables, chairs and other such furniture. You will be responsible for setup and placement of such tables, chairs and equipment that you use in connection with event. You agree to provide [Private Venue] with a description of electrical requirements two weeks prior to event.

You agree that you will conduct all activities on the property in compliance with all applicable laws. [Private Venue] may designate certain areas as off limits on your event date. You will be responsible for guests upholding these restrictions. [Private Venue] will monitor volume of music played, and may require a reduction in volume if it will cause a disturbance to neighbors.

You agree that only decorations that have met with the approval of [Private Venue] will be installed. Your plans must be submitted at least two weeks prior to the event.

[Private Venue] will provide security guard(s) to help with parking and for the safety of the guests. An additional charge may be required for certain events with special security requirements. [Private Venue] makes no representation that such security will be adequate to prevent injury, loss or theft during your event.

Catering cleanup shall be completed within one hour of the scheduled conclusion of your event. The property, including all floors, walls, equipment and grounds, must be cleaned and restored to the condition in which they were given to you. [Private Venue] maintains the right to charge you for the cost of completing any inadequate or incomplete work.

You agree that you will be responsible for any repairs done to the property or to [Private Venue]'s personal property, if the need for repairs arises in connection with your event.

By signing this contract, you agree to all contract rules and regulations between you and [Private Venue]. By signing this contract, you acknowledge that you have read the Guidelines for Caterers.

All payments must be made by credit card, certified check or bank check, payable to the order of [Private Venue, Inc.]. Payment of the Patron or Grand Patron Membership will entitle you to one [Private Venue] membership for a period of one year, commencing on the date following your event. Please speak to the Event Director for details.

[Private Venue] may amend or supplement the rules and regulations at any time without giving you prior notice of such amendment or supplement.

Form 9-8:
A sample contract for a private venue or catering hall. (Page 3 of 5)

[PRIVATE VENUE, INC.]

Guidelines for Caterers, Musicians and Vendors

The rental fee provides use of the house and grounds for 9 hours; 3 hours of setup, 5 hours for the event, and 1 hour for cleanup. The caterer may use the [Private Venue] kitchen.

Additional space for a cook tent is allowed, set up behind kitchen area.

Catering services are the responsibility of the host. [Private Venue] will provide the rental of chairs, tables, tableware and the like when feasible. When our rentals are used, [Private Venue] will provide personnel to wash tableware. Caterer will bring tableware to dish area and make said tableware "dish-machine ready," i.e., emptying glasses, scraping food from plates.

Music, entertainment and flowers are the responsibility of host. Musicians are expected to adhere to volume-level restrictions determined by [Private Venue] staff.

[Private Venue]'s Event Coordinator must approve all decorating.

Breakdown should occur immediately following function. Caterers and Vendors must remove everything they bring on premises at the conclusion of the event. Any area used by guest/vendor must be left as clean as it was found. Garbage may be left on premises; it must, however, be sorted as follows: garbage bagged and placed in Dumpster. Cardboard boxes broken down and placed alongside Dumpster; Glass and plastic sorted and placed alongside Dumpster.

Form 9-8:
A sample contract for a private venue or catering hall. (Page 4 of 5)

[PRIVATE VENUE, INC.]

> For certain off-premise venues, part of the rental fee will be listed as a membership fee. This may be tax deductible.

Patron Membership

Only Patron and Grand Patron Members of [Private Venue] are eligible to schedule weddings at [Private Venue]. Membership contributions must be received prior to, or together with, the signed copy of this contract, to schedule a wedding date. Membership contributions are income tax deductible to the extent allowed by law and non-refundable. A Patron or Grand Patron Member may opt to pledge $_____ of the membership contribution. Such pledges are payable 90 days prior to the wedding date.

Contract Modifications

Changes made to this contract shall require mutual approval in writing.

Financial Obligations

The rental fee and all other fees under this contract are payable 60 days prior to scheduled wedding.

Enforcement of this Contract

This contract shall become effective between the parties when signed by each party in the spaces indicated below. It shall be construed under the laws of the State of (State). In the event of any dispute between the parties, including but not limited to civil litigation, the parties agree that the prevailing party shall be entitled to all costs incurred to enforce this contract, including but not limited to reasonable attorney's fees, expert witnesses fees, disbursements and court costs, including appeal.

[Lessor]   Date

[Private Venue, Inc.]

By:
        Manager, [Private Venue]

Form 9-8:
A sample contract for a private venue or catering hall. (Page 5 of 5)

A Sample Institutional or Public Space Contract

The Really Historical Center

SPECIAL EVENT RENTAL AGREEMENT

WEDDINGS, PRIVATE PARTIES AND RECEPTIONS

The Really Historical Center ("The Center") is pleased that (Client) has selected The Really Historical Center (RHC) for an event held on [date] (Event). To ensure the safety of your guests and the security of our museum grounds, the Client hereby agrees to comply with the terms and conditions set forth below:

1. The intended scope and nature of the Event, including but not limited to, the number of people expected to attend, duration, activities, type of music, use of tents, and food and beverages to be served, must be fully disclosed by the Client and approved in advance by the Center.

2. The Center reserves the right to refuse rental and/or cancel an Event for any reason.

3. [Special Building] may not be used for receptions, gatherings, or meetings of any kind. Docent led tours of [Special Building] may be conducted in conjunction with the Event. Arrangements for tours must be made at the time of the signing of this agreement.

> For museums or other large spaces, you may have the choice of using only certain areas.

4. The Client has chosen rental plan [X] and the rental fee is $(amount) which must be paid in full at least thirty (30) days prior to the Event. A deposit of $(amount) is required at the time of the signing of this agreement. The deposit shall be refunded if cancellation occurs at least ninety (90) days prior to the date of the Event. If the Event is canceled with less than ninety (90) days notice, no refund will be made. The signing of this agreement and the payment of the deposit guarantees the reservation of the date of the Event as set forth herein.

5. The number of guests is limited to (n).

6. Unless otherwise determined by the Center, the minimum number of security guards on duty in each building will be RHC – (n), [Special Building] – (n), and [Other Building] – (n). In addition, the site will maintain a minimum of (n) security guards for the grounds. At the discretion of the Center, additional security, docents and/or supervising personnel will be assigned to the Event.

7. Use of RHC piano is prohibited unless permission has been obtained in advance of the Event. There will be a charge of $(amount) for the use of the piano.

8. Client agrees to conduct the Event in an orderly manner in full compliance with applicable laws, regulations and the Center policies and procedures. Client's responsible for damage to property and personal injury occurring during rental term which results from acs, default or negligence of the Client, Client's guests, or independent contractors to the extent permitted by law.

Form 9-9:
A sample contract for the use of an institutional or public space. (Page 1 of 3)

9.   The Event may not start prior to [time] and must conclude by [time]. Client will have access to the Center facility for one hour prior to the start of the Event for setup and one hour after the termination of the Event for cleanup and take down.

10.   Client is responsible for hiring vendors and caterers. Please note that the Center provides no kitchen facilities. Client will provide in advance of the Event a list of names and addresses of all vendors providing services at the Event. The Center reserves the right to limit the participation of any vendor who fails to adhere to Center policies and procedures.

> This space has an area where an outside tent may be erected contiguous with the event space to serve a seated meal for a larger number of guests.

11.   In accordance with Center policy, location of tent(s) will be determined in collaboration with [Party & Tent Rental Company], the Center, and Sponsor to mitigate damage to the Center grounds.

12.   The Center will provide a list of approved caterers to the Client. Client must select a vendor from this list.

13.   Client is responsible for all fees charged by vendors for rentals of furnishings, tents, linens, glasses, plates, equipment, etc. Billing and payment is handled directly between the Client and the rental company. All rentals, other than tents, must be delivered and removed the day of the Event. Tents must be removed on the day following the Event.

14.   All deliveries by independently hired contractors must be arranged in advance.

15.   If requested the Center will provide electrical and heater services for outdoor venues.

16.   Decorations and/or signage are not allowed unless approved in advance by the Center. All invitations and/or advertising and promotional copy must be submitted to the Center for review and approval prior to printing and distribution.

17.   All facilities are to be cleared of debris prior to leaving the premises. Caterers and/or Client assume full responsibility for preparation of food service areas and cleanup procedures before, during and after the Event.

Form 9-9: A sample contract for the use of an institutional or public space. (Page 2 of 3)

18.   No alcoholic beverages are to be served on the premises unless specifically approved in advance by the Center. If approved, white wine and/or champagne are the only alcoholic beverages permitted in the RHC. Other alcoholic beverages are permitted at outdoor venues. The Client is responsible for controlling the consumption of alcohol by members of the Client's party and may not serve minors. All [State] Liquor Control Board laws must be observed. No fee may be charged for alcoholic beverages.

19.   Dancing is not permitted in the RHC or [Special Building].

Sites in residential areas often have rules about music.

20. Amplified music is permitted only at low decibel levels in consideration of local ordinance and neighborhood residents. Client agrees to limit noise levels to those permitted by city ordinance, to particularly limit noise levels between the hours of [times] and further agrees to immediately reduce sound levels upon the request of the representatives of the Center.

21. No food or drink is permitted in [Special Building] or [Other Building] or in the RHC galleries or auditorium. All beverages served in the RHC must be clear and uncolored.

22. Coffee may not be served in the RHC.

23. Smoking is not permitted in any building on the premises.

24. The Center reserves the right to terminate the Event or to remove any individual from the premises for behavior considered to be objectionable; such a determination will be made solely by at the discretion of Center personnel.

25. An adult must closely monitor children at all times.

26. Throwing rice, birdseed or confetti is not permitted in the RHC, [Other Building] or outdoors.

27. Because exposure of high levels of light and heat may contribute to the deterioration of works of art, taking videos inside [Special Building] or the RHC galleries is prohibited. In the RHC, photography and videotaping is permitted only in the rotunda and auditorium. Clients must supply to the Center, in advance of the Event, the name and address of the photographer and/or videographer and the Center will furnish them with a copy of the Guidelines for Photography.

28. No admission fees or fees for any other purpose may be collected on the premises. No sale of any merchandise is permitted on the premises.

Intending to be legally bound, the undersigned Client hereby acknowledges and agrees to the terms and conditions set forth herein.

Client	The Really Historical Center
_____	_____
	[Name]
Authorized Signature	Authorized Signature
_____	_____
	Director of Visitor Services and Communications
Dated _____	Dated _____

Form 9-9:
A sample contract for the use of an institutional or public space.
(Page 3 of 3)

A Typical Lighting Contract
[X] LIGHTING CONTRACT

PROPOSAL TO:	SITE LOCATION:
John Man/ Jane Woman	Woman
100 Any Street	11 Home Street
Town, US 10000	Other Town, US
	555-555-5555
ATTN: [ ] Office Phone	
Home Phone Facsimile	Caretaker: [ ] Telephone

TODAY'S DATE	DATE(S) REQUIRED	HOUR(S)	INSTALLATION DATE	REMOVAL DATE

PROPOSED CONTRACT FOR THE FOLLOWING:

COST

ENTRANCE

Glass hurricanes with candles lining one side of the driveway to the street for direction.

250 watt floods to wash over rock-ledge areas of driveway in front of house.

[*To light an outdoor ceremony and tented cocktail hour.*]

CEREMONY

Wash of ambient lighting over ceremony area.

COCKTAILS- PAVILION

Uplighting on the two center poles.

Bright wash of light to highlight the steps for safety.

OPTIONAL

Downlighting in the canopy installed due to inclement weather.

2-arm sconces with shades on selected sidepoles.

Men on site to effect the changeover.

DINING AND DANCING- CLEAR PAVILION

[*Lighting in the dinner tent.*]

Soft washes of light of gelled ambient lighting to provide the overall lighting required.

Double-pin beam spotlighting of the table centers.

Washes of moonlighting over the dance floor to change colors throughout the evening.

Spotlighting of the band.

20AMP receptacle for the Band.

Ambient lighting in the resting tents.

Ceiling fans to help circulate the air.

Landscape lighting to create some dramatic interest throughout the property.

ACCIDENTAL DAMAGE WAIVER (ADW) Accepts_____Declines_____(initial one) Lessee accepts declines Lessor's waiver of Lessee's responsibility for accidental damage to Lessor's equipment. WAIVER FEE IS FIVE PERCENT (5%) OF CONTRACT PRICE. See terms and conditions.

TOTAL PRICE: **DEPOSIT:**

SPECIAL NOTES: [Prices include all costs of [X] Lighting Personnel only.]

[X] LIGHTING COMPANY	ACCEPTED
By: _____	By (Lessee) _____
NAME DATE	DATE

THIS PROPOSAL IS SUBJECT TO THE TERMS AND CONDITIONS AS STATED IN THE CONTRACT. PLEASE SIGN AND RETURN ONE COPY.

Form 9-10:
A typical lighting contract. (Page 1 of 5)

[X] LIGHTING CONTRACT

PROPOSAL TO:	SITE LOCATION:
John Man/ Jane Woman	Woman Residence
100 Any Street	11 Home Street
Town, US 10000	Other Town, US
	555-555-5555
ATTN: [ ]	
Office Phone	Caretaker: [ ]
Home Phone	Telephone
Facsimile	

TODAY'S DATE	DATE(S) REQUIRED	HOUR(S)	INSTALLATION DATE	REMOVAL DATE

PROPOSED CONTRACT FOR THE FOLLOWING:

GENERAL SERVICES

Functional lighting in the service tent to include the connecting canopy.

15 AP receptacles for coffee makers, 1 for sound, 1 for video etc.

30 AMP electrical hook up for porta-trailer.

Wiring to facilitate all of the above to include dimmer controls on all appropriate lighting.

Operational generator to provide all of the necessary power required for the above lighting and electrical services.

[State] electrical inspection and permits to include bonding and grounding of all metal frames.

Emergency and exit lighting as per [state] codes.

Lighting technician on site (required).

Delivery, removal, transportation and any applicable special service charges.

*Estimated Subtotal:

*Special Discounted Price:

(n)% [state] sales tax

> For a tented wedding, it's a good idea to have at least one generator.

ACCIDENTAL DAMAGE WAIVER (ADW) Accepts_____Declines_____(initial one) Lessee accepts declines Lessor's waiver of Lessee's responsibility for accidental damage to Lessor's equipment. WAIVER FEE IS FIVE PERCENT (5%) OF CONTRACT PRICE. See terms and conditions.

TOTAL PRICE: **DEPOSIT:**

SPECIAL NOTES: [Prices include all costs of [X] Lighting Personnel only.]

[X] LIGHTING COMPANY	ACCEPTED
By:_____	By (Lessee)_____
NAME DATE	DATE

THIS PROPOSAL IS SUBJECT TO THE TERMS AND CONDITIONS AS STATED IN THE CONTRACT. PLEASE SIGN AND RETURN ONE COPY.

Form 9-10:
A typical lighting contract.
(Page 2 of 5)

[X] LIGHTING CONTRACT

PROPOSAL TO:	SITE LOCATION:
John Man/ Jane Woman	Woman Residence
100 Any Street	11 Home Street
Town, US 10000	Other Town, US
	555-555-5555
ATTN: [ ]	
Office Phone	Caretaker: [ ]
Home Phone	Telephone
Facsimile	

TODAY'S DATE	DATE(S) REQUIRED	HOUR(S)	INSTALLATION DATE	REMOVAL DATE
	PROPOSED CONTRACT FOR THE FOLLOWING:			
	ADDENDUM			
		Addendum Subtotal:		
		Previous Subtotal:		
		Total Price:		
		(n)% [state] sales tax		

ACCIDENTAL DAMAGE WAIVER (ADW) Accepts_____Declines_____(initial one) Lessee accepts declines Lessor's waiver of Lessee's responsibility for accidental damage to Lessor's equipment. WAIVER FEE IS FIVE PERCENT (5%) OF CONTRACT PRICE. See terms and conditions.

TOTAL PRICE: DEPOSIT:

SPECIAL NOTES: [Prices include all costs of [X] Lighting Personnel only.]

>Estimated balance of $_____ due _____ .

>This proposal will expire unless confirmed by deposit and signed contract before (date).

>*Excludes these items marked TBD (to be determined)

[X] LIGHTING COMPANY   ACCEPTED
By:_____   By (Lessee) _____
NAME   DATE   DATE

THIS PROPOSAL IS SUBJECT TO THE TERMS AND CONDITIONS AS STATED IN THE CONTRACT. PLEASE SIGN AND RETURN ONE COPY.

Form 9-10: A typical lighting contract. (Page 3 of 5)

LEASE AGREEMENT

Terms and Conditions

[X] Lighting ("Lessor") hereby agrees to lease to Lessee the equipment described on the face of this agreement or in attached schedules in accordance with the following terms and conditions:

> This information is boilerplate often found on lighting or tent rental contracts to specify that the hardware is being "leased" for the event, not sold.

Title and Ownership

1. The leased equipment shall be and remain the sole and exclusive property of Lessor. Lessee shall have only the right to use the equipment in accordance with the terms and of this agreement. Lessor shall have the right to display notice of its ownership of the equipment by display of an identifying stencil, plate or other marking and Lessee agrees that it will not remove or cover such markings without the written permission of Lessor. It is expressly intended and agreed that the equipment shall be personal property even though it may be affixed or attached to real estate. The equipment shall not be removed from the place of installation without the express written permission of Lessor.

2. Lessee assumes all responsibility for loss of or damage to equipment (unless due solely to negligence of Lessor or an act of God) during the period from delivery of the equipment to removal thereof (the "lease period"). Lessee will pay for all equipment lost or damaged in an amount equal to, in Lessor's discretion, the replacement or repair cost of the equipment provided, however, that if the ADW "ACCEPTED" is initialed by Lessee (on front of this agreement) and the Lessee had paid the ADW fee, then Lessor shall waive any and all claims it may have against Lessee for accidental loss or damage to Lessor's equipment. ADW IS NOT INSURANCE. Lease shall provide adequate security for the protection of the equipment.

Indemnity

3. Lessee shall indemnify, protect and save and keep harmless Lessor, its agents, servants, successors and assigns, from and against all losses, damages, injuries, claims, demands and expenses, including legal expenses, of whatsoever nature, arising out of the use, condition or operation of the leased equipment during the terms of this agreement. Lessee shall assume the defense of any suit or suits or other legal proceedings brought to enforce all such losses, damages injuries, claims demands and expenses, and shall pay all judgments entered in any such suit or suits or other legal proceedings. The indemnities and assumptions of liabilities and obligations herein provided for shall continue with full force and effect notwithstanding the termination of this agreement, whether by expiration of time, by operations of law, or otherwise.

Waiver of Liability

4. Although Lessor will endeavor to use its best efforts at all times to minimize the danger of damage to Lessor's property from the installation of the equipment, Lessee assumes the risk of such damage and expressly releases Lessor from liability for any such damages that may occur.

Modification of Agreement

5. In the event that the Lessee changes any of the arrangements relating to the services to be performed or to equipment to be leased, Lessor shall have the right to add or subtract such equipment, service or servicemen as in its discretion may be necessary to maintain the safety and quality of the work to be formed. Lessee shall pay for any additional equipment, service or servicemen (or shall receive credit for any reduction thereof) at Lessor's customary charge therefor. No such modification may occur without the written approval of Lessor.

Form 9-10:
A typical lighting contract. (Page 4 of 5)

Payment

6.   Lessee shall pay the contract price, plus such additions thereto as may be agreed upon or chargeable pursuant to the terms hereof within the period of specified herein. If the balance due is not paid at that time, an amount equal to 1% (18% annually) of the outstanding balance due shall be charged every month thereafter until final payment is made by Lessee. In the event that Lessee has directed that the lease charges hereunder be billed to another person or organization, and payment is not made by such person or organization within the terms specified, Lessee shall, promptly upon receiving notice of non-payment, pay such lease charges and such additional charges as may be added to the outstanding balance pursuant to the terms hereof.

Inspection by Lessor

7.   Lessor shall at all times, after prompt and reasonable notice to Lessee have the right to enter any premises where the equipment may be located for purposes of inspecting it or observing its use.

Alterations

8.   Lessee shall make no alteration whatsoever in the leased equipment without having obtained the prior written permission of Lessor.

Default

9.   The occurrence of any of the following events shall, at the option of the Lessor, terminate this lease and Lessee's right to possession of the property leased: (a) the non-payment by Lessee of the deposit required hereunder to be paid by Lessee. (b) The noncompliance by Lessee with any other term, covenant, or condition of this lease, which if not, cures within reasonable time after notice thereof from Lessor. (c) Should any execution or other writ or process of law be issued in any action against the Lessee, whereby the said equipment might be taken or destined, or if a proceeding and bankruptcy, receivership or insolvency shall be instituted by or against Lessee or his property, or if Lessee shall enter into any agreement or composition with creditors, or if Lessor shall deem itself insecure.

Choice of Law

10.   This agreement shall be governed by and construed under the laws of the state in which the office as Lessor hereunder is located.

Suspension of Lessor's Obligations

11.   Lessor's obligations hereunder shall be suspended to the extent Lessor is hindered or prevented from complying therewith because of labor disturbances, including strikes and lockouts, acts of God, fires, storms, accidents, government regulations, or interferences or any cause whatsoever beyond the control of Lessor.

Entire Agreement Severability

12.   This agreement embodies the entire agreement of the parties. It may not be modified or terminated except as provided therein or by other written agreement of the parties. If any provision herein is declared invalid, it shall be considered deleted from this lease and shall not invalidate the remaining provisions hereof.

Sales Contract

In the event that this contract provides for the sale of equipment, [X] Lighting Company hereby agrees to sell to the buyer the equipment described on the face of this agreement or on attached schedules in accordance with the above terms and conditions: 4, 5, 6, 10, 11, 12.

Form 9-10:
A typical lighting contract. (Page 5 of 5)

A couple days before your wedding, fill out and make two copies of Form 9-11. Keep one copy and fax the other to your caterer or site manager, ask him or her to initial it and send it back. It serves as a flash-card version of timing and details. A blank version of Form 9-11 can be found on the CD-ROM.

A Typical Day-of Details Checklist for the Caterer or Site Manager

To: Ms. Irma La Duce, Site Manager

Very Hip Photo Loft

Via fax 445 555 0090

Re: The Hunter-Fawn Wedding

Sunday March 12, 2003

Confirmation

Time	Activity	Details
9:00 a.m.	Caterer arrives for setup	Please have white chairs moved to library and piano tuned.
12:30 p.m.	Guests arrive	Parking attendants on duty. Guests shown to ceremony in library by catering staff.
1:00 p.m.	Ceremony	Over by 1:30.
1:30-2:00 p.m.	Receiving line in vestibule	Please make sure sconces are dusted.
2:00-4:00 p.m.	Lunch in Tyler Room	Please show finished room to bride and groom a few minutes before guests are seated.
4:00 p.m.	Guests leave	
4:00-6:00 p.m.	Caterer breaks down and cleans up	

Form 9-11: Keep your caterer or site manager informed.

Please note: When we say the "caterer breaks down" in Form 9-10, we are referring not necessarily to the caterer's emotional state but rather to the chore of packing up equipment and supplies.

Forms on the CD-ROM

Form 9-1	Evaluating Reception Sites Worksheet	Evaluate reception sites.
Form 9-2	Evaluating Combination Ceremony-Reception Sites Checklist	Evaluate combination ceremony-reception sites.
Form 9-3	Evaluating an On-Premise-Reception Site Checklist	Evaluate on-premise reception sites.
Form 9-4	Evaluating an Off-Premise-Reception Site Checklist	Evaluate off-premise reception sites.
Form 9-5	Caterer Interview Checklist	Interviewing prospective caterers
Form 9-6	The Bid Picture: Reception Venues	Compare on- and off-premise reception venues.
Form 9-7	The Bid Picture: Off-Premise Caterers	Compare cost estimates from caterers.
Form 9-11	A Typical Day-of Details Checklist for the Caterer or Site Manager	Keep your caterer or site manager informed.

Chapter 10

Dance to the Music

. . . .

In This Chapter
▶ Interviewing a band or DJ
▶ Creating a reception playlist
▶ Making some musical requests

. . . .

You've gracefully executed your first dance, both sets of parental units have taken their requisite spins around the dance floor, and your reception is really starting to rock. But now, what's this? The band is launching into the opening strains of "Always and Forever." You and your spouse freeze in each other's arms, both uncomfortably aware that this Commodores classic was your theme song — when you were dating someone else, whom your partner despises. You smile weakly and try to ignore the pit in your stomach. You mentally curse the bandleader, but how could he have known, short of calling the psychic hotline?

In this chapter, we explain how to get the music you want—and only the music you want, played the way you like it—at your reception.

Putting Your Reception to Music

For starters, you need to understand that different parts of the reception call for different types of music. Here we offer some ideas for each phase of the reception; please bear in mind that these are only suggestions and that music preferences are highly subjective.

Cocktail reception

If you have classical music played at the ceremony and your budget permits, consider having something different played at the cocktail reception. Even if it's jazz from a CD player, it works well to change the mood from serious to festive. Consider one of the following options:

- ✔ **Two or three pieces from the band:** Usually composed of one or two guitars, an electric keyboard, and trumpet or sax (these instruments are the easiest to move to the room where the main reception is). Think in terms of a jazz lounge — Miles Davis, Herb Alpert, Sinatra, Tony Bennett.

- ✔ **Piano and singer:** If the site has one or you have the budget to rent it, this combination works best with a baby grand piano. Think cabaret, a la Billie Holiday or Sarah Vaughn. Be conscious of acoustics; this duo shouldn't be loud enough to take over the cocktail reception.

- ✔ **Something unusual:** Cocktail receptions can be great fun with zydeco, klezmer, doo-wop, or an a cappella group.

As guests enter main reception space

After the cocktail reception, guests are escorted to the main reception area. If you have hired a band, the full band should be playing as guests come into the room. The music should be something upbeat and recognizable; many guests may want to dance before the first dance of the bride and groom, and these first songs should encourage such dancing.

Here are a few tunes that may fit the bill:

- ✔ **The Glenn Miller Orchestra:** *In The Mood*
- ✔ **Original Cast Recording or Tony Bennett:** *Anything Goes*
- ✔ **Nat King Cole:** *Just One of Those Things or Our Love Is Here To Stay*

First dance

Some couples prefer to dance their first dance to a CD even if they have hired a band. They feel that only the original artist can do "their" song justice.

If you decide to play your first song on a CD, it's imperative that the timing is down-to-the-minute so the music blends seamlessly. Of course, that means having someone there to operate the sound system.

Some popular choices for this memorable moment include:

- ✔ **Rod Stewart:** *Have I Told You Lately*
- ✔ **Louie Armstrong:** *What a Wonderful World*
- ✔ **Whitney Houston:** *I Will Always Love You*

- **Eric Clapton:** *Wonderful Tonight*
- **The Beatles:** *In My Life*
- **Jimmy Cliff/ Gladys Knight & The Pips:** *I Can See Clearly Now*
- **Paul McCartney/The Beatles:** *Maybe I'm Amazed*
- **Frank Sinatra:** *Just in Time*
- **Nat King Cole:** *Unforgettable*
- **Johnny Mathis:** *Chances Are*
- **The Flamingos:** *I Only Have Eyes For You*
- **Bob Dylan:** *If Not For You*
- **The Cure:** *Lovesong*
- **Berlin:** *Take My Breath Away*
- **Katrina & The Waves:** *Walking On Sunshine*
- **Stevie Nicks:** *Leather and Lace*
- **Nancy Wilson:** *Sweet Love*

Second dance

The second dance is usually when the parents dance with the bride and groom (see *Weddings For Dummies* for more information on format), and then the guests are invited to join them. If you find this awkward (because of divorced or widowed parents or for other reasons), instruct the wedding party to join you on the dance floor as the second piece of music starts. Other guests will inevitably join in.

The second dance is usually a little faster paced in order to "break the spell." However, any of the following songs would be lovely for a first dance:

- **James Taylor:** *You've Got A Friend*
- **Joe Cocker & Jennifer Warnes:** *Up Where We Belong*
- **James Taylor:** *How Sweet It Is (To Be Loved By You)*
- **Foreigner:** *Waiting For A Girl Like You*
- **Whitney Houston:** *Saving All My Love For You*
- **Temptations:** *My Girl*

Ethnic dances

Don't assume that the band or DJ has a full repertoire of traditional or ethnic selections. Most likely, they can play a Hora or a Tarantella or *Danny Boy* (a traditional Irish tune), but if you want a full set of ethnic dancing, you need to arrange this with the musicians or DJ far enough in advance for them to find or learn the music.

Dances with parents

Occasionally, the father of the bride and the mother of the groom wish to dance a special song with their son or daughter during the reception. While the usual suspects over the years have included such ditties as *Sonny Boy* (Al Jolson), *Sunrise, Sunset* (*Fiddler on the Roof*, Original Cast), and *Daddy's Little Girl* (Al Martino), you should choose something meaningful for you. One bride and her father spent weeks choreographing a tango and then performed it with great flair, much to the surprise and delight of all the wedding guests.

Special requests

On occasion, a couple has friends who are talented singers or musicians who will add to the festivities by performing a number with the band. Not only does the band need to know about this in advance so they have the music, but it's a good idea to have the friend rehearse the special performance, which can be done while other guests are in another room having cocktails.

GAME RULES

Your band leader should understand that no special requests are to be played without clearing them with one of you — unless, of course, you don't mind a rousing *Hokey-Pokey*!

As a surprise for your new spouse, your guests, or your parents, consider having someone perform a song written expressly for your wedding. To find a songwriter who specializes in customized lyrics, do an Internet search with the keywords *custom songs*.

Background music

While people eat, you want something soothing and not distracting. You may request showtunes or instrumentals, or can play just a CD or tape by a mellow artist such as Bonnie Raitt, Joni Mitchell, or Emmy Lou Harris. If you decide to play a CD or tape, the entire band can then slip away for a bite to eat as well.

Cake cutting

When it's time to cut the cake, music (or a drum roll and confetti canon) notifies the guests that something is about to happen. You may reprise the music used for the first dance, and continue the song while you cut the first slice.

If you really want to make an event of this ritual, an energetic rock-and-roll version of "The Bride Cuts the Cake" (played to the tune of "The Farmer in the Dell") brings the house down.

Keep 'em dancing

If you've hired both a band and a DJ or if you've decided to keep the band for late-night dancing (after many of your guests have left), this is when you may have both louder and more contemporary dance music.

People usually like to kick back and have fun during this part of the reception, and many people will want to sing along with the tunes. Ask the band leader or DJ to always play full renditions, no medleys. This will avoid the dreaded *musicus interruptus*. It's frustrating to be in the middle of lip-synching *Natural Woman* when it suddenly segues into *Respect* without warning.

The following is a highly subjective list of wedding tunes that are appropriate for this phase of the reception. We could have cranked out a thousand more, but in the interest of ecology, we pared it down. We left out some obvious selections, such as Motown hits, because they will inevitably get played anyway. This list is just to help you get your creative juices flowing.

- **David Bowie:** *Let's Dance, Fame*
- **Michael Jackson:** *Thriller, Wanna Be Startin Somethin, Billie Jean, Don't Stop 'til You Get Enough*
- **Cyndi Lauper:** *True Colors, She Bop, Girls Just Want to Have Fun*
- **John Mellencamp:** *R.O.C.K. in the U.S.A.*
- **Steely Dan:** *Reelin' In the Years*

- **B52s:** *Rock Lobster, Love Shack*
- **Meatloaf:** *Paradise by the Dashboard Light*
- **Dire Straits:** *Money for Nothing*
- **Bruce Springsteen:** *Cover Me, Fire, Glory Days, Dancing in the Dark*
- **The Police:** *Every Breath You Take, Wrapped Around Your Finger*
- **Prince:** *1999, Little Red Corvette, Let's Go Crazy, Purple Rain*
- **Madonna:** *Vogue, Like a Virgin, Papa Don't Preach, Material Girl*
- **Stevie Wonder:** *Boogie on Reggae Woman, Living For the City, Made to Love Her, Signed, Sealed, Delivered, Brand New Day (with Sting), Superstition, Higher Ground*
- **Culture Club:** *Do you Really Want to Hurt Me?, Karma Chameleon*
- **Tina Turner:** *What's Love Got to Do with It?, Proud Mary*
- **Lauryn Hill:** *That Thing*
- **Human League:** *Don't You Want Me?*
- **Al Green:** *Livin' For You, I'm Still in Love With You, How Can You Mend a Broken Heart*
- **Pointer Sisters:** *Jump, Slow Hand*
- **Other Disco:** *Lady Marmalade, Don't Leave Me This Way, I Will Survive, Turn The Beat Around, She Works Hard for the Money, Never Gonna Give You Up, I Feel for You, Jungle Boogie, Ring My Bell*
- **Fine Young Cannibals:** *She Drives Me Crazy*
- **Blondie:** *The Tide is High*
- **Talking Heads:** *Burning Down the House*
- **Will Smith:** *Miami, Gettin' Jiggy Wit It*
- **Garth Brooks:** *Friends in Low Places*
- **Bob Marley:** *Jamming, One Love/People Get Ready*
- **UB40:** *Red, Red, Wine*
- **Rolling Stones:** *Honky Tonk Woman, Brown Sugar, Jumpin' Jack Flash, Wild Horses*
- **The Kinks:** *Lola, You Really Got Me*
- **Sister Sledge:** *We Are Family*

If you're trying to find a particular song, go to an Internet search engine, such as www.snap.com or www.excite.com, and plug in the keywords *audio music selections*.

Creating Your Own Play List

To make sure your wedding sounds as good as it looks, give your band leader or DJ not one list, but two succinct lists. The first is a *play list*, which indicates the general times when you want certain kinds of music — and a few specific requests — to be played. The second is a *don't play list*, which should head off any awkward or undesirable musical interludes.

Enter Forms 10-1 and 10-2, blank versions which you also find on the CD-ROM for you to fill out in Microsoft Word and print out. Don't worry about the boxes looking small. Because the forms are created in Microsoft Word, the more you type (and then hit return), the bigger each "cell" or box gets.

Under "Notes," indicate who you want to announce specific songs. For example, you may have the person who gives the first toast segue into announcing the first dance; in which case, in the far right column you can write "Best man, after first toast." If you have someone who doesn't know you well, such as the band leader or vocalist, announce a song, make sure that the person knows how to pronounce your name. In fact, even if your name is Smith, you may want to indicate the phonetic pronunciation.

Sample Music Play List

Music Play List for the Wedding of Brook Troutiwitz & Rhett Snapperella

Date: August 12, 2001
Location: The Blue Space
Start time: 6:00 p.m.

Event and Approximate Time	*Music*	*Notes*
Full band sound check: 5:00 p.m.		Please okay piano tuning. Full band sound check
Cocktail Hour: 6:00-7:00 (please have musicians in place by 5:45)	*Cole Porter tunes* *Show tunes including Cabaret, Sound of Music (NO-Beauty and The Beast)*	As agreed: Electric piano, guitar and bass
Guests entering ballroom: 7:10	*New York, New York* *As Time Goes By*	Full band, vocals
First Dance: 7:20	*Have I Told You Lately*	Please have handheld mike ready now. Best Man (Marvin Limpjaw) will propose first toast and introduce couple
Second dance	*Crazy Love*	No announcements; cut-ins will take place automatically
Ethnic dances	*Third piece: Hora (approximately 10 minutes)* *Fourth piece: Tarantella (10 minutes)*	Ask guests to be seated after Tarantella
Special requests After main course: approx 9:00 p.m.	Maid of Honor (Shannon O'Leary) *Danny Boy*	As rehearsed with band – sings
Cake cutting: 10:30	*Reprise of Have I Told You Lately*	
Dancing in between courses all night	*Please see Play and Don't Play lists attached*	
Other Last Dance: 11:30	*We Are Family*	Please play tapes as dismantling equipment

Form 10-1: Tell the bandleader or DJ exactly what you want to hear and when.

Don't Play List for _____ & _____ Wedding

Form 10-2:
Tell the bandleader or DJ what *not* to play during the reception.

Note to Bandleader/DJ: Please do NOT play the following songs at the reception:

_____
_____
_____
_____
_____

Thank you!

Strike Up the Band — Without Striking Out

Before you begin interviewing bands, ask friends as well as your caterer or banquet manager for references. (For other ideas on where to find bands, see *Weddings For Dummies*.)

Take a look at your guest list and think about what kinds of music will get most of them up and dancing. The two of you may be partial to a great swing band, but if a lot of your friends have no idea how to dance to this genre, you might consider a more eclectic band.

When shopping for a band, look for someone who knows the importance of flexibility and reading a crowd. Any experienced bandleader will tell you that a minute-by-minute play list for your wedding just doesn't work. Hire a band whom you trust to read the room and change the music accordingly.

The Band Interview Checklist, Form 10-3, will help you search and find the band that's right for you. You can also find Form 10-3 on the CD-ROM.

Band Interview Checklist

Date of Interview: Band:

Contact Person: Phone Number: E-mail:

❑ Can you review an audiotape, video, and photograph of the band?

❑ Does the contract stipulate that the performers you have listened to will be the ones who will perform at your wedding?

❑ Is the audiotape or videotape recorded live? Is the sound technically enhanced?

❑ Do they have a play list that they will supply?

❑ How many pieces are in the band you've heard?

❑ How many vocalists, guitars, and so on are in the band? Is it possible to hire more or fewer? (If you wanted a big band sound, for example, you might ask for more brass pieces.)

❑ Does the band supply its own sound system? Who sets it up and when will they arrive? (If not, are you responsible for the contracting of a sound company or are they?)

❑ What is the cost and for how many pieces, how many hours? How is overtime calculated? Is overtime available for your date?

❑ Is continuous music part of the agreement? If not, is it negotiable or do they play tapes during breaks?

❑ What does their equipment look like? Do they have music stands, for example? (If you have an aversion to the band or company's name on the music stands, mention it now.)

❑ Who is the bandleader? If that is not who you are meeting with, can you have a pre-wedding meeting or phone conversation with him or her?

❑ Will they learn/arrange any special requests in advance? Is there a charge for this?

❑ What will they wear?

❑ Have they worked at the venue before, are they familiar with the acoustics, load-in arrangements, and other details? If not, will they either visit the space or have a conversation with the site director before the wedding?

❑ Do they have a rider that has special stipulations?

❑ How much time do you have to make up your mind? Will they give you right of first refusal or do you need to leave a deposit to ensure that they don't get booked by someone else?

Form 10-3:
Ask the right questions when interviewing a band for the reception.

Discussing Details with the DJ

Finding the right DJ is often a matter of asking the right questions — about the equipment, their costs, flexibility and willingness to accommodate your requests.

Form 10-4, the DJ Interview Checklist, which you also find on the CD, tells you all the important questions to ask a potential DJ. Have this checklist handy when you talk to prospective spinners or their representatives.

DJ Interview Checklist

DJ:

Contact Person:

Phone Number:

E-mail:

❑ Are you talking to an agent or the person who will be spinning at your wedding?
   (If it's an agent, ask if it's possible to have a conversation with the actual DJ.)

❑ How do they charge? Is overtime available and at what rate?

❑ Do they come with an assistant?

❑ How do they handle taking breaks?

❑ Do they have a play list?

❑ If you have special requests, will they furnish the CDs?

❑ Have they worked at the space before? Do they know load-in requirements, electrical capacity, and logistics? If not, will they visit the space beforehand?

❑ How do they usually see music for a wedding progressing?

❑ What do they wear?

❑ What does their equipment look like? Do they need tables draped or other equipment supplied by the caterer?

❑ Do you need to leave a deposit now? How much?

❑ How much time do you have to decide?

Notes:

Form 10-4:
Get the information you need from prospective DJ's.

Sorting Out the Contracts

Before you agree to hire a band or DJ, review their contract, including the proverbial fine print. Even though the legalese might be unbearable, read it closely anyway and make sure you understand every word before signing.

To give you an idea of what to expect in a music contract, we include samples of the following types of contracts:

- **Artist (Form 10-5):** This Artist Engagement Contract can be used for a vocalist, pianist, or other solo performer.

- **Band (Form 10-6):** This sample Band Contract keeps it simple — just who, when, where, and how much money.

- **Band rider (Form 10-7):** This is a key addendum when hiring a large ensemble or one that has complicated equipment issues. Many bands will not have a rider because their requests are not very complicated; all necessities will be included in the contract.

- **Sound and instrument (Form 10-8):** Most bands bring their own sound equipment and instruments. We include this contract (which also covers the sound for the ceremony) because it applies if you're bringing a band to a destination wedding or if you're hiring a big-name orchestra. Note that this document includes sound for the band as well as a stereo set-up so the couple can dance to a special CD for their first dance.

- **DJ (Form 10-9):** The example of a DJ Services Contracts is very simple. If you want the DJ to give away party favors such as lightsticks and sunglasses on the dance floor, specify this in the contract. You can find other versions of DJ contracts on the Web at sites such as Party Professionals Online (www.partypros.com).

These contracts are adapted from standards used throughout the industry. If a group doesn't provide a contract, you can print out Form 10-5, or 10-6, or 10-9 from the CD-ROM and use it. Forms 10-7 and 10-8 show what a filled out contract might look like.

If something doesn't apply to your situation, you can delete it or cross it out. Just make sure it's not something crucial. And you certainly can't cross out or change anything after the contract has been signed unless both parties agree and initial the change.

Artist Engagement Contract

AGREEMENT made this _____ day of _____ 20 _____

Between _____(hereinafter referred to as "ARTIST")
and _____(Hereinafter referred to as "PURCHASER")

It is mutually agreed between the parties as follows:

The PURCHASER hereby engages the ARTIST and the ARTIST hereby agrees to perform the engagement hereinafter provided, upon all the terms and conditions herein set forth, including those hereof entitled "Additional Terms and Conditions."

1. PLACE OF ENGAGEMENT _____

2. DATE(s) OF ENGAGEMENT _____

3. SHOW SCHEDULE _____

4. REHEARSAL(s) _____

5. FULL PRICE AGREED UPON $ _____

All payments shall be paid by certified check, money order, bank order, or cash as follows:

(a) $ _____ shall be paid by PURCHASER to and in the name of the ARTIST agent. Not later than _____ day of _____ 20 _____.

(b) $ _____ shall be paid by PURCHASER to ARTIST not later than _____ day of _____ 20 _____.

6. SPECIAL PROVISIONS

| Specify breaks, travel expenses, and meals. |

_____
_____
_____
_____

Signed:

(ARTIST)
_____

(PURCHASER)
_____

Full Address _____

Phone _____

Form 10-5:
Example of an artist contract.

Band Contract

It is hereby agreed by and between the undersigned that _____ orchestra will provide music for the function as indicated below.

Event_____ Date_____

Place_____ Hours_____

Number of musicians_____

Price $_____
Overtime per $^1/_2$ ____ hour or part $_____

Orchestra_____

Special
Provisions _____ Specify breaks, music stands, and meals.
_____
_____
_____

Client agrees to consult organization prior to engaging any additional entertainment such as Dancers, Disc Jockeys, etc., to ensure proper coordination and quality control.

This contract shall be paid in three (3) installments. The first payment, due upon signing, shall consist of 25% of the contract price, 75% of the balance shall be due not less than eight (8) weeks prior to the engagement date. The remainder shall be payable **PRIOR TO THE PERFORMANCE** by cash, certified check, or money order. Failure to pay the balance according to the terms of this contract shall make the purchaser liable for all court costs and attorney's fees necessary to satisfy any indebtedness.

Deposits nonrefundable_____   ACCEPTED BY_____
_____   X_____
_____   Name_____
Date_____   Address_____
Accepted By_____   Home Phone_____
Address_____
Business Phone_____   Be sure to have balance for day
                                                 of wedding in form specified.

Form 10-6:
An example
of a band
contract.

MUSICAL ORCHESTRAS, INC.

RIDER DATED _____,20___ , IS HEREBY MADE PART OF THE CONTRACT BETWEEN MUSICAL ORCHESTRAS, INC. (HEREAFTER CALLED SERVICE) AND Ms. Mammoth (HEREAFTER CALLED CLIENT).

FOR: _____, 20____

CLIENT EXPRESSLY AGREES TO FURNISH AT ITS SOLE COST AND EXPENSE THE FOLLOWING:

1. PIANO: A grand piano, preferably Baldwin (Steinway or Yamaha also acceptable) in excellent condition; 5'8" if possible. Piano must be tuned to a perfect A-440 pitch after it is placed on stage as per the stage plot.

2. SOUND: A first class, professional sound system (including delivery and set up) for engagement shall meet Service's requirements foe the performance. This sound system shall be capable of giving distortion free, balanced sound mix to all areas of the performance site (suitable for size for room and number of guests in attendance) at all times during the band's performance.

    a. TEN (10) Microphones with stands.

    b. TWO (2)   Speakers (placed one on each side of the band stage).

    c. ONE (1) Mixing board with operator (operator shall start with levels down and bring up slowly).

    d. TWO-THREE (2-3) monitors, one for lead guitarist and one or two for either additional vocalist or horn section & 1 – 2 monitor mixes.

    e. ONE (1) power amplifier.

3. ELECTRICAL OUTLETS AND CHAIRS:

A minimum of FOUR (4) outlets close to the stage for band's equipment, and one comfortable (preferably padded) without arms for each musician (total number of musicians stated in contract).

4. STAGE: A stage for band and leader with platforms which approximate the dimensions outlined in stage plot. (Stage plot will follow.)

Form 10-7:
A sample
band rider.
(Page 1 of 2)

5.   LIGHTING: Client shall provide Service, at Client's sole cost and expense, with a high quality lighting system and adjustable spotlights to meet Service's reasonable requirement for stated engagements.

Ask if this means hiring a lighting company.

6.   MERCHANDISING: It is truly understood that there will be absolutely no merchandising of any product(s) directly or indirectly related to Musical Orchestra without a written permission from Artist to Artist's representatives. This merchandise shall include but not be limited to Records, Pictures of Musical Orchestra alone or with another person or persons, any instant photographic reproductions, T-shirts, Pennants, Program Books or any other materials bearing the Musical Orchestra name or resemblance.

This is usually for a "big name" orchestra.

7.   A hot meal, identical or equal to the meal being served to the party guests.

ACCEPTED AND AGREED TO

_____   _____

[NAME]   CLIENT: MUSICAL
                                                               ORCHESTRA, INC.

DATE:_____

Please note: If there are any difficulties meeting any of the rider requirements, please contact my office at the above telephone number to discuss possible alternatives. Also, please call to discuss details associated with rider to ensure that technical requirements meet those specifications best suited for your engagement.

Form 10-7:
A sample
band rider.
(Page 2 of 2)

Proposal

Generic Sound Systems, Inc.

1 Main Street Township, US 10000

PROPOSAL SUBMITTED TO	PHONE		DATE
Olive Otterz & Barry Badger	555-555-5555		6-1-02

STREET	JOB NAME
12 Any Road	Otterz-Badger Wedding

CITY, STATE, and ZIP CODE	JOB LOCATION
Weddingland, US 00001	**Acme Country Club**

SOUND ARCHITECT	DATE OF EVENT		JOB PHONE
I.M. Johnson			

We hereby submit specifications for estimates for:

Sound System for Wedding on 06/00/00
COST

Ceremony

1- 8 ch Mixer

1- Carver amp

1- 1/3 oct EQ

4- Small "Headlamp" type speakers

> To invisibly get sound at the altar or under the chuppah.

2-3 Wireless Mics (Handheld or Levalier)

Form 10-8:
A sample music equipment contract. (Page 1 of 3)

All necessary spares

Cocktail Reception ——— For a jazz quartet.

1- 24 Ch. Mixer/ amp

2- Full Range Speakers

3-4 Wired Mics

Wedding Reception

1- 24 Ch. Mixer

4- Full Range Speakers

2- Sub Woofers

4- Monitors

2-3 Wireless Handheld Mics

1- CD Player for First Dance

1- Spare CD player for back-up

1- Cassette

All nesc. Microphones, stands and cables

We shall deliver, setup and remove the above equipment on _____ (date).

The company must arrange delivery
and removal with site manager at your venue.

(2)- Technicians will be on site (in Tuxedo) to operate and oversee the equipment
for the duration of the event.

Very important in case of sound glitches.

Labor $

We propose hereby to furnish material and labor - complete in accordance with
above specifications, for the sum of: $

Form 10-8:
A sample
music
equipment
contract.
(Page 2 of 3)

Total $

PAYMENT TO BE MADE AS FOLLOWS:

Net (n) Days upon Completion

All material guaranteed to be as specified. All work to be completed in workmanlike manner according to standard practices. Any alteration or deviation from above Specifications involving extra costs will be executed only upon written orders, and will become an extra charge over and above the estimate. All agreements contingent upon strikes, accidents or delays beyond our control. Owner to carry fire, tornado and other necessary insurance. Our workers are fully covered by Workman's Compensation Insurance.

Authorized Signature_____

Note: This proposal may be withdrawn by us if not accepted within _____ days.

Acceptance of Proposal

The above prices, specifications and conditions are satisfactory and are hereby accepted. You are authorized to do the work as specified. Payment will be made as outlined above.

Signature_____

Signature_____

Date of Acceptance_____

Form 10-8:
A sample
music
equipment
contract.
(Page 3 of 3)

DJ Services Contract

WHEREAS _____ (known hereafter as ARTIST), has offered to perform services, and WHEREAS, the undersigned, has agreed to employ ARTIST to perform the services explained herein, and by its signature below or signature of its authorized agent hereby accepts the terms or this offer, now therefore.

IT IS HEREBY AGREED between the parties that ARTIST on the _____ day of _____ 20____, perform for the below signer between the hours of _____ and _____ at _____ (hereafter referred to as VENUE). ARTIST will provide the use of his equipment, cds, lights and the performance of a disc jockey. The type of engagement for the performance by ARTIST shall be as follows: Wedding Reception. The wage and/or cost of the performance of ARTIST shall be $_____ as a retainer or deposit for faithful performance of said duties by ARTIST.

IT IS FURTHER AGREED that the above scheduled event shall take place at VENUE _____.

IT IS FURTHER AGREED that after payment of the binder upon acceptance of this by _____ (hereafter referred to as CLIENT) the remaining balance of $_____ is payable at completion of Wedding Reception and, if applicable, excess hours to be charged at $_____ per hour or portion thereof.

IT IS FURTHER AGREED between the parties that unless after accepting this Contract this Contract is cancelled by client within (30) days prior to the performance date, then at the option of ARTIST the binder as above stated may be retained by ARTIST.

IT IS FURTHER AGREED and intended by both parties that the terms and conditions as set forth herein are the total terms and conditions of the Agreement and that they shall be binding upon both parties and interpreted under the laws of State of _____ that any additional terms, conditions, modifications not expressly stipulated herein shall be null and of no force and effect unless said stipulation or additional terms or conditions shall be in writing attached hereto and executed with the same authority as this document.

We the undersigned, do agree to accept the terms and conditions of this offer made by the ARTIST.

NOTE: PLEASE READ ALL TERMS AND CONDITIONS OF THIS CONTRACT PRIOR TO SIGNING AND BE SURE THAT ALL BLANK SPACES ARE FILLED IN WITH APPROPRIATE INFORMATION OR n/a (FOR NOT APPLICABLE FOR YOUR SITUATION).

CLIENT
SIGNATURE_____DATE_____

ARTIST
SIGNATURE_____DATE_____

Form 10-9:
An example
of a DJ
contract.

Forms on the CD-ROM

Form 10-2	Don't Play List	Tell the band leader or DJ what not to play during the reception.
Form 10-3	Band Interview Checklist	Ask the right questions when interviewing a band for the reception.
Form 10-4	DJ Interview Checklist	Get the information you need from potential DJ's.
Form 10-5	Artist Engagement Contract	Example of an artist contract.
Form 10-6	Band Contract	An example of a band contract.
Form 10-9	DJ Services Contract	An example of a DJ contract.

Chapter 11

A Taste of Things to Come

*I*n Chapter 9 of this book, we provide a worksheet for interviewing prospective caterers. Although that might seem premature, the fact is that whether you have your reception at an on-premise or off-premise site, selecting a venue and the caterer go hand in hand. You often can't make a decision about where to have your reception until you get all the variables into place.

In this chapter we focus less on *who* is doing the cooking than *what* they're cooking. In other words, we're talking content — planning the menus, selecting the cake, and figuring out the liquid refreshments to accompany them. We walk you through the steps of planning an exquisite menu that suits your wedding style, and provide a few tantalizing menus to give you some ideas.

Getting a Reception Reality Check

First thing's first: What *type* of meal do you envision serving? Are you planning on a wedding brunch or breakfast? And does that entail everyone sitting at assigned tables? If you're having a seated dinner, do you want it fully served or buffet style? Will you have a cocktail reception before dinner, and for how long? All these fundamental questions need to be taken into account before you decide the actual items on the menu. (See "Planning the Menu" later in this section for more information on sorting out these issues.)

Planning your reception menu is about choosing what your guests may like. Remember this rule and resist the temptation to make every single dish one of your favorites. Most likely, you'll be too busy greeting and speaking to guests to eat the food anyway. Ask the banquet manger to wrap up an entire meal for you to take with you after the reception — you'll probably be starving later on.

To help focus the level of hospitality you plan to offer, ponder the following:

✔ What time of day are you planning on getting married? Do you plan on serving your guests directly after the ceremony, or will there be hours in between?

✔ What are the price differentials? A lavish breakfast or brunch may be less expensive than even a skimpy cocktail party, due to the liquor consumption. Don't assume a buffet is less expensive than a served meal.

✔ Who are your guests? As much as you may love the idea of a partially seated reception, older guests feel uncomfortable without an assigned seat.

✔ Is there a wide variation of ages, food tastes, or dietary restrictions among the guests? If so, food stations may be a good idea because they offer the most options.

✔ What is the level of sophistication of the majority of your guest list? Would they enjoy a salad and cheese course after the main course, for example, or would such culinary delight go unappreciated?

✔ For a seated meal, how many courses do you want to serve?

✔ For a buffet or station meal, consider serving a seated first course to eliminate lines.

✔ At an off-premise space, what are the kitchen facilities? What sorts of things have to be pre-cooked? What can be cooked to order?

✔ Do you want a plated meal, or do you want it served from silver platters by waiters?

✔ Is there room on your table to serve any family-style courses, such as an antipasto appetizer or breads and dips? For an informal reception, family-style courses can be a fun alternative to a traditional served course. Would your guests enjoy helping themselves?

✔ What season will your wedding be held in? Is there seasonal produce? Can the chef suggest preparations that go with the time of year?

✔ For a cocktail party, either preceding a meal or as the entire wedding reception, might you have both passed and stationary hors d'oeuvres? What are the choices and the price differentials? What sort of trays or serving dishes would the hors d'oeuvres be served on? How would the food be garnished?

✔ Ask to see the possible place settings in-house. For an off-premise caterer, make a trip to the rental showroom. You may find mix-and-match china patterns that work beautifully together, or other props they rent that the caterer may not be aware of.

✔ Ask the caterer about donating leftover food to a homeless organization. Make sure the arrangements are made for this well in advance.

✔ What does the caterer and/or banquet manager suggest as their most popular dishes, and what do they think you should stay away from?

Make sure to discuss what the wait staff will wear. For a leisurely brunch, for example, you may prefer the waiters in khakis, pressed striped shirts, and bistro aprons, rather than having them wear black tuxedos.

Tasting and Testing

After you pick a caterer (see Form 9-5 in Chapter 9 for tips on the selection process), it's time to schedule a tasting, which can be one of the high points of your wedding planning.

Make sure that a tasting is spelled out in your catering contract or in an oral agreement. The majority of facilities, as well as off-premise caterers, include a tasting after they receive your deposit. Some caterers provide tastings before you have committed to hiring them, but the dishes they present to you will not be your personal menu choices.

For the tasting, ask to have the table set with your final place setting choices. It's also a good time to ask your florist to see the centerpiece and linens.

When preparing for the tasting, bear in mind the following points:

- Peruse a variety of sample menus from the facility or caterer before you decide what to taste.

- For your tasting, even if you think you are definite about a particular dish, taste a few different choices in each category. You may be surprised at what you prefer.

- Ask to taste a variety of starches and vegetables, not only the ones that come with each dish. You may opt to choose things to serve together that aren't listed the same way on the menus.

- For your final menu, choose varied flavors, colors, and ingredients. For example, don't serve asparagus puffs as an hors d'oeuvres, and asparagus vinaigrette as an appetizer.

- Make a detailed tasting sheet, with a line for each item tasting and a place for notes and "final grade." List each hors d'oeuvre, each side dish, main courses, and desserts.

- If applicable, taste the wines that can be served with the different courses.

- Ask to have the dishes served exactly as they would be served at your wedding — not on a plate if they would be served from a tray, for example.

- For buffets or food stations, choose a combination of hot and room temperature dishes so the food can be displayed in a more interesting manner than a row of chafing dishes. Ask what props and serving pieces are available to offset the foods. Caterers and banquet facilities often have baskets, small fountains, bamboo steamers, giant urns, or other items that add to the beauty of the presentation.

For smaller weddings, peruse your own treasures for items (such as vases or platters) to present the food. Make sure that such items can stand the jostling that catering entails. Also assign someone to retrieve them afterwards, so you don't need to go on a treasure hunt at the site after your honeymoon.

As you sample the delectables, use Form 11-1, the Tasting Worksheet (which you can print out from the CD-ROM), to make notes about the food. Give a copy to each taster. Under Presentation, note whether the dish is an hors d'oeurve, entrée, side dish, and so on. Record your impressions under the Taste column (like "too salty" or "substitute almonds"). In the Doodles column, sketch what the actual plate or display looks like; these visual notes will help you recall dishes as you make your selections later.

A Tasting Worksheet

Dish	Presentation	Taste Impressions	Doodles

Form 11-1:
Record your thoughts about the food during your tasting.

Considering the Cake

For many people, a wedding cake is a major part of their reception. In recent years, cakes have come to be as meticulously created as couture wedding dresses — and often as stylized. In any case, the cake may be the only thing you get to sit down and eat the entire day, so make sure it's delicious. (For more information on cake flavors and fillings, see Chapter 9 in *Weddings For Dummies*.)

Take into account the following points as you scope out bakers·and their wares:

✔ Even if the cake is included with your menu, ask if you can talk to the baker about options. You're bound to get something more suited to your individual tastes this way. Ask to see photos, and tell them how long and where your cake will be on display so they can advise on the type of icing.

✔ How many people are you serving? Are you having another dessert? Is it a complicated dessert or just berries or sorbet? Cakes are priced per slice, and you may not need to order a full slice per person if you are having a second dessert.

✔ Ask to taste cake flavors at the same time you taste the desserts you are considering. Seasonal possibilities, such as light lemon cakes filled with fresh strawberries in the summer, or chestnut puree in the fall, will complement seasonal menus.

✔ Consider serving a small wedding cake as a part of an extravagant dessert table rather than as the main dessert. This option gets guests up and moving again after a seated dinner.

✔ Individual wedding cakes for each guest are in vogue. They are sometimes displayed on round platters in wide tiers to resemble a large wedding cake. A small cake as a dessert "centerpiece" for each table is another possibility.

✔ Consider a cake composed of different flavors on each tier, and serve a few slices of each flavor to each table.

✔ Jazz up a simple cake by decorating the cake table with several layers of cloths, garlanding, or flowers around the perimeter.

✔ A talented baker can replicate any part of your wedding on the cake, from sugar flowers that echo the real ones to marzipan shells for a beach wedding, or recreate the lace pattern on the wedding dress.

✔ Take a whimsical cake topper a step further by having a cake that's off-kilter, has vibrant colors, or is an unusual shape, such as the traditional French tower of cream puffs known as the croquembouche, a cupcake pyramid, stacks of gift boxes, or a castle.

Coordinate times and specific delivery entrances with your baker and the banquet manager. Most cakes are delivered ready to be placed on the table; large cakes of more than three tiers are often assembled on-site. Request to have the cake table dressed and ready so that the cake can be set up upon delivery.

Fielding Catering Proposals

The following forms are two typical reception catering proposals. Form 11-2 is for an off-premise weekend wedding. (For a quick reminder on the difference between on- and off-premise sites, see Chapter 9.) The proposal is from the caterer and consists of meals, rentals, and staff, and lasts for three days at a rented mansion. The wonderful and varied menus are courtesy of Great Performances Catering in New York City. Form 11-3 is for an elaborate cocktail reception and a seated, formal dinner at an elegant hotel. The menu selections are courtesy of The St. Regis Hotel in New York City.

After you go over the proposed menus, discuss changes and suggestions with your caterer or banquet manager. The final proposal becomes the "contract."

A Sample Weekend, Off-Premise Caterer's Proposal

MENU & CATERING, INC. CONTRACT

Proposal Designed for A Wedding Celebration

For

[Bride]

&

[Groom]

At [Private Venue]

On [Date]

Picnic Lunch On [Date 1] for [n] Guests

Rehearsal Buffet Dinner On [Date 1] for [n] Guests

Wedding on [Date 2] for [n] Guests

Breakfast On [Date 3] for [n] Guests

Note that menu, staff and rentals have been carefully outlined for each event.

Proposal Revised on

[Date]

By

[Name]

Event Coordinator

Form 11-2:
A sample weekend wedding proposal from an off-premise caterer.
(Page 1 of 9)

Mr. [Name] & Ms. [Name]
Menu & Catering, Inc.
Wedding Celebration for [Date 1]

LUNCHEON MENU

FOR [DATE 1]

Assorted Sandwiches, Chips & Dips and Salads
Served Picnic Style in Front of [Venue]

Chips & Dips
Hummus, Babba Ghanoush, Guacamole and Salsa

Served with Pita Triangles and Tortilla Chips

Baskets Overflowing with Assorted Terra Chips

Sandwiches
Grilled Chateaubriand on Baguette with Spicy Baby Arugula and Onion Confit

All American Tuna Salad with Red Leaf Lettuce and Vine Ripe Tomatoes on Sliced Challah Pullman Bread

Roasted Vegetables and Fresh Mozzarella Drizzled with Balsamic Vinegar and Brushed on Rosemary Focaccia

Tomato, Cucumber, Alfalfa Sprouts, Shredded Carrots and Chive Cream Cheese On Multi Grain Bread

Grilled Chicken Sandwich on Focaccia with Saffron Aioli, Roasted Peppers and Alfalfa Sprouts

Salads
Wild Rice Salad with Diced Fruit & Slivered Almonds in a Citrus Vinaigrette Dressing

Mixed Baby Greens with Julienne Vegetables tossed with a Light Lemon Tarragon Vinaigrette

Fresh Summer Fruit Arrangement
Honeydew Melon, Pineapple, Cantaloupe, Oranges and Grapes Garnished with Fresh Seasonal Berries

Assorted Canned Sodas, Bottled Juices and Mineral Water

Form 11-2:
A sample weekend wedding proposal from an off-premise caterer.
(Page 2 of 9)

Mr. [Name] & Ms. [Name]
Menu & Catering, Inc.
Wedding Celebration for [Date 1]

REHEARSAL DINNER MENU

FOR [DATE 1]

Stationary Hors d'oeuvres

Satay Skewers

Skewered Medallions of Grilled Tandoori Chicken

Grilled Tuna, Calamata Olive & Red Pepper Kebabs

*Grilled Vegetable Skewers of Portabello Mushrooms, Button Mushrooms,
Artichoke Hearts, Red Peppers and Baby Squash*

Tropical Dipping Sauces Including Coconut Rum and Citrus Yogurt

Crudite – Fresh Vegetables Served with Roasted Red Pepper Dip

Entrée

*Free Range French Cut Chicken Breast Grilled over Oak Charcoal, Sprinkled
with Fresh Herbs, and served with a Portabello Mushroom
& Dijon Mustard Sauce*

*Boneless Salmon Filet Marinated in Five Fruit Juices and Grilled Over Oak
Charcoal – Served with Papaya Salsa and Fresh Lime Wedges*

Corn on the Cob Fresh off the Grill, Served with Seasoned Butter

*Baby Red Potatoes Brushed with Olive Oil and Fresh Herbs, Salt and Pepper and
Served Fresh off the Grill*

Green Beans and Rosemary Smoked Oyster Mushroom Salad

Traditional Caesar Salad

*Romaine Tossed with Focaccia Croutons, Shaved Imported Parmesan and
Our Homemade Caesar Dressing*

Baker's Basket of Assorted Breads and Rolls

Ramekins of Sweet Creamery Butter Topped with Fresh Herbs

Dessert

*Amaretto Peach Crisp Baked Under a Crisp Almond Biscotti Crust Topped with
Rich Vanilla Bean Ice Cream*

Freshly Brewed French Roast and Decaffeinated Coffee

Form 11-2:
A sample
weekend
wedding
proposal
from an
off-premise
caterer.
(Page 3 of 9)

Mr. [Name] & Ms. [Name]

Menu & Catering, Inc.

Wedding Celebration for [Date 1]

WEDDING DINNER MENU

Butlered Hors d'oeuvres Garnished with Bouquets of Spring Flowers

Napoleon of Smoked Salmon with Horseradish Cream & Fresh Dill

Thai Beef Salad with Lemongrass and Ginger, Served in Endive Petal

Peppered Yellowfin Tuna on Pickled Daikon Wafer with a Sweet Pepper and Wasabi Sauce

Grilled Salmon Satay With a Spicy Peanut Dip

Duck Breast Quesadilla with Guacamole & Pico de Gallo (Without Cheese)

Escargot Champignons with Sauteed Wild Mushrooms, Shallots and Herbs served in a Crispy Croustade

Herb Smoked Crimini Mushroom with Balsamic-Port Wine Marinade

First Course

Grilled Halibut Topped with Sauteed Spinach and Garlic Confit, Garnished with a Baby Holland Pepper Stuffed with Yukon Gold Mashed Potatoes and Served on a Plate "Painted" with Balsamic Reduction

Entrée

Sweet Roasted Garlic and Peppercorn Crusted Tenderloin of Beef Served with a Merlot Wine Sauce
~Served with~
Matchstick Potato and Sweet Potato Tart Wedge with Leeks & Herbs
&
Asparagus Bundles Tied with a Poached Leek Accented with Bok Choi Sprinkled with Orange & Yellow Pepper Dice

Assorted Breads & Rolls from the Finest Bakeries

Sweet Creamery Butter

Salad Course

Mixed Baby Green Salad Accented with Hudson Valley Goat Cheese Croustades Garnished with Dried Cranberries and Spiced Pecans, Tossed with a Light Lemon Tarragon Vinaigrette

Dessert

Wedding Cake
(Can be supplied by Menu & Catering or an Outside Vendor. Please Advise.)
Summer Berry Pastry Basket Filled with Bavarian Cream and Seasonal Berries Presented on a Plate "Painted" with Raspberry Coulis and Garnished with a Beautiful Butterfly

Freshly Brewed French Roast & Decaffeinated Coffee

Form 11-2:
A sample weekend wedding proposal from an off-premise caterer. (Page 4 of 9)

Mr. [Name] & Ms. [Name]
Menu & Catering, Inc.
Wedding Celebration for [Date 1]

CASUAL BRUNCH

FOR [DATE 3]

Served from 11 a.m. to 1 p.m.

~

Smoked North Atlantic Salmon Platter

Fresh Smoked Salmon with Bagels and Cream Cheese,
Tomatoes, Red Onion, Capers, and Lemon

Vegetable & Chive Cream Cheese Spreads

Vegetable and Chive

Belgium Waffle

Offered with Fresh Seasonal Berries, Roasted Pears,
Freshly Whipped Cream, Sweet Creamery Butter & Vermont Maple Syrup

Breakfast Bakery Basket

A Delicious Selection of Homemade Miniature Muffins,
Scones, Croissants, and Danish
Offered with Butter and Preserves

Sliced Seasonal Fresh Fruit Platter

Melons, Pineapple, Citrus, Strawberries, and Grapes

Freshly Brewed Regular and Decaffeinated Coffee

Served with Hot Water and Assorted Herbal Teas

Milk, Sugar, Lemon, Honey, and Equal

**Orange Juice, Cranberry Juice, Grapefruit Juice, Tomato Juice, and
Mineral Water**

Form 11-2:
A sample
weekend
wedding
proposal
from an
off-premise
caterer.
(Page 5 of 9)

Mr. [Name] & Ms. [Name]

Menu & Catering, Inc.

Wedding Celebration for [Date 1]

STAFF: Your staff will be attired in khaki pants with white button down shirts and festive ties for [dates 1 and 3]; white Summer Jackets will be the attire for [date 2] Wedding Celebration. Kitchen Personnel will be attired in Chef's Whites.

Party Staff for [Date 1]

Daytime Activities, Lunch [time]

___ Working Captain ___ Beverage Attendant ___ Buffet Attendant/Waiter
___ Activity Attendant

Estimated
@...$_____

As this wedding had several games on the lawn (baseball, volleyball and soccer) there was an activity attendant.

Rehearsal Dinner from [time]

The contract states the number of personnel.

___ Captain ___ Bartenders ___ Buffet Attendants ___ Waiter ___ Chef
___ Kitchen Attendants ___ Sanitation Attendant

Estimated
@...$_____

Party Staff for [Date 2]

Dinner from [time]

___ Captain ___ Hors Captain ___ Bartenders ___ Waiter ___ Wine Steward
___ Chef ___ Kitchen Assistants ___ Sanitation Attendant

Estimated
@...$_____

Party Staff for [Date 3]

___ Working Captain ___ Buffet Attendant/Waiter ___ Beverage Attendant
___ Chef ___ Kitchen Assistant ___ Sanitation Attendant

Estimated
@...$_____

Note the time of setup and break down is clearly delineated.

Arrival time is 3 hours prior to guest arrival with estimated staff departure time of one hour past guest departure. If you wish service to continue past estimated departure times, additional costs will be incurred.

A 25% administrative charge has been included in the estimate. It is applied to the cost of labor and insures that our entire staff is covered under Disability and Workman's Compensation, Unemployment Compensation, Social Security Contribution and Complete Liability Coverage.

Form 11-2:
A sample weekend wedding proposal from an off-premise caterer. (Page 6 of 9)

Mr. [Name] & Ms. [Name]
Menu & Catering, Inc.
Wedding Celebration for [Date 1]

BAR SETUPS

Your bar setups would include the following and be supplied for the Rehearsal Dinner on [Date 1] and the Wedding Celebration on [Date 2]:

Mineral Water, Tonic, Water, Soda, Orange Juice, Cranberry Juice, Grapefruit Juice, Ice for Chilling and for Drinks.

Bar Fruit: Lemons, Limes, Cherries and Onions.

NOTE: We will Also Supply Keg Beer for the Luncheon on [Date 1] and Keg Beer and White Sangria for [Date 1] Rehearsal Dinner.

RENTALS: Classic Selections

> The couple would be purchasing the liquor and the caterer supplying the rest of the items for the bar.

Luncheon on [Date1]

White Paper Plates
Stainless Steel Forks & Serving Utensils
White Wood Folding Chairs
Round Tables for Guest Seating
White Cloths for Guest Seating
Tables for Stations
All Serving, Presentation and Kitchen Equipment

Estimated
@ ....$_____

Rehearsal Dinner on [Date 1]

Cloths for Dinner Tables
Plates for Stationary Hors d'oeuvres
Serving Platters and Utensils for Stationary Hors d'oeuvres and Buffet
Classic White Rim China for Dinner & Dessert
Silver Plated Flatware
All-Purpose Glassware for Cocktails
White Wood Folding Chairs for Dinner Seating
Round Tables for Dinner Seating
Tables for Bars and Buffets
Cloths for Cocktail Tables, Cloths for Stations, Cloths for Bars, Cloths for Dinner Tables
Guest Napkins
All Bar Equipment, All Serving, Presentation and Kitchen Equipment

Estimated
@ ....$_____

Form 11-2:
A sample weekend wedding proposal from an off-premise caterer.
(Page 7 of 9)

Mr. [Name] & Ms. [Name]
Menu & Catering, Inc.
Wedding Celebration for [Date 1]
RENTALS: *Continued...*

Wedding Celebration on [Date2]:

Celedon Linen or Celery Stripe for Dinner Tables

Classic White Rim China for first course, dinner, salad, bread, dessert and coffee service

Silver Plated Flatware for first course, dinner, salad, bread, dessert and coffee service

All-purpose Glasses for Cocktails

At Each Place Setting: White Wine Glass, Red Wine Glass, Water Goblet and Champagne Flute

White Wood Folding Chairs for Ceremony & Cocktail Seating

Ballroom Chairs for Dinner Seating

Petite Glass Salt and Pepper Shakers

Votive Candles for Guest Tables

Cocktail Tables, Dinner Tables, Bar Tables, and Cake Table

Cloths for Cocktail Tables, Cake Table, Bars, Dinner Tables and Guest Napkins

All Serving, Presentation and Kitchen Equipment

Estimated
@ ....$_____

Breakfast on [Date 3]

Classic White Rim China

Coffee Cups and Saucers

Silver Plated Flatware and Serving Utensils

All-Purpose Glasses for Juices and Water

Cloths for Buffet

Cloths for Guest Tables

Guest Napkins

All Serving, Presentation and Kitchen Equipment

Estimated
@ ....$_____

Form 11-2:
A sample weekend wedding proposal from an off-premise caterer.
(Page 8 of 9)

MENU & CATERING, INC.

[Date]
Ms. [Name]
Mr. [Name]
Address

SUMMARY OF ITEMIZED COSTS

STAFF:
Total Estimated @ ....$_____

MENU: **[Date 1]**
Lunch @ $_____ per person x _____ people.....................$_____
Rehearsal Dinner @ $_____ per person x _____ people........$_____

[Date 2]
Wedding Menu @ $_____ per person x _____ people.........$_____

[Date 3]
Breakfast @ $_____ per person x _____ people..................$_____

BAR SET-UPS: ———— As client purchased own liquor, this is for fruit, ice and mixers.

Luncheon @ $____ per person..$_____
Rehearsal Dinner @ $_____per person...$_____
Wedding @ $____per person..$_____

CATERER DELIVERY:
4 @ $_____ per delivery...$_____

SUB TOTAL: Estimated @...$_____

TAX: ....$_____

TOTAL: Estimated @...$_____

LESS DEPOSIT: Estimated @...$_____

AMOUNT DUE: Estimated @...$_____

Note: Please make check payable to Menu & Caterer, Inc. Amount due in the form of a Cashiers or Bank Check by [Date]. A separate check is due to Party rental upon arrival on [Date 1] for the estimated total of $____ .

Form 11-2:
A sample
weekend
wedding
proposal
from an
off-premise
caterer.
(Page 9 of 9)

A Sample On-Site Caterer's Proposal

The Hotel Fabulosity

We are pleased that you have chosen the Hotel Fabulosity for your upcoming function. We are looking forward to hosting this important event and would like to acknowledge the following reservation:

In Honor of Ms. Bride & Mr. Groom

Date

Reystion

> The ceremony for this wedding took place in a church; therefore, the contract denotes only the reception details.

> "Hotel speak" for cocktail hour.

5:00– 6:00 p.m.

Penultimate Penthouse

Dinner/Dance

6:00–10:00 p.m.

Tip Top Terrace

Attendance: 200 Guests

This reservation shall be considered definite upon receipt of your signed copy of this contract by [date] and will guarantee the space designated. Along with the reservation confirmation, please enclose a deposit check in the amount of $_____ which will be subject to the standard terms and conditions on the reverse side of this letter. Total prepayment will be required by [date].

Form 11-3: A sample proposal for a wedding where the catering operation is part of the venue, or "on-premise." (Page 1 of 6)

<u>**PROPOSAL**</u>
MS. BRIDE & MR. GROOM   *[date]*
In Charge: Ms. Wedding Coordinator   *555-5555*

Event	*Time*	*Room*	*Guests*
Reception	*5:00–6:00 p.m.*	*Penultimate Penthouse*	*200*
Dinner/Dance	*6:00–10:00 p.m.*	*Tip Top Terrace*	*200*

Reception
An excellent selection of hot hors d'oeuvres & cold canapés – passed butler style on silver trays.

Hot Hors d'oeuvres
Miniature Dim Sum
Miniature Crab Cakes, Creole Sauce
Thai Chicken Satay, Peanut Dipping Sauce
Beggar's Purses with Eggplant and Goat Cheese
Shish Kebob of Lamb with Mint Yogurt Sauce

Cold Canapés
Smoked Salmon Rosette with Fresh Dill
Foie Gras Canapé

Buffet Items
Ice Bowls of Jumbo Shrimp, Cocktail Sauce, Lemon Wedges

Pasta Station
Penne Pasta di Pomodoro, Tortellini Primavera

Risotto Station
Wild Mushroom Risotto
Asparagus & Lobster Risotto
(Additional $__ per person)

Vol-Au-Vent Station
Wild Mushroom
Seafood
Vegetarian
(Additional $___ per person)

Sushi Station
Japanese Chef to Prepare Sushi & Sashimi to Order
Wasabi, Pickled Ginger, and Soy Sauce
(Additional $___ per person)
(No waitress needed)

Form 11-3:
A sample proposal for a wedding where the catering operation is part of the venue, or "on-premise." (Page 2 of 6)

PROPOSAL

MS. BRIDE & MR. GROOM

In Charge: Ms. Wedding Coordinator

[date]

555-5555

Event	Time	Room	Guests
Reception	5:00–6:00 p.m.	Penultimate Penthouse	200
Dinner/Dance	6:00–10:00 p.m.	Tip Top Terrace	200

Dinner

First Course

Grilled Jumbo Shrimp on a Bed of Julienne Vegetables
Citrus Vinaigrette

Entrée

Dry Aged Prime Strip, Cabernet Reduction Truffle Sauce
Sautéed Spinach
Phyllo Bundle of Ratatouille
Sweet and Yukon Gold Pommes Dauphinoise

Salad Course

Frisée Salad with Warm Lardon Dressing, Blue Cheese, and Tossed Walnuts

Dessert

Apple Tart with Apple Sorbet and Vanilla Ice Cream
Calvados Cider Sauce
Wedding Cake Provided by:
[Pastry Chef]
Petits Fours
Coffee Service

Beverages

Full Premium Open Bar to Include Red and White Wine; Champagne; Cordials
and Brandy; and Special Liquors to be Decided
White Wine: Chateau Such-And-Such
Red Wine: Nice Merlot
Champagne: Fizzy French, Brut
Cordials: To Be Served After Dinner

Form 11-3:
A sample proposal for a wedding where the catering operation is part of the venue, or "on-premise." (Page 3 of 6)

PROPOSAL

MS. BRIDE & MR. GROOM   *[date]*

In Charge: Ms. Wedding Coordinator   *555-5555*

Event	Time	Room	Guests
Reception	*5:00–6:00 p.m.*	*Penultimate Penthouse*	*200*
Dinner/Dance	*6:00–10:00 p.m.*	*Tip Top Terrace*	*200*

Room Arrangements

Penultimate Penthouse

Set Reception Style with Bars, Buffet, Cocktail Seating
Provide Baby Grand Piano

Tip Top Terrace

__ Tables with Dance Floor — See diagram

Extra items & arrangements

Escort cards: Provided by guest.   *Place cards: Provided by guest.*

Menu cards: Provided by guest.   *Captain: Provide escort with card table in penthouse.*

Coat room/lounge attendants: Fully staffed.   *Linen: Provided by florist. Please advise.*

Flowers: Client's own arrangements.   *Candles: Hotel to provide votives.*

Photography: Client's own arrangements.   *Audio Visual: To be arranged through other company.*

Complimentary Suite/Room: Bridal Suite and Groom's Changing Room Available On [Date].

Charges

Food & beverage: $_____per person as per contract

___% sales tax   *___% service charge*

Additional reception charges to be advised.

Deposit: $_____ received. Thank you.   *Payment: Total payment due on [date]*

Overtime policy

Overtime is charged at $___ per man hour for every additional hour or fraction thereof. Bar charged at $___ per person for every additional one hour or fraction thereof.

Guarantee policy

A guaranteed attendance of (n) must be given to the hotel at least two (2) days before prior to your function. The hotel will be set for and prepared to serve 3% over the guaranteed attendance.

Billing

Full Payment Prior to Function   *Ms. Wedding Coordinator*
Tel: *Fax:*
Address   *City, State:*   *Zip:*
ARRANGEMENTS WITH: Hotel Manager   *MAITRE D'HOTEL: Hotel Maitre d'*
DATE: *FILE:*
AGREED AND ACCEPTED BY: _____
DATE: _____

Form 11-3:
A sample proposal for a wedding where the catering operation is part of the venue, or "on-premise." (Page 4 of 6)

PROPOSAL

MS. BRIDE & MR. GROOM   *[date]*
In Charge: Ms. Wedding Coordinator   555-5555

Event	Time	Room	Guests
Reception	5:00–6:00 p.m.	Penultimate Penthouse	200
Dinner/Dance	6:00–10:00 p.m.	Tip Top Terrace	200

Hotel Fabulosity Contract Terms and Conditions

1. Billing and Deposit

Billing arrangements must be made in accordance with Hotel policy at the time of booking. All requests for direct billing must be authorized by the Hotel's Credit Department. A non-refundable deposit of $___ per estimated attendees is required along with the signed contract. An additional deposit of up to ___% of all estimated charges is required ___ days in advance of the event. The balance of all charges is due at the time the guaranteed attendance figure is submitted. If direct billing is approved, full payment is due upon receipt of invoice.

2. Guarantee

A specific attendance figure is required three business days prior to the event. This figure will be considered the guarantee, not subject to reduction, and charges made accordingly. If no guarantee figure is given, you will be charged for this number of guests or the number served, whichever is greater. The Hotel will be prepared to serve ___% above the guarantee. Reasonable increases to the guarantee may be accepted up to (n) hours in advance prior to the function. Groups submitting guarantee figures of (n) persons or less are subject to a $___ service charge. (All food charges are subject to a ___% service charge and ___% sales tax. Alcoholic beverages charges are subject to a ___% service charge only.)

3. Guarantee of attendance

Should your guest count fall below ___% of your estimated attendance, a set-up fee will be applied. This fee will be equal to the difference between your guaranteed attendance and ___% of your contracted attendance above, multiplied by the menu price.

4. Cancellation

Groups submitting written cancellations will be responsible for charges based on the following guidelines:

Prior to six months (180 days) — responsible for ___% of total food, beverage and rental charges.

Within three to six months (90 to 179 days) — responsible for ___% of total anticipated food, beverage and rental charges.

Within one to three months (30 to 89 days) — responsible for ___% of total anticipated food, beverage and rental charges.

Within 29 days to 3 days — responsible for ___% of total anticipated food, beverage and rental charges and (n)% of room charge.

Within zero to three days — responsible for ___% of total anticipated food, beverage and rental charges and room charge.

Form 11-3:
A sample proposal for a wedding where the catering operation is part of the venue, or "on-premise." (Page 5 of 6)

Please note that food, beverage, and room rental charges are based upon expected attendance as outlined in this agreement, multiplied by prevailing rental charges and menu prices.

Any collected non-refundable deposit fees will be applied toward applicable cancellation charges.

5. Liability and Damage

The Hotel Fabulosity reserves the right to inspect and control all private functions. The Hotel shall not be liable for any damage to or loss of equipment, merchandise or articles left in the Hotel prior to, during or following the function. The client will be held responsible for any damages to the building, equipment, decorations or fixtures belonging to the Hotel, lost or damaged during the affair due to the activities of its guests. Any damage will be billed to the client at replacement cost.

6. Signs/Displays/Decorations

All signs, displays and/or decorations proposed by the client are subject to the Hotel's approval. All registration, directional or advertisement signs must be printed in a professional manner with signature size limited to a maximum of 22 x 28 inches. No signs, banners, displays or exhibits will be permitted in the public areas without prior Hotel approval. All decorations must meet approval of the City Fire Department. Flammable substances are not permitted in the building or anywhere on the Hotel's premises. The Hotel will not permit the affixing of anything to the walls, floors or ceiling with nails, staples, adhesives or other substance without prior Hotel approval. Any damages resulting from this will be placed on the group's master account.

> Make sure your floral designer is cognizant of the details in this part of the contract.

7. Labor Charges

For meal events requiring setup of tables, linens, silverware and glassware more than 1 _ hours prior to the scheduled event start time, a charge of $___ per waitstaff person per $^1\!/_2$ hour will be applied.

For set up of table linens only, more than 1 _ hours prior to scheduled start time, the following charges will apply: 1-20 tables = $___ charge, 21-40 tables = $___ charge, 41 or more tables = $___ charge.

Resetting of meeting rooms from previously agreed setups will cost $___ for all rooms, except, the Ballroom, the Other Ballroom, which will be a $___ charge per room.

> For an on-premise facility, such as this one, labor charges are delineated as additional fees.

8. Storage

The Hotel Fabulosity will hold and store items left after an event in public meeting rooms for up to ___ hours after the event. It is the responsibility of the contracting party to pick up and remove these articles. After ___ hours, the hotel will discard these materials with no liability to the hotel, its employees or agents.

Additional comments

The person executing this agreement expressly represents that he/she is over 21 years of age and that he/she is authorized to execute this agreement on behalf of said organization. Where the client is a corporation, unincorporated association, partnership, political, social or private group or other legal entity, this agreement shall be binding on such legal entity.

Performance of these conditions are contingent upon the ability to complete the same. We cannot be held responsible for conditions beyond the control of Hotel management which prevent or interfere with performance such as labor disputes, strikes, government restrictions upon travel, transportation, food, beverage or supplies and other cause whether enumerated herein or not.

Form 11-3: A sample proposal for a wedding where the catering operation is part of the venue, or "on-premise." (Page 6 of 6)

Planning the Menu

If you decide to serve any of the following possibilities at your wedding reception, write your invitation accordingly so guests are aware of the timing and have an idea of what kind of meal or refreshment they will be served and when. We include generally accepted times for the different options.

Breakfast

A breakfast reception usually follows a morning ceremony and should start between 9 and 11 a.m. If you choose any later time, you're serving a luncheon reception.

Luncheon

After a late-morning or high noon ceremony, a luncheon reception generally starts around 11:30 a.m. or 12:30 p.m. and goes until 2 p.m. These affairs may include a brief cocktail hour.

In Figure 11-1, we show a menu for a bridesmaid's luncheon although it would be appropriate for a luncheon reception as well. It was created for us by the legendary food guru (and mother of a lovely bride to be) Sheila Lukins.

Figure 11-1:
A menu for
a luncheon
reception.

> ### *Blushing Bridal Luncheon*
>
> *Champagne Punch*
>
> *Demitasse of Sweet Pea Soup*
>
> *Luscious Lobster Salad*
>
> *Delicate Garden Potato Salad*
>
> *Confetti of Corn, Tomato and Avocado*
>
> *Strawberry Shortcake*

VALUE TIP

A tea party is a good solution for a large guest list with budget considerations. These events run about three hours, usually from 2 to 5 p.m. You can serve light finger foods, cookies and cakes — as well as a wedding cake.

Cocktail party

A two-hour cocktail reception with heavy hors d'oeurves (also known as finger food) is less expensive than a full-service seated dinner. However, the food needs to be tasty and somewhat substantial because these events generally run into the dinner hour, usually from 4 to 6 p.m. or 5 to 7 p.m.

The reception menus in the contracts in this chapter provide excellent examples of heavy hors d'oeuvres.

Dinner

In this book, as well in *Weddings For Dummies,* we include several comprehensive menus for seated dinner receptions. The starting times are 5:30 p.m. at the earliest and 9 p.m. at the latest.

Figure 11-2 shows a menu that's innovative because it requires only three ingredients for each dish. It is courtesy of the award-winning chef and cookbook author Rozanne Gold. All the recipes can be found in her book, *Recipes 1-2-3 Menu Cookbook* (Little Brown & Company).

Figure 11-2:
A simple menu for a dinner reception.

A Wedding Supper

Sweet Corn Soup with Scallion Butter

Smoked Salmon Quesadillas

Stuffed Tenderloin with Black Olives and Sun-Dried Tomatoes

Potato Silk

Gelato D'Arancia, Candied Orange Peel

Dessert

If you're trying to save money, a champagne- or dessert-wines-and-dessert reception is a lovely way to go. These generally start around 8:30 p.m. or 9:00 p.m. Write the invitation along these lines: "Please join us for dessert and cocktails to celebrate our marriage at such-and-such time and location." This way, no one will starve all day in anticipation of a late-night dinner feast.

Figure 11-3 shows an assortment of exceptional dessert wines that you may serve with a dessert and cheese buffet to create a festive after-dinner celebration. The list, courtesy of Roberta Morrell, a friend and renowned wine expert, is culled from the extensive selection served at the Morrell Wine Bar and Café in Rockefeller Center.

Figure 11-3:
A fantasy
dessert
wine menu.

Muscat de St. Jean de Minervois, Val d'Orbieu, NV, France
Tastes of apricots and peaches
Banyuls, Clos des Paulittes 1998, Southwestern France
Red and sweet (but not cloying) with an amazing flavor that clicks
with chocolate and coffee
Muscat, Vin de Glaciere, Bonny Doon 1998, California
Spicy, intense, delicious!
Passito, Tenuta Sant'Antonio, Colori d'Autunno, 1995, Verona Italy
Thick and powerful, nutty and sweet
Taylor-Floodgate 30-Year-Old Tawny Port
Notes of oranges and raisins
Pinot Gris, Mendelson, 1998, Napa Valley, California
Creamy texture, fresh fruit flavors and exotic spices
Sauternes, Chateau Lafaurie Peyraguey 1995, Bordeaux, France
Creamy, classy, gorgeous texture with lemon, honey,
and dried apricot flavors.

Tending Bar

With some exceptions, most people serve alcohol at their wedding. If you have rented a site and are working with a caterer, or if you are hosting a wedding at your home, you may be purchasing all the liquor yourself at a supplier. We give you tons of information on stocking your own bar in Chapter 10 of *Weddings For Dummies*. In this section, we give you some other methods for determining how much to purchase as well as the quantities of non-alcoholic beverages to buy.

Laws that relate to liquor licenses for caterers at off-premise sites have been rewritten recently in many states, so it's possible that your caterer can supply your liquor for you. In any case, he or she can advise you on quantities to buy as well as types of liquor that are popular in your area or with your guests. Rum and tequila, for example, are more popular with younger crowds.

A growing number of states are passing "social host" laws where everyone from the vendor to the host is responsible if an intoxicated person injures himself/herself or others. Specify that the bartenders may not serve minors, obviously intoxicated guests, or known alcoholics.

As you estimate how much liquor you will need, keep in mind the following guidelines on average guest consumption:

- ✔ For a liter bottle of alcohol, estimate 20 to 22 drinks.
- ✔ For a one-hour cocktail reception before dinner, estimate two drinks per person.
- ✔ For a two-hour cocktail party, estimate three drinks per person.
- ✔ For a four-hour dinner party, estimate four drinks per person.
- ✔ There are approximately five glasses in a bottle of wine.
- ✔ A liter of soda has five to seven glasses depending on glass size and ice.
- ✔ For a champagne toast, figure on 75 glasses per case.
- ✔ For wine with dinner preceded by a cocktail party, you need two or two and a half glasses per person. The proportion of red to white will depend on the season, the wine served, and your guests.

For elegant service of drinks at tables, individual bottles of soda or mixers, along with the alcohol in an iced glass, are a spiffy touch.

Form 11-4, the Bar Setup Checklist, which you can also find on the CD-ROM, is a checklist of things to take into account whenever you are hosting a party that includes bars.

Bar Setup Checklist

❑ Does the caterer charge a service or corkage fee on top of the bar "setup" fee that includes ice and fruit?

❑ Is it possible for the hosts to personally supply any wines or champagne at an in-house venue? If so, what is the corkage fee?

❑ Will the liquor supplier take back unopened bottles of liquor and unchilled bottles of wine?

❑ Do you wish to have blended drinks, specialty drinks, or drinks that require special preparation? (For example: drinks such as cosmopolitans, martinis and margaritas that require shaking and particular glasses.) What ingredients and equipment do you need to arrange in advance? Are any of those included in the regular bar setup?

❑ What non-alcoholic beverages will be available? (These might include fruited iced teas, fresh squeezed juices, sangria without alcohol filled with slices of fresh lemons, limes, and oranges and served in glass pitchers, or nonalcoholic beers.)

❑ If you're using a full-service facility, what brands will the banquet manager provide? What is the price difference between inexpensive "well" brands and "premium" or "top shelf," the most expensive?

❑ Are liquor stores allowed to deliver in your state? What arrangements can you make with the caterer to pick up the liquor?

Form 11-4:
Work out a beverage strategy with the caterer regarding the bar.

❑ Will your site accept liquor deliveries in advance of your reception? Do they have a secure place to keep it?

❑ If you're supplying the liquor, where should leftover open bottles of liquor be left? Who will pick them up for you after the wedding?

❑ Do you feel comfortable serving liquor to vendors such as musicians and photographers? How do you want to instruct the caterer regarding this matter?

In Form 11-5, which you can also find on the CD so you can modify the list to fit your needs, we show you a typical order of what would be needed for 100 guests with a four-hour open bar including a cocktail hour. Note that these amounts are only estimates. It's always better to have returns than to be caught short with no liquor store open within 100 miles.

Bar Checklist

❑	Scotch	4 liters
❑	Vodka	6 liters
❑	Gin	5 liters
❑	Rum	2 liters
❑	Bourbon	1–2 liters
❑	Blended whisky	1–2 liters
❑	Tequila	1 liter
❑	Campari	1 liter
❑	Dry Vermouth	2 750-ml bottles
❑	Sweet Vermouth	2 750-ml bottles
❑	Assorted beers	2 or 3 cases
❑	Lite beer	2 cases
❑	White Wine during cocktails	1½ cases
❑	Red Wine during cocktails	6 bottles
❑	Champagne during cocktails	1½ cases
❑	Cola	14 liters
❑	Diet cola	12 liters
❑	Lemon lime soda	7 liters
❑	Diet lemon lime	7 liters
❑	Ginger ale	7 liters
❑	Club soda	9 liters
❑	Tonic	1 case
❑	Juices (cranberry, orange, grapefruit)	8 quarts each

Form 11-5:
Figure out how much liquor you need.

If you wish to serve after-dinner drinks or are hosting a dessert, coffee, and liqueur party, here's a list of various possibilities. For elegant service, use brandy snifters and cordial glasses:

- ✔ **Cognac:** From the Cognac region in France, brands such as Hennessy and Courvoisier

- ✔ **Sambuca:** Licorice flavor, often served with coffee beans in the bottom of the glass

- ✔ **B&B:** Benedictine and brandy

- ✔ **Kahlua:** Mexican coffee liqueur, Tia Maria-Jamaican coffee liqueur

- ✔ **Cointreau or Grand Marnier:** Orange flavored liqueur

- ✔ **Cordials:** May include either inexpensive or name brands with flavors such as Crème de Cacao (chocolate), Crème de Menthe (mint), peach, apricot, pear, peppermint, and banana

In some states, you can't buy beer where you buy liquor, so make separate arrangements with your caterer.

Keeping the Food and Drink People Informed

A couple of days before your wedding, fill out and make copies of Form 11-6, A Day-of Details Food Worksheet, and Form 11-7, A Day-of Details Beverage Worksheet, of which you can also find blank versions on the CD. Keep one and give the others to your liquor supplier and baker. Fax the forms and then get them back initialed to confirm they have received them.

A Day-of Details Food Worksheet

To: Patty Cake Bakery

Re: The Hurly-Burly Wedding

Time: 1 p.m.

Date: Saturday, August 24, 2001

Place: The Mansion on Lake Gandolf

Address: 810 Tolkien Drive

Phone: 477-555-8888

Directions: Go left on Main street until Route 33. Exit at Hobbitville N. Take road 10 miles to interpass. Right under bridge, enter at left-service entrance.

Time	Item	Delivered To
3:00 – 3:30 p. m.	Wedding cake: Four-tier mocha and raspberry cheesecake iced with whipped mocha cream. Cake top: Blonde bride in riding ensemble and groom with brown ponytail and glasses. Groom's cake: Chocolate CD player	See above; see Mr. Golum at service entrance (ext. 234)

Form 11-6: Make sure your baker knows where to deliver the cake.

A Day-Of Details Beverage Worksheet

To: Les Vins de Pays Wines and Liquors

Re: The Hurly-Burly Wedding

Time: 1 p.m.

Date: Saturday, August 24, 2001

Place: The Mansion on Lake Gandolf

Address: 810 Tolkien Drive

Phone: 477-555-8888

Directions: Go left on Main street until Route 33. Exit at Hobbitville N. Take road 10 miles to interpass. Right under bridge, enter at left-service entrance.

Time	*Item*	*Delivered To*
Thursday, August 22; between 12 and 2 p.m.	1 ltr. Johnny Walker Black 1 ltr. Johnny Walker Red 6 ltrs. Dewars 1 ltr. MacCallan	See above; see Mr. Golum at service entrance (ext. 234)

Form 11-7:
Give your liquor supplier all the details.

Forms on the CD-ROM

Form 11-1	A Tasting Worksheet	Record your thoughts about the food during your tasting.
Form 11-4	Bar Setup Checklist	Figure out a beverage strategy with the caterer regarding the bar.
Form 11-5	Bar Checklist	Figure out how much liquor you need.
Form 11-6	A Day-Of Details Food Worksheet	Make sure your baker knows where to deliver the cake.
Form 11-7	A Day-Of Details Beverage Worksheet	Give your liquor supplier all the details.

Chapter 12

A Bed of Roses

Here we go again with another subject to challenge your Trivial Pursuit skills — the art of floral decor. A wedding just isn't a wedding without flowers, but it's a big blossoming world out there, so you need to narrow down the field.

In this chapter, we facilitate that process by providing tips and worksheets for interviewing floral designers and comparing their services. We also give you a bunch of ideas about various flowers and arrangements to help get you started on designing the look of your wedding.

Getting a Sense of What You Want

Before you start interrogating florists, get a sense of the kinds of flowers you like. Begin by perusing all sorts of magazines (not just wedding ones) and by clipping photographs of rooms that entice you and convey the feeling you want for your wedding. If a floral designer is credited in a photo you like, be sure to jot down the name; if a florist is familiar with the designer's work, it may help the florist think about the look you want. You don't need to be a horticulturist to think about colors, mood, or style such as romantic, modern, or rococo. Focus on these things first and then find the flowers that go with the image you want.

As you do your initial dreaming and research, be sure to read the sections "Do Pick the Flowers" and "Let Your Flowers Do the Talking" in this chapter to get some ideas about where you want your flowers to appear and what your flowers symbolize.

To further your expertise, take a look at www.aboutflowers.com, which is sponsored by the Society of American Florists and has photographs of just about every flower under the sun.

Do Pick the Flowers

Filling out Form 12-1, the Flower-Décor Worksheet, helps you crystallize your ideas before you meet with a florist. Form 12-1 also gives the prospective florist a basis on which to submit realistic proposals, and ensures that you get to compare apples to apples. Anyway, the florist will think you're so smart and organized. (See the section "Finding a Fabulous Florist" later in this chapter for more information on selecting a florist.)

As you tick off the arrangements you want, keep in mind that some of the following items won't pertain to you. For example, linens may be included at the banquet hall, but if you're interested in which kind the florist would suggest and the price, check the box anyway.

Flower-Décor Worksheet

Altar or ceremony platform flowers_____

Chuppah_____

Aisle arrangements_____

Pew flowers/bows_____

Aisle runner_____

Entrance flowers_____

<u>Personals</u>

Bridal bouquet_____

Tossing bouquet_____

Maid of honor's bouquet_____

Bridal attendants' bouquets_____

Petal baskets_____

Ring bearer flowers_____

Other bouquets (corsages, tussie mussies, mothers' flowers)

_____

Groom's boutonniere_____

Other boutonnieres_____

Hair or head piece flowers_____

Form 12-1:
Figure out
your flower
needs.
(Page 1 of 2)

Cocktail Reception

Entrance décor _____

Escort card table _____

Cocktail table arrangements _____

Cocktail table linens _____

Buffet station flowers _____

Bar flowers _____

Station/bar linens _____

Hors d'oeuvres-tray flowers _____

Candles _____

Other background arrangements _____

Restroom flowers _____

Amenities basket(s) _____

Reception Arrangements

Entrance _____

Table numbers _____

Centerpieces _____

Table linens _____

Napkins _____

Napkin flowers/tying _____

Band stand flowers _____

Candles _____

Chair treatments _____

Other room décor _____

House flowers _____

Cake flowers _____

Cake table flowers/linen _____

Miscellaneous

Ceiling treatment _____

Tent poles _____

Tree rentals _____

Flowering plants _____

Prop rentals (urns, furnishings, and so on) _____

Garden ceremony items _____

Other _____

Form 12-1:
Figure out
your flower
needs.
(Page 2 of 2)

Let Your Flowers Do the Talking

Since Roman times, people have ascribed various meanings to flowers and herbs. The Victorians took floriography to new heights by producing several books on the subject, the most famous being *La Langue de Fleurs*. A search on `www.abebooks.com` or `www.bookfinder.com` will turn up many of the versions that have been published since the 1850s, including Kate Greenaway's classic *Language of Flowers* (London, Routledge), published in 1884.

In times gone by, a man may have sent a woman a red chrysanthemum (which means "I love you") only to have the object of his affection respond with a striped carnation (which symbolizes refusal). Of course, both parties needed to refer to the same book in order to know what the other was talking about. Today, one of the few places where the language of flowers has any relevance is at a wedding.

As you choose your flowers, keep in mind their potent traditional meanings. It's also fun to indicate the meanings on menu cards and ceremony programs, or to use flowers rather than numbers to designate your tables.

Table 12-1 helps you sort out the various meanings of some popular flowers.

Table 12-1	Popular Flowers and Their Traditional Meanings	
Flower	*Symbolizes*	*Description*
Alstromeria (*Istromeria*)	Devotion	Also known as the Peruvian lily. Carmine, orange, yellow, and pink flowers, flecked with tawny tints. Bloom traditionally from early to mid summer. Last well in water, growing paler as they age gracefully.
Amaryllis (*Hippeastrum hybrids*)	Splendid beauty	Showy red, pink, and white flowers clustered at the top. Long, hollow stems that need supports for complicated arrangements. Another option: Cut off stems and use the heads only for a cocktail arrangement.
Baby's breath (*Gypsophila*)	Innocence	Tiny, white, lighter-than-air sprays. Inexpensive. Used primarily as filler, but an entire bouquet can look dramatic.
Calla lily (*Zantedeschia aethiopica*)	Magnificent beauty	Pure white, pink, or yellow folded trumpets with a long central spike. Large, glossy leaves. Used for funerals in England, but appropriate for American weddings. Miniature hybrids now available in colors that border on Day-Glo.
Camellia (*Camellia*)	Unpretending excellence (red); perfect loveliness (white)	Hardy despite fragile, fluffy blooms. Glossy green foliage.

Flower	Symbolizes	Description
Carnation (*Dianthus caryophyllus*)	Devotion	Frilly basic flower for any wedding need, including boutonnieres, bouquets, or arrangements. Inexpensive. New varieties are less trite than the traditional pink, red, and white. In the hands of a talented designer, can be innocuous, but shouldn't be focal point of arrangement.
Daisy (*Leucanthemum vulgare*)	Innocence	White petals surrounding a yellow eye. Flowers in late spring and throughout summer. Closes at dusk. Inexpensive and hardy. Use in loose bouquets or tie into "chains" for bracelets and head wreaths.
Freesia (*Freesia*)	Innocence	Snowy white, pink, mauve, cream, and golden flowers. Fragrant, elegant, and somewhat delicate. Flowers throughout winter, spring, and summer. Popular for sprays.
Gillyflower (*Dianthus Caryophyllu*)	Bonds of affection	A fancy name for any flower in the genus *dianthus,* such as the carnation. Can also refer to stocks and wallflowers. Frilled formal blooms. Colors range from white to peach to scarlet. Very hardy and inexpensive.
Honeysuckle (*Lonicera Periclymenum*)	Generosity	Semi-evergreen white flowers.Heady fragrance. Blooms in latewinter. To make them last in water, strip off leaves below water line and crush the end of the stem.
Hydrangea (*Hydrangea*)	Boaster or heartlessness (but don't let that deter you from using this versatile, fairly inexpensive flower)	Tiny florets in large, delicatelace caps. Bloom in early summer, turning from a green-tinged white to pink or blue. Used in bouquets andarrangements, either fresh or dried to a warm-tea color.
Larkspur (*Delphinium ajacis*)	Laughter	Smaller cousin of delphinium. Spikes of tightly knit florets. Pink, lilac, violet, blue, and white shades.

(continued)

Table 12-1   (continued)

Flower	Symbolizes	Description
Lily *(Lilium)*	Happiness, honor, truth, purity, and majesty	Fragile, beautiful, and heavily scented. Trumpet-shaped flowers. Last well in water. Ranging from white with yellow throat (White Lady) to yellow and pink. Some-times flecked. Caution: the intense odor drives some people berserk. Lily of the Valley (*Convallaria majalis*) features white, bell-like flowers and rich green foliage. Madonna Lily (*Lilium candidum*) is the original wedding flower.
Mock orange *(Philadelphus)*	Brotherly love	Pure white flower clusters with a terrific scent that can perfume an entire room. Less expensive and more available than orange blossoms.
Orange blossoms *(Citrus)*	Fertility and love	The tree can flower during any season and bear fruit at the same time. Delicate white flowers. Given by Juno, Roman goddess of marriage, to Jupiter on their wedding day. Queen Victoria wore an orange blossom wreath in 1840, and Jacqueline Kennedy carried them when she married Aristotle Onassis in 1968. Rather rare and very expensive.
Orchid *(Orchidaceae)*	Love and beauty	Delicate but, amazingly, stay fresh for hours out of water. Hundreds of varieties and colors. With lavish sprays in pink, white, yellow, red, and striped and spotted flowers, *Phalaenopsis,* or Moth Orchid, is the most popular. Dendrobium have long flower spikes. Cymbidium are the most popular for weddings. Cattleyas, used for classic corsages, are large, open, and available in virtually every color but black.
Peony *(Paeonia)*	Bashfulness	Large, bold flowers. Intense shades of white, pink, red, or yellow as well as hybrid shades, such as coral. Used for centerpieces and bouquets. Increasingly available year round via import.

Flower	Symbolizes	Description
Rose *(Rosa)*	Love (red rose) and worthiness (white rose)	The year-round, favorite flower of romance. Fragrant, luxurious, hardy. Available in a variety of colors and varieties. Hybrid tea roses are densely petalled and less hardy with a long growing season. Floribundas, a cross between hybrid tea roses and dwarf polyanthas, feature clusters of small blooms. Old roses or musk roses have a less formal look and a sweet musk scent. Sweet-scented China roses are often bright pink but darken with age. Used either closed or blown open, depending on desired effect.
Stephanotis *(Stephanotis floribunda)*	Marital happiness	An evergreen flower with white, waxy, star-like flowers. Very traditional. Last well in water and used in bouquets or as trailers in large arrangements. Sometimes called Madagascar jasmine.
Tulip *(Tulipa)*	Love, fame, and passion	Turban-shaped spring flower increasingly available year-round and in a variety of colors from plain white to striped purple. French tulips have a ruffled edge. Somewhat fragile. Light, sweet scent. In arrangements, allow for slight natural elongation of stem as the flower matures.

A few blurbs on herbs

The language of flowers encompasses the language of herbs as well. Since ancient Greece, where brides carried herbs and grains as signs of fertility, many a bride has slipped a sprig of herbs into her bridal bouquet to either convey a special meaning or to fool the evil eye. Consider an herb sprig in your attendants' bouquets, the men's boutonnieres, or on each guest's napkin.

Table 12-2 acquaints you with some popular herbs commonly used at weddings.

Table 12-2	**Popular Herbs and Their Meanings**	
Herb	*Symbolizes*	*Description*
Borage *(Borago officinalis)*	Courage	Opens in summer. Flowers open pink and then turn blue.
Mint *(Mentha)*	Wisdom	Fragrant decorative leaves. Peppermint, *M. piperita*, has purple stem and purple-tinged leaves. *M. citrata* has sharp, lemony scent. Thought to stir up amorous feelings.
Myrtle *(Myrtus odorata)*	Love and remembrance	Known in Europe as Sweet Cicely. A flowering herb. Divided green leaves. Umbels of white flowers, similar to Queen Anne's Lace. Flowers in early spring. Varieties include periwinkle (*Vinca minor*), California laurel, and moneywort.
Parsley *(Petroselinum crispum)*	Rejoicing or beginnings	Green, finely dissected, smooth or curly leaves. Breath freshener but can cause tell-tale trace on teeth.
Sage *(Salvia)*	Immortality, domestic virtue, and esteem	Perennial. Long spikes of blue or purple flowers. Aromatic. Lasts well in water.
Rosemary *(Rosemarinus officinalis)*	Friendship, love, fidelity, and remembrance	Gray, needle-like leaves. Pale blue flowers. superstitions. In Slovak weddings, guests wear sprigs attached to lapels. In some countries, people stick a sprig in the hands of the dead. As Ophelia said, distributing her herbs, "There's rosemary, that's for remembrance — pray you, love, remember."

Herb	Symbolizes	Description
Sweet basil *(Ocimum basilicum)*	Good wishes	Fragrant, green, and sometimes purplish. Tuck into small bunches of flowers. A tasty snack between ceremony and reception.
Thyme *(Thymus)*	Courage or activity	Fragrant. Pink, mauve, or purple flowers. Short stems.

Leaf all your worries behind

Even the greenery you use to offset flowers is imbued with meaning — or at least some species are, as Table 12-3 indicates.

Table 12-3	Popular Greens and Their Meanings	
Greenery	Symbolizes	Description
Boxwood *(Buxus)*	Stoicism	Sometimes called *box*. Small, dense, glossy, shrub-like leaves. Long-lasting in water. Sometimes smells like bruised leaves. Available all year. Use for topiaries and garlands.
Ivy *(Hedera H. helix)*	Fidelity and friendship	Hardy, leathery evergreen leaves. Variegated ivies edged in gold, silver, or rose make nice ornamental statement. Used as filler or to wind around pillars or poles. Looks best trailing and twining naturally rather than wired stiffly into sprays. Tip: To improve appearance, fully immerse in cold water for up to four hours.

Finding a Fabulous Florist

After you have some idea of what sort of flowers you want and where you want them (see the previous sections), it's time to stop and smell the roses — or at least sniff out the best floral designer for the job. Ask around for the names of florists; get recommendations from friends and the other vendors of your wedding.

Form 12-2, the Floral Designer Interview Checklist, provides you with a handy-dandy list of questions to ask prospective florists when you interview them. Print out a version from the CD-ROM and take it along for reference and to scribble notes on.

At the interview, look at photographs of weddings, individual bouquets, and events for which the florist has supplied flowers or décor. Judge the quality of the designs rather than the quality of the photographs.

Afterward, if you and the florist seem to be on the same wavelength, ask her to submit a design plan and estimate for your wedding.

Take Form 12-3, a bid sheet, with you as well when you go off to interview a floral designer. Floral and décor costs run the gamut from inexpensive to "if you have to ask, you can't afford it."

Don't play guessing games about your floral budget when you meet with prospective florists. Be up front about your budget and see what the designer can do within your price range. It's a waste of your time (and theirs) to have them work up a proposal that is outlandish by your standards.

Floral Designer Interview Checklist

❑ Have they worked at your venue(s) before? If not, will they make a site visit before sending you a proposal?

❑ Look at photographs of weddings, individual bouquets, and events for which they've supplied flowers or décor. Judge the quality of the designs, not the quality of the photographs.

❑ What props, tablecloths, floral containers, and other "extras" does the florist own? What would need to be rented and by whom?

❑ Do you like the environment in their space or shop?

❑ Are their concepts original? How do they respond to your ideas? If you've brought clippings are they interested in them?

❑ How do they handle substituting flowers if the ones you've decided upon are unavailable?

❑ Will they do a sample centerpiece/table set up for you?

❑ What are the set up and break-down fees?

❑ How soon can you expect a proposal?

❑ What are their payment terms?

❑ How long do you have to make up your mind?

❑ When do they need a deposit?

Form 12-2:
Know what
to ask when
interviewing
florists.

The Bid Picture: Floral Designers

Florist and Contact Information	Price Estimate	Notes
Company: Contact Name: Phone: Address: E-mail:	$	
Company: Contact Name: Phone: Address: E-mail:	$	
Company: Contact Name: Phone: Address: E-mail:	$	
Company: Contact Name: Phone: Address: E-mail:	$	

Form 12-3:
Compare wedding flower estimates.

Getting Down to Dollars and Scents

After finding a florist whose talent enthralls you, it's time to talk turkey — or tulips. A full-service florist/event designer will send you a proposal that looks something like Form 12-4. (We omit prices because they vary so widely depending on where you live, the time of year, and the caliber of florist; any numbers we made up would seem naively low or exorbitantly high.) If you're contracting for a simple set up — just centerpieces, for example — you'll probably just receive an invoice.

Sample Proposal from a Full-Service Floral Designer

May 10, 2010

Dear Ms. Ella Fant:

We are delighted that you have asked Hot New Florist Ltd., (HNF) to submit a proposal for your wedding on Sept. 25, 2010. The following is based on our conversations with you as well as our experience in working at your site, The Old World Club.

Foyer

1 exquisite arrangement composed of flowering quince branches and white amaryllis in a faux marble urn. $_____

Ceremony — Rotunda

1 8-by-12-foot platform, covered with ecru taffeta, rental included. $_____

4 arrangements of white tulips in clear glass urns on white marbleized pedestals. $_____

16 candle stanchions (approx. 8 ft. tall) decorated with ivy, to line the aisle for first 8 rows of chairs. $_____

4 ficus trees (rentals) outfitted with bee lights for room corners. $_____

Cocktails —The Governor's Lounge

12 cocktail tables outfitted with green dupioni silk cloths (rentals). $ _____

12 arrangements on cocktail tables. Gardenias floating in water in glass bubble bowls, 4 green glass votive candles on each table. $_____

**Note: 4 gold chairs with green cushions for each table (supplied by club)

Form 12-4:
What you can expect in a proposal from a full-service floral designer. (Page 1 of 3)

2 bars and 2 hors d'oeuvres stations outfitted with green dupioni cloths. $ _____

4 tall glass cylinders filled with various shades of green flowers and vines (euphorbia, hydrangea, ivy, smilax) **as per photo shown. $_____

1 escort card table (no cloth, use the large wood table from club). 24 assorted candles, 6 white orchid plants in green terra cotta pots. $ _____

Dinner — The Hunt Ballroom

Entrance: Exquisite, large (3 ft. at top) arrangement in glass urn filled with shades of white, champagne, rose, deep pinks, tulips, roses, peonies, (if available). $ _____

20 centerpieces:

Option #1-Iron candelabra entwined with greenery, center filled with an abundance of roses, freesia, parrot tulips, ranunculus (no green in center). Each table will be in the same palate, but will be different in shades and shape. $ _____

Option #2-Combination of tall and low centerpieces. Tall (will be above eye level) with center airy, constructed of metal "branches"(as per our discussion and enclosed sketch). Each table one color arrangements of flowers — some white, some pink, some rose. The low centerpieces will not go above 12 inches in height and will be constructed in invisible containers. $ _____

Candles — Each table will have 5 to 7 assorted height pillar candles and 5 votive candles $_____(votives supplied by club) $ _____

Linens — Use club underlays (white) and cover with rental ecru damask squares (20). $ _____

200 club napkins tied with ecru wired ribbons. $ _____

12 trees, approximately 8-10 feet tall, palm and ficus for corners of room (rental). $ _____

Note: 210 wooden chairs supplied by club from lower ballroom.

Form 12-4:
What you can expect in a proposal from a full-service floral designer. (Page 2 of 3)

Personals

1 bride's bouquet: Hand wired, all champagne roses, finished with gold ribbon. $_____

1 maid-of-honor bouquet: Hand wired, slightly smaller than brides bouquet, all pink roses, finished with silver ribbon. $ _____

4 attendants' bouquets: Tied bouquets. One white roses, one red roses, one pink freesia, one deep rose tulip. All tied with silver ribbon. $ _____

1 groom's boutonniere: champagne rose. $_____

8 gentlemen's boutonnieres: white freesia. $ _____

Miscellaneous

2 ladies' room vases: pink ranunculus. $_____

1 men's room vase: same $_____

1 amenities basket: $_____ n/c

1 bride's tossing bouquet: $_____ n/c

Other Requests

Set up and break down. $_____

Escort card table arrangement, entrance arrangement, 3 centerpieces delivered to bride's mother's home by 10 a.m. Sunday for post-wedding brunch. (Mrs. Swan, 633 Park Avenue, Apt. 12 D). $_____

Total with option 1. $_____

Total with option 2. $_____

Estimate does not include sales tax.

Form 12-4:
What you can expect in a proposal from a full-service floral designer. (Page 3 of 3)

After you receive the proposal, you can work with the florist to add and delete items, tweak and re-tweak, obsess about tulips versus roses, and so on. Usually, the proposal becomes the basis for the contract — to which the essential legal jargon is added. An example of this contract is shown in Form 12-5. The invoice that you actually pay will be an itemized bill.

Sample Floral Contract

[Date]

Dear _____:

Thank you for selecting Hot New Florist Ltd., (HNF) to supply the decor for your wedding on _____ at the _____. We find that a full explanation of company practices in advance of the event helps to eliminate any unnecessary misunderstanding. Please take time to read the following paragraphs carefully.

Terms of Agreement   If someone takes a candelabra, you pay for it!

All materials provided for parties (except flowers and flowering plants, which must be purchased) are provided on a rental basis, unless explicitly agreed otherwise. From delivery at the party site until pick-up within a reasonable amount of time (given delivery schedules, weekend closings, etc.), clients assume full responsibility for all materials provided for a party. Repair when possible of any damaged items will be billed to clients unless the damage was due to the negligence of HNF employees. Lost, stolen, or completely damaged items will be charged to the client at retail value less the rental fee.

Changes   Custom items are made far in advance.

In order to have sufficient time to acquire supplies and custom made necessary items for your event, quantities described on the enclosed proposal will be considered FINAL seven (7) days before your event. With reasonably short notice we can provide suitable items when you are faced with unexpected increases. We will do our best to obtain additional IDENTICAL items for you when asked to accommodate increases. Additional charges for increases will be made; however, we are unable to reduce our charges for tablecloths, chairs, centerpieces, posters, lighting, or signage if your count decreases after the seven (7) days before your event.

Payment

Upon your agreement to the enclosed proposal, we require a nonrefundable deposit minimum of 50% of the total as confirmation of the order. The remaining 50% balance is due one week prior to the event. The agreed cost for floral and decor services to be provided by HNF is $_____. Payment for any other costs (last-minute changes) is due ten (10) days after receipt of an itemized bill. Please sign both copies of this agreement and return one signed copy with your 50% payment of $_____.

We look forward to working with you on this special occasion.

Sincerely,

_____   for Hot New Florist Ltd.

Accepted by: _____   Date: _____

Form 12-5:
An example
of a floral
contract.

Confirming Your Plans

A couple of days before your wedding, make two copies of Form 12-6, the Day-of Details Florist Worksheet. Keep one and give the other to your florist. A blank version appears on the CD-ROM for you to customize.

Day-of Details Florist Worksheet

To: Stellar Floral And Design Company

Event: The Montague-Capulet Wedding

Date: Saturday August 24, 20001

Ceremony: Our Holy Lady, 233 Feud Street; 11:30 a.m. SHARP

Reception: Trendoid Hotel, 810 Edgy Street; 1 p.m.

Flowers	Time	Delivered To
Bride's and attendants' bouquets, brides mother's corsage, bride's father's boutonniere	10 a.m. (for pre-wedding photos)	Hotel: The Charisma Suite, 2nd Floor
All other boutonnieres and groom's mother's corsages	11 a.m.	Church: Front entrance. Florist to pin on all men's boutonnieres and corsage for groom's mother
All cocktail and reception flowers. **Don't forget tossing bouquet!**	To be announced	Cocktail flowers: The Nouveau Room Terrace Reception: The Grand Ballroom. Give tossing bouquet to Maitre d', Sharon
10 centerpieces	After reception	The Manor Room, 2nd floor (for brunch the next day)

Form 12-6: Give your florist a concise plan to use on the big day.

Making Alternative Arrangements

One of the biggest costs in the flower universe is labor. If you have the time and the inclination (or a posse of doting aunts dying for a wedding assignment), consider going into do-it-yourself mode. Or you may ask your florist to come up with some simpler decorating ideas that require fewer stems and helping hands. See Figure 12-1 for examples of centerpieces.

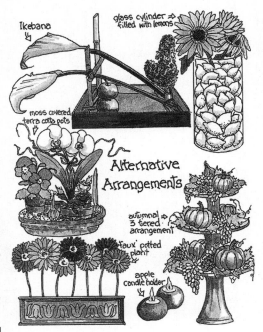

Figure 12-1:
Lavish floral
centerpieces
aren't the
only way
to go.

The following tips will help you create a unique look for a reasonable price:

✔ Consider using long banquet tables instead of rounds. It can be an interesting look with a row down the center of votive candles interspersed with bud vases.

✔ Use other elements to create centerpieces that use fewer flowers: glass bowls of green apples with ivy, tiered plates laden with varieties of grapes, miniature pumpkins, and acorns, or highly stylized, minimalist arrangements such as ikebana (see Figure 12-1). The look of the room comprises all the tables together, so alternating tables that have ornate arrangements with those that have smaller ones won't diminish the beauty of your reception.

✔ Fill glass cylinder vases with an inexpensive material such as whole or sliced lemons (line the outside of the cylinder with slices), colorful birdseed, tiny pinecones, or lentils, and top with a couple of sunflowers or bird of paradise stems.

✔ Use the available banquet cloths for underlays and top them with a square of contrasting color or more lavish fabric.

- Instead of mixed cut flowers, use a moss-covered terra cotta pie dish (used under large flower pots) as a base and fill it with small pots of flowering plants such as primroses, pansies, African violets, and one orchid for height.

- Use petals and greens in lieu of flowers to decorate the cake table.

- To accent an escort card table, use small pots of herbs or flowering plants rather than an oversized floral piece.

- Scoop out apples or pears to make a small well in the top, drop in a disc candle (sold as "floating candles") or votive, and use them to add polish to tables that have small arrangements. Tip: Rub lemon juice on cut parts to prevent browning.

- Create "faux" potted plants by pressing soaked floral foam in the bottoms of long or round terra-cotta planters, fill with moss or dirt, and stick in flowers that have sturdy stems (wire them if necessary), such as gerber daisies, sunflowers, and calla lilies.

- Put scented candles, rather than flowers, in the ladies' and men's rooms.

Forms on the CD-ROM

Form 12-1	Flower-Décor Worksheet	Figure out your flower needs.
Form 12-2	Floral Designer Interview Checklist	Know what to ask when interviewing florists.
Form 12-3	The Bid Picture: Floral Designers	Compare wedding flower estimates.
Form 12-6	Day-of Details Florist Worksheet	Give your florist a concise plan for use on the big day.

Part V
Gifts, Garb, Pics, and Tips

In this part . . .

Among the myriad details a wedding entails are the joys (and headaches) of registering for gifts, selecting clothes for the big day, hiring a photographer or videographer, and tackling paperwork. You'll find out the best way to finesse these tasks and more in this part.

Chapter 13

Greed Expectations and Registry Realities

- -

In This Chapter

▶ Figuring out what you need

▶ Registering on the Net

▶ Keeping track of the goodies

- -

*W*e don't know why, but for some reason, an impending wedding suddenly makes the normally mundane task of setting the table seem as complicated as mapping the human genome. Suddenly you're not just looking at plates but discussing esoterica such as electroplating techniques, the translucency of bone china, and the percentage of chrome in stainless steel. What's more, you're forced to ponder questions like "What's a charger?" and "What's the difference between a dinner plate and a luncheon plate?" — things hardly anybody has given a hoot about since the Harding administration.

While it may seem shallow, look at registering for gifts as one of the rewards of going through the stress of planning a wedding. Registering for gifts may seem like a chore, but it can save time and prevent misunderstandings. If handled adroitly, you may get better results than if you wrote a letter to Santa, clicked your heels three times, or uncorked a genie in a bottle. In this chapter, we give you advice (and a plethora of worksheets) to make the process of registering for gifts go smoothly.

Creating Your Wish List

Despite the variety and audaciousness of registries these days, it's difficult to find one store that sells everything you need for your new life together. Many couples find it useful to divide their registry among two or three retailers — for example, a home furnishings store for decorative items and casual glassware and china; a department store for linens, formal china, stemware, crystal, and kitchen appliances; and a home improvement center for house and garden supplies.

Don't forget boutiques, artisan crafts shops, and galleries. Many of them allow you to set up a registry for select items.

Registering a la carte is even easier with the help of the Internet, and now many stores offer online registries. You can sign up from home, and gift givers who live anywhere in the world can shop at your favorite store. (See the section "Surfing for Gifts" later in this chapter for more information.)

No matter where you register, it's helpful to keep all the contact info in one place. Form 13-1, the Registry Contact Info Worksheet, which you can find on the CD, helps you organize the data. If you register at more than one shop, you may want to remind yourself of what you've asked for where with a note such as "barware" under "Item Categories." Be sure to list the store's 800 number if it has one.

Registry Contact Info Worksheet

Store and Contact Person	Address	Phone	Web Site	Item Categories

Form 13-1:
Keep track of all your registry contacts.

If people ask where you're registered, give them a filled-out copy of Form 13-1. However, don't hand it to them voluntarily and never include it with an invitation of any kind.

Setting the table for everyday and special occasions

Tabletop items are the most popular registry category for couples, and they include the following items:

- **Dinnerware:** A five-piece place setting consists of a dinner plate, salad plate, soup/pasta bowl, cup, and saucer. You may want to order additional salad plates and a set of bread-and-butter plates because they're so versatile. In addition, there are *completer* pieces, including serving dishes, sugar bowls and creamers, and salt and pepper shakers. Many people like to have two sets of dinnerware — casual and formal — so we provide worksheets for both.

- **Flatware:** Generally sold as five-piece place settings consisting of a dinner knife and fork, salad fork, soup/table spoon, and teaspoon. A *hostess set* comprises a butter knife, pierced tablespoon, serving fork, and serving spoon. Formal sets are made of sterling silver, silverplate, or goldplate. Stainless steel can take everyday use and is dishwasher safe. We provide registry worksheets for both casual and formal flatware because many people register for one set of each.

- **Stemware:** This term refers to any glass on a stem. A basic setting includes a water glass and a wineglass, such as a balloon and a Bordeaux. A complete set includes glasses for red and white wines, water, and champagne. Nice extras are glasses for serving sherry, port, and liqueurs. If you often have a glass of wine with dinner, you should consider getting a set of molded glasses for everyday use. For special occasions — and especially for drinking champagne — crystal or full-lead crystal adds sparkle and pizzazz.

- **Glassware or barware:** These terms are used interchangeably and refer to any glass with a solid flat base. The shapes include highball glasses and double old-fashioneds, which are suitable for everyday beverages as well as for mixed drinks. A complete set includes glasses for beer, martinis, and liquors.

- **Bar accoutrements:** Ice buckets and wine racks aren't necessities for everyone (shocking, isn't it?), but they're nice to have, especially if you entertain, and they're quintessential wedding gifts.

- **Table linens:** In addition to tablecloths and napkins, don't forget to register for placemats, coasters, trivets, and other useful items for the table. Although it's doubtful that anyone will give you just a trivet or a set of coasters as a gift, some people like to bundle several small gifts rather than give one big one.

When considering the quantity of each item, get enough to host a dinner party for 8 to 12 people, which figures up to a dozen place settings, cutlery, napkins, and so on. For stemware and barware, register for at least the same number of settings as your dinnerware and perhaps include a few extras to allow for breakage.

If you're not the kind of people who host formal dinner parties, you might consider mixing and matching several patterns of dinnerware. However, understand that many people like the idea of giving you a full place setting, and they may be confused that your salad plates don't match your dinner plates.

The following registry worksheets appear on the CD-ROM. You can fill them out in Microsoft Word on your computer or print them and fill them out by hand.

Figure 13-1 shows what a five-piece place setting plus extras looks like.

Figure 13-1:
A five-piece place setting plus completer pieces.

China choices

When choosing dinnerware, there are actually four types to consider:

✔ **Porcelain:** Many people use the word *china* to refer to any kind of dinnerware, but true china is actually made of porcelain, a combination of fine clay and quartz that's fired at very high temperatuers. Although china is vitrified (fused like glass), it looks delicate. Porcelain is nonporous, chip resistant, and very durable. Except for styles decorated with gold or silver, porcelain is oven, microwave, and dishwasher safe.

✔ **Bone china:** Made like porcelain, bone china contains bone ash, which makes it look whiter and translucent. Dishes made of bone china are thin, lightweight, and durable. Modern versions are dishwasher and microwave safe, but gently handwash any handpainted or vintage pieces.

✔ **Stoneware:** Made from coarser clays than porcelain, high-fired stoneware has a more relaxed feel but is just as sturdy and chip resistant. The material is opaque and nonporous. Perfect for casual entertaining as well as everyday meals, it is oven, microwave, and dishwasher safe.

✔ **Earthenware:** This casual country-style dinnerware is made of natural or terra-cotta clay. Because it's fired at a lower temperature than porcelain or stoneware, earthenware is fairly fragile and heavy. An ideal medium for glazes, earthenware is often hand painted in appealing colors and designs — majolica, faience, delftware, and slipware are examples. It is oven safe at low temperatures when indicated.

Many people register for two sets of dinnerware — a formal set in porcelain or bone china, and a casual or everyday set in stoneware or earthenware. However, depending on your lifestyle, you may find that one good set of porcelain dishes is adequate for all occasions.

Casual Dinnerware Registry Worksheet

Item	Manufacturer	Pattern/Style	Quantity	Price	Notes
Dinner plate					
Salad plate or dessert plate					
Bread and butter plate					
Bowl					
Pasta bowl					
Cup and saucer					
Mug					
Coffeepot					
Teapot					
Serving bowl					
Serving platter					
Pitcher					
Sugar bowl and creamer					
Salt and pepper shakers					
Other					

Form 13-2: Lay out your casual dinnerware desires.

Formal Dinnerware Registry Worksheet

Item	Manufacturer	Pattern/Style	Quantity	Price	Notes
Dinner plate					
Salad plate or dessert plate					
Luncheon plate					
Bread and butter plate					
Cream soup bowl					
Soup or cereal bowl					
Rim soup bowl					
Fruit bowl					
Pasta bowl					
Coffee cup and saucer					
Teacup and saucer					
Demitasse cup and saucer					
Coffeepot					
Teapot					
Covered dish					
Serving platter					
Gravy boat					
Egg cup					
Sugar bowl and creamer					
Salt and pepper shakers					
Other					

Form 13-3: Contemplate formal dinnerware possibilities.

Do you ever get confused on which utensil is used for what? Take a look at Figure 13-2 for examples of different flatware.

Figure 13-2:
A five-piece flatware setting plus serving utensils and specialized pieces.

Casual Flatware Registry Worksheet

Item	Manufacturer	Pattern/Style	Quantity	Price	Notes
Knife					
Butter knife					
Fork					
Salad fork					
Teaspoon					
Tablespoon					
Serving spoon					
Serving fork					
Other					

Form 13-4:
Decide what casual flatware you need.

Formal Flatware Registry Worksheet

Item	Manufacturer	Pattern/Style	Quantity	Price	Notes
Knife					
Steak knife					
Fish knife					
Fork					
Salad fork					
Butter knife					
Soup spoon					
Teaspoon					
Dessert spoon					
Tablespoon					
Iced tea or sundae spoon					
Serving spoon					
Pierced serving spoon					
Serving fork					
Other					

Form 13-5: Register for formal flatware.

There's a glass for almost every type of beverage out there; Figure 13-3 shows you what they look like.

Figure 13-3:
A stemware
and
barware
wardrobe.

Stemware Registry Worksheet

Item	Manufacturer	Pattern/Style	Quantity	Price	Notes
Champagne					
Claret					
Cocktail					
Iced tea					
Liqueur or sherry					
Red wine					
Water goblet					
White wine					
Other					

Form 13-6:
Outline what
stemware
you want.

Glassware and Barware Registry Worksheet

Item	Manufacturer	Pattern/Style	Quantity	Price	Notes
Beer mug					
Cocktail					
Fruit juice					
Highball					
Iced tea					
Margarita					
Martini					
Old-fashioned					
Red wine					
Tumbler					
Water goblet					
White wine					
Other					

Form 13-7: Get your glassware and barware together.

Time to set up the bar. For examples of what items a bar requires, look at Figure 13-4.

Figure 13-4: Accessories for the bar.

Bar Accoutrements Registry Worksheet

Item	Manufacturer	Pattern/Style	Quantity	Price	Notes
Coasters					
Cocktail shaker					
Corkscrew					
Decanter					
Ice bucket					
Ice tongs					
Jigger					
Punch bowl set					
Tray					
Wine bucket					
Wine rack					
Other					

Form 13-8:
Don't forget the bar accoutrements.

Table Linens Registry Worksheet

Item	Manufacturer	Pattern/Style	Quantity	Price	Notes
Casual napkins					
Casual tablecloth					
Coasters					
Cocktail napkins					
Formal napkins					
Formal tablecloth					
Place mats					
Napkin rings					
Trivet					
Other					

Form 13-9:
Pin down your table linens.

Covering the kitchen

When registering for your kitchen equipment, try to assess what you might actually use in the coming years. While in the throes of wedding planning, it may seem like enormous amounts of fun to spend your days making gallons of homemade ice cream or whipping up a few batches of whole wheat bread, but be realistic about your lifestyle. If you will really use items like ice cream freezers and bread machines, go ahead and register for them; they can be great to use. Just remember that basements all over the world are littered with appliances that seemed like a good idea once upon a time.

The following is a list of items that you might want for your kitchen:

- **Appliances:** These aren't limited to blenders anymore — big-ticket appliances, such as professional-calibre ranges and Sub-Zero refrigerators, are showing up on registries more and more.

- **Gadgets, equipment, and utensils:** Besides being useful, small items — like canister sets — are relatively inexpensive, which might be appreciated by guests whose dot-com stocks have tanked or by guests who can't make up their minds and want to give you multiple gifts. Such items are also good for bridal showers.

- **Cookware and bakeware:** This includes pots and pans, tins, and kettles in every shape and size. Although it's possible to buy a complete set-in-a-box, you may be better off having a variety of materials, finishes, and styles depending on your level of culinary expertise, the dishes you like to make, and how much you loathe doing dishes by hand.

- **Cutlery:** A quality set of knives makes cooking a pleasure and will last you a lifetime. You also want a variety of knives for different purposes: a chef's knife for chopping; a carving knife (perhaps serrated) for meats; a cleaver for cutting through bones, sinewy meats, and hard vegetables; a paring knife for delicate cutting; a semiflexible boning knife for cutting around and removing bones from meats and poultry; and serrated knives for cutting bread, tomatoes, and other foods you don't want to squish. Carbon steel blades maintain the best edge, but stainless steel blades are easier to care for. Look for handles that are sealed, seamless, and riveted to the tang (the extension of the blade).

You can find the following registry worksheets on the CD-ROM. Fill them out in Microsoft Word on your computer or print them and fill them out by hand.

Appliance Registry Worksheet

Item	Manufacturer	Pattern/Style	Quantity	Price	Notes
Blender					
Bread maker					
Coffee bean grinder					
Coffeemaker					
Convection oven					
Electric skillet					
Espresso/ cappuccino maker					
Deep fryer					
Food processor					
Hand mixer					
Stationary mixer					
Ice cream maker					
Indoor grill					
Juicer					
Microwave oven					
Percolator					
Pressure cooker					
Rice cooker					
Steamer					
Toaster					
Toaster over					
Waffle maker					
Dishwasher					
Trash compactor					
Refrigerator					
Stove					
Other					

Form 13-10:
Organize
your small
and large
appliance
needs.

Gadgets, Equipment, and Utensils Registry Worksheet

Item	Manufacturer	Pattern/Style	Quantity	Price	Notes
Baker's rack					
Bread board					
Butcher's block					
Can opener					
Canister set					
Cookbooks					
Cutting board					
Dish rack					
Dish towels					
Fruit basket					
Juicer					
Measuring spoons and cups					
Potholders					
Pot rack					
Salad spinner					
Scale					
Sifter					
Spatula					
Spice rack					
Storage containers					
Timer					
Utensils					
Whisk					
Wooden salad bowl					
Other					

Form 13-11: Register for all the little things you need in the kitchen.

Stocking the kitchen requires lots of cookware. See Figure 13-5 for examples of what you might need.

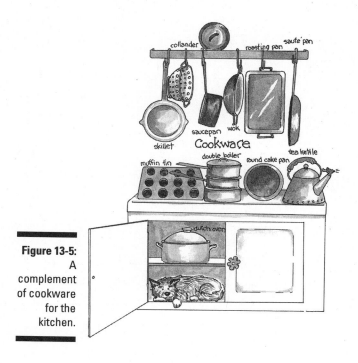

Figure 13-5:
A complement of cookware for the kitchen.

Pots and Pans Registry Worksheet

Item	Manufacturer	Pattern/Style	Quantity	Price	Notes
Colander					
Double boiler					
Dutch oven					
Fondue pot					
Frying pan					
Griddle					
Omelet pan (7")					
Omelet pan (8")					
Omelet pan (10")					
Oval gratin dish					
Roasting pan (10" x 14")					
Roasting pan (12"x 16")					
Roasting rack					
Saucepan (1 qt)					
Saucepan (2 qt)					
Saucepan (4 qt)					
Flare-sided saucepan (1 qt)					
Flare-sided saucepan (2 qt)					
Flare-sided saucepan (4 qt)					
Saute pan (3 qt)					
Saute pan (5 qt)					
Saute pan (7 qt)					
Skillet (8")					
Skillet (10")					
Skillet (12")					
Steamer basket					
Stockpot					
Tea kettle					
Wok					
Other					

Form 13-12:
Clean out
the stores of
pots and
pans.

Bakeware Registry Worksheet

Item	Manufacturer	Pattern/Style	Quantity	Price	Notes
Baking sheet					
Baking stone					
Cake pan, rectangular					
Cake pan, round					
Cake pan, square					
Casserole					
Cookie sheet					
Cooling rack					
Loaf pan					
Mixing bowls					
Muffin tin					
Pie pan					
Pizza stone					
Souffle dish					
Other					

Form 13-13: Bring on the bakeware.

Man cannot live by a butter knife alone! See Figure 13-6 for examples of different types of knives.

Figure 13-6:
Knives for
all your
needs.

Cutlery Registry Worksheet

Item	Manufacturer	Pattern/Style	Quantity	Price	Notes
Boning knife					
Bread knife					
Carving fork					
Carving knife					
Chef's knife					
Cleaver					
Kitchen shears					
Knife block set					
Paring knife					
Serrated knife					
Sharpening steel					
Steak knives					
Tomato knife					
Other					

Form 13-14:
Slice and
dice through
cutlery
options.

Outfitting the rest of the house

Beyond the tabletop and countertop, you have an entire household to fill up. Don't forget these items that your new home together may need:

- **Housewares and furnishings:** It never fails — no matter how badly you need a toaster oven, 14 people give you bud vases. And who knew there were so many ugly bud vases to choose from? That's why it pays to register for decorative items.

- **Bath:** Bath towels, hand towels, and washcloths aren't the half of it. As long as you're in the bath department deciding between flat woven and jacquard, you may as well toss in a few other accessories.

- **Bedroom:** This pertains mostly to the bed, of course. After you get started with fitteds and flats, you're a goner for shams, skirts, and pads.

- **Yard and garden:** Why do people always assume newlyweds need picnic hampers? As if you have time for a moveable feast when there's all that composting to do.

- **Home maintenance:** Hardware and home-improvement products are the sexy new categories cropping up on wedding registries.

- **Electronics:** Life has gotten a lot more complicated since the days when your parents registered. Now there's hardly an aspect of your multi-tasking life that doesn't require a computer chip. Consumer electronics stores are responding by setting up gift registries.

You guessed it — we give you worksheets a plenty to help you organize your registry of these household items. You find these worksheets on the CD; they're just waiting for you to fill them out electronically in Microsoft Word or to print them and fill them out by hand. Enjoy!

Housewares and Furnishings Registry Worksheet

Item	Manufacturer	Pattern/Style	Quantity	Price	Notes
Bed					
Bookends					
Cabinet					
Candlesticks					
Chair					
Clock					
Desk					
Hamper					
Lamp					
Luggage					
Mirror					
Picture frame					
Pillow					
Rug					
Vase					
Wastebasket					
Other					

Form 13-15: Organize your housewares and furnishings needs.

Bath Registry Worksheet

Item	Manufacturer	Pattern/Style	Quantity	Price	Notes
Bath accessories					
Bath mat					
Bath rug					
Bath sheet					
Bath towel					
Beach towel					
Guest towel					
Hand towel					
Mirror					
Scale					
Soap dish					
Storage					
Vanity set					
Washcloth					
Wastebasket					
Other					

Form 13-16:
Register for
bathroom
linens and
accessories.

Bedroom Registry Worksheet

Item	Manufacturer	Pattern/Style	Quantity	Price	Notes
Bedspread					
Bed skirt					
Blanket					
Box spring					
Duvet					
Duvet cover					
Electric blanket					
Fitted sheet					
Flat sheet					
Mattress					
Mattress pad					
Pillow					
Pillowcase					
Pillow sham					
Quilt					
Throw					
Other					

Form 13-17:
You may need bedroom linens and accessories, too.

Yard and Garden Registry Worksheet

Item	Manufacturer	Pattern/Style	Quantity	Price	Notes
Barbecue					
Birdhouse/feeder					
Cachepot					
Garbage can					
Garden tools					
Hammock					
Hose					
Ladder					
Lawn mower					
Patio furniture					
Pavers					
Planter					
Picnic hamper					
Plant					
Pool equipment					
Pot					
Rake					
Shovel					
Spreader					
Sprinkler					
Tree Trimmer					
Watering can					
Other					

Form 13-18: Don't forget your yard and garden needs.

Unfortunately, not every new couple will be getting a maid service as a wedding gift. General home maintenance and cleaning items are needed (see Figure 13-7), too.

Figure 13-7:
Items every
couple
needs to fix
up, clean,
and
maintain
their home.

Home Maintenance Registry Worksheet

Item	Manufacturer	Pattern/Style	Quantity	Price	Notes
Adjustable wrench					
Air purifier					
Allen wrench					
Clothes dryer					
Clothes washer					
Drill					
Fastener kit (nails, nuts, bolts, screws)					
Iron					
Ironing board					
Hammer					
Hand vacuum					
Humidifier					
Level					
Lighting fixtures					
Measuring tape					
Paint and supplies					
Plumbing fixtures					
Room fan					
Saw					
Screwdriver					
Toolbox					
Tool kit					
Vacuum cleaner					
Other					

Form 13-19:
You can also register for home maintenance needs.

Electronics Registry Worksheet

Item	Manufacturer	Pattern/Style	Quantity	Price	Notes
Answering machine					
Boom box					
Calculator					
Camcorder					
Camera					
CD player					
Clock radio					
Computer					
DVD player					
Fax					
Flatbed scanner					
Net appliance					
Personal organizer					
Printer					
Security system					
Smoke detector					
Software					
Speakers					
Stereo					
Surge protector					
Telephone					
TV					
VCR					
Other					

Form 13-20:
You don't have to be a geek to register for consumer electronics.

Taking a personal interest

Asking for "non-essentials" for wedding gifts is a trifle self-indulgent but not out of the question. After all, who's to say that an annual membership to the Metropolitan Museum of Art or a new set of golf clubs isn't exactly what you need to get your marriage off on the right foot?

As for cash gifts, the same rules of etiquette apply when it comes to hobby-gifts: Even though they might be what you truly want or need, you should drop the hint (and only a hint) to only your closest friends and relatives — and only if they ask.

Living large (in your dreams)

In recent years, there's been a lot of talk about registries for very unconventional wedding gift items such as mortgages, honeymoons, cars, or personal debt relief. However, the idea hasn't really caught on. Few, if any, companies know how to market this seemingly crass concept in a palatable manner, and much of the wedding-going public isn't ready to give up the box-tied-with-a-bow tradition. If you're able to pull it off, more power to you. While you're at it, see if your guests want to give you venture capital for that dot-com idea you have.

Or you can fill out Form 13-21 and leave it casually in plain view the next time your friends or relatives come over!

Personal Interests Registry Worksheet

Item	Name/details	Store	Quantity	Price	Notes
Books					
Camping gear					
Charity					
Game					
Museum membership					
Sports equipment					
Sports tickets					
Theater tickets					
Travel					
Other					

Form 13-21: You can register for personal items.

Surfing for Gifts

Wedding registries are getting increasingly high tech. A few years ago, it was big news when stores such as Target and Home Depot began letting couples fill out their registries using bar-code scanners as they roamed the aisles. Now the trend is online registries, which have numerous advantages:

- You and your intended can argue about flatware patterns in the privacy of your home as opposed to in the housewares section of a department store.

- People can purchase gifts for you from anywhere in the world 24 hours a day, seven days a week.

- You can check on the status of your registry or edit your gift list at any time from your personal computer.

- Many registries are affiliated with Web sites that offer other planning tools, tips, and information.

- You can have several registries for different items and have them all linked on one site such as the Wedding Channel, The Knot, or eWish.

- You and the people buying can usually see the goods displayed onscreen.

- You can e-mail your registry to close family members or intimate friends (your maid of honor, for example) even if they live far away, and then "go shopping" together through the sites.

At this writing, the e-commerce industry is undergoing rapid changes. Although some obscure registry sites may offer wonderfully offbeat items, you want to be reasonably sure they'll be around by the time you get married. Companies such as Williams-Sonoma and Crate and Barrel already have brand recognition and a winning combination of bricks, clicks, and slicks (catalogs). And as the dot-com dust settles, chances are they'll still be around. You want to find an Internet registry that has the "five Cs" — content, customer service, customization, convenience, and commerce. And remember: Don't necessarily expect a store's online registry to be hassle-free. If a store is dysfunctional, what makes you think its Web site will be any better? If you have doubts about a site, look it up on a rating service such as www.bbb.org, www.gomez.com or www.bizrate.com.

Although registering from home is convenient, you should still check out the goods in person at brick-and-mortar stores. The click-and-buy lifestyle can streamline your life, but it helps if you're an educated consumer and have done your fieldwork.

Even though some sites offer to e-mail your registry list to all your guests, please refrain unless someone you know makes a specific request.

It seems that everyone is getting in on the online registry business. Bridal magazines, department stores, specialized e-commerce sites, and other ventures are hanging out cybershingles and making alliances with each other to capture a piece of this market. Even as we write this book, new sites are popping up and others are consolidating; so before you go with any one site, do your homework to make sure it's viable through your wedding day! There are different ways to approach online registries. The major contenders include:

- **All-inclusive sites:** These are the top comprehensive wedding sites such as The Knot (www.theknot.com), Wedding Channel (http://weddingchannel.com), The Wedding List (theweddinglist.com), and Wedding Network (weddingnetwork.com). Many of these sites have relationships with retailers for registries and bridal magazines for content. Wedding Channel, for example, merged with della.com and incorporated the latter's extensive registry component.

- **Department stores:** Many of the major chains such as Federated, May, and Nordstrom have added online components to their in-store registries and have forged alliances with particular wedding Web sites.

- **Niche retailers:** Specialized shops are linking up with wedding Web sites and launching their registries as part of their online operations. To see if your favorite store has joined the pack, type in the name with a dot-com appendage or go to a search engine and do a keyword search on the store's name.

- **Web-based wish lists:** One of the most interesting trends in the e-commerce revolution is the development of consolidated registries or wish lists. You register at several different stores through one site that does nothing but offer registry services. The idea has merit, judging by the number of wish-list sites (such as ewish.com and wishlist.com) vying for top rung. It's anyone's guess which few will survive the inevitable dot-com shakeout.

In most cases, it's not necessary to type www or .com — just the online store or site name.

If by now you're suffering from registry overload, you still have time to forget the whole thing and get what's coming to you in stock. At www.stockgift.com, you can create a registry that's a brokerage account. You list the publicly traded securities that you'd like to receive and the preferred date of purchase. Friends and family can contribute to your account without knowing your Social Security or account numbers. You can also personalize your StockGift registry page with announcements and photographers. It's enough to make online trading seem warm and fuzzy.

Who Gave Us That and Where Did It Come From?

We hope that as your wedding day draws closer, the gifts are arriving fast and furiously. Even if you're knee-deep in cellulose peanuts, it's imperative that you keep up with your thank-you notes. If this sounds like an alien concept, please read the registry chapter in *Weddings For Dummies*.

To aid you in the gift management department, we also refer you to Chapter 3 of this book, where we explained about creating the master guest list spreadsheet. You can use that list to help you keep track of who sent which gift and whether you've sent a thank you.

You'll find the Excel template for gifts, Form 3-1, on the CD-ROM (see Chapter 3 for details).

Finally, one bit of advice: If you're an eBay fanatic (join the club), you already know exactly what to do with that hideous Pelican-shaped ashtray from Aunt Gertie. But before you put it up for sale on the world's largest online auction site, you better make sure that ol' Gert isn't an eBaysian herself.

Gifting Unto Others

Now, while we are on the subject of gifts, how about a little sharing of the wealth? You know, the 'tis nobler to give than to receive idea. One way to show you have special affection for every one of your attendants is to give them something specially chosen for each of them (see Figure 13-8). If that's more than you can handle or you think it might cause unrest among the troops, there are ways to personalize gifts so they are true keepsakes.

Some items are suitable for engraving or etching monograms or a few personal lines. Others can be embroidered or calligraphed. Do give yourself enough time in advance to have this done and also to write a personal note to enclose with each gift. Send a thank you gift to each set of parents as well. If one parent has basically carried you through the entire wedding planning process, consider presenting something to him or her during your toast at the reception.

Don't forget your guests! Offering favors gives you the chance to show your guests how much you appreciate their participation in your wedding. Figure 13-9 shows some ideas of what to give.

Forms on the CD-ROM

Form 13-1	Registry Contact Info Worksheet	Keep track of all your registry contacts.
Form 13-2	Casual Dinnerware Registry Worksheet	Lay out your casual dinnerware desires.
Form 13-3	Formal Dinnerware Registry Worksheet	Contemplate formal dinnerware possibilities.
Form 13-4	Casual Flatware Registry Worksheet	Decide what casual flatware you need.
Form 13-5	Formal Flatware Registry Worksheet	Register for formal flatware.
Form 13-6	Stemware Registry Worksheet	Outline what stemware you want.
Form 13-7	Glassware and Barware Registry Worksheet	Get your glassware and barware together.
Form 13-8	Bar Accoutrements Registry Worksheet	Don't forget the bar accoutrements.
Form 13-9	Table Linens Registry Worksheet	Pin down your table linens.
Form 13-10	Appliance Registry Worksheet	Organize your appliance needs.
Form 13-11	Gadgets, Equipment, and Utensils Registry Worksheet	Register for all the little things you need in the kitchen.
Form 13-12	Pots and Pans Registry Worksheet	Clean out the stores of pots and pans.
Form 13-13	Bakeware Registry Worksheet	Bring on the bakeware!
Form 13-14	Cutlery Registry Worksheet	Slice and dice through cutlery options.
Form 13-15	Housewares and Furnishings Registry Worksheet	Organize your housewares and furnishings needs.
Form 13-16	Bath Registry Worksheet	Register for bathroom linens and accessories.
Form 13-17	Bedroom Registry Worksheet	You may need bedroom linens and accessories, too.
Form 13-18	Yard and Garden Registry Worksheet	Don't forget your yard and garden needs.

Form 13-19	Home Maintenance Registry Worksheet	You can also register for home maintenance needs.
Form 13-20	Electronics Registry Worksheet	You don't have to be a geek to register for consumer electronics.
Form 13-21	Personal Interests Registry Worksheet	You can register for personal items.

Chapter 14

The Best-Dressed List

After our dissertation on wedding gowns in Chapter 3 of *Weddings For Dummies*, we didn't think there was much more to say on the subject. There's not, actually. What we provide here are some tools for making the process of choosing and buying your wedding ensemble easier. And we don't stop at that. In this chapter, we also map out a plan for shopping for clothes for the groom and all your attendants. (For dos and don'ts on this subject, we refer you to Chapter 4 of *Weddings For Dummies*.) Finally, although our goal is to not regurgitate information from *Weddings For Dummies*, we do reprise our famous Bridal Emergency Kit as a checklist because, as crisis diva Jacqueline Susann says, once is not enough.

My Mama Told Me: "You Better Shop a Gown"

One of the best places to start shopping for the perfect dress is on the Web. Although you'll be hard-pressed to find out actual prices until you go to a retail shop, these sites offer a lot of food for thought as you browse by designer, style, price, or silhouette:

✔ **theknot.com:** You can peruse more than 20,000 gowns on The Knot and find links to stores. You can plug in your price, neckline, designer, or silhouette, and search for gowns that fit your criteria. This site also features exclusive couture designers such as Carolina Herrera and Yumi Katsura. Depending on where you live, The Knot can direct you to local bridal shops.

- **weddingchannel.com:** A nice selection and a tool that allows you to do a "custom sketch" of the gown of your dreams. The site also features local vendors for certain metropolitan areas.

- **modernbride.com:** An easy-to-use site that enables you to create your own showroom in which to store pages of your favorite gowns for quick reference. You can also use this site to find a local bridal shop, bridesmaids' dresses, mothers-of-the-bride dresses, and tuxedos.

- **tncweddings.com:** Pamela Fiori, the editor in chief of *Town & Country* magazine, personally selects the best wedding gowns from the current fashion collections. The results are presented in an easy-to-click format with links to the manufacturer/designer Web sites.

- **Bridesmaids.com:** This New York City showroom features a handful of good designers of bridesmaids dresses, notably Nicole Miller, ABS by Allen Schwartz, and Watters & Watters. Dresses ordered directly from the site take up to 12 weeks for delivery. There are no extra charges for plus sizes. However, order carefully because there are no exchanges or returns.

- **BridalStoreSearch.com:** Once you get an idea of what you're looking for, go here to find a retail store in your state. For each store, the site also tells you whether it carries Dessy and After Six, the two companies affiliated with the site. We found more options here than when we searched for "bridal stores" in the Yahoo! yellow pages.

As you head out to brick-and-mortar shops to try on and evaluate, take along Form 14-1, a price comparison worksheet, which you can find on the CD-ROM.

As you schedule fittings and alterations, be sure to get the store's policies in writing. You want to know about special charges for large sizes, rush orders, fitting, bustling, style modifications, and cancelled orders. In general, alterations shouldn't cost more than about 10 percent of the cost of the dress.

Of course, the gown is just the beginning. You also need all the little accessories and undergarments (see Chapter 3 of *Weddings For Dummies* for more information on these items). Use Form 14-2, the Bride's Clothing Worksheet (on the CD-ROM), to organize your bridal wardrobe. You can also use Form 14-2 as a quick checklist for the day of your wedding, when your mind just might be on other things.

The Bid Picture: Wedding Gowns

Store and Contact Info	Possible Styles or Designers	Cost Estimate	Notes
Store: Salesclerk: Phone: Address: E-mail:			
Store: Salesclerk: Phone: Address: E-mail:			
Store: Salesclerk: Phone: Address: E-mail:			
Store: Salesclerk: Phone: Address: E-mail:			

Form 14-1: Compare bridal gowns store by store.

The Bride's Clothing Worksheet

Item	Details	Cost	Pick-Up Date	Picked Up
Gown	Manufacturer/Designer: Style #: Fabric: Color: Train length: Sleeve: Silhouette: Store: Contact #: Fitting date/time: Final fitting: Alterations person:			
Headpiece	Manufacturer/Designer: Style #: Store: Contact #:			
Veil	Manufacturer/Designer: Style #: Length: Color: Store: Contact #:			
Slip or Petticoat	Manufacturer: Style # Size: Color: Store: Contact #:			
Bra	Manufacturer: Style # Size: Color: Store: Contact #:			

Form 14-2: Organize your bridal wardrobe. (Page 1 of 2)

Now, back by popular demand, we bring you the Bridal Emergency Kit, Form 14-3. A few weeks before the big day, start assembling the following list of goodies in a nice, multi-compartmented satchel or gym bag. Even if you don't end up using any of this stuff, you'll feel more relaxed knowing it's there for you.

Item	Details		Cost	Pick-Up Date	Picked Up
Under things	Manufacturer: Style # Size: Color: Store: Contact #:				
Stockings	Manufacturer: Style # Size: Color: Store: Contact #:				
Garter	Color: Store: Contact #:				
Shoes	Manufacturer: Style # Size: Color: Dye to: Store: Contact #:				
Gloves	Manufacturer: Style # Size: Color: Store: Contact #:				
Jewelry	Earrings: Bracelet: Necklace: Other: Store: Contact #:				
Handbag	Manufacturer: Style # Store: Contact #:				
Hair	Stylist: Contact #: Style # Be sure to bring:				
Makeup	Artist: Contact #: Be sure to bring:				

Form 14-2: Organize your bridal wardrobe. (Page 2 of 2)

Bridal Emergency Kit Checklist

- ❑ Satchel or gym bag
- ❑ Thread in white, black, and bridesmaids' dress colors
- ❑ White chalk
- ❑ Studs and cufflinks
- ❑ Pins (bobby, safety, straight, and hair)
- ❑ Ballet slippers
- ❑ Brush and comb
- ❑ Blow-dryer
- ❑ Toothpaste
- ❑ Breath mints
- ❑ Clear nail polish
- ❑ Emery board
- ❑ Crotchet hook
- ❑ Antacid
- ❑ Contact lenses and solution
- ❑ Tampons and sanitary napkins
- ❑ Earring backs
- ❑ Extra copies of wedding day and transportation schedule

- ❑ Sewing kit
- ❑ Smelling salts
- ❑ Bow ties
- ❑ Makeup
- ❑ Stockings (two pairs)
- ❑ Hairspray
- ❑ Toothbrush
- ❑ Mouthwash
- ❑ Dental floss
- ❑ Nail glue
- ❑ Tweezers
- ❑ Aspirin
- ❑ Eye drops
- ❑ Sedatives
- ❑ Straws
- ❑ Masking tape

Form 14-3: Assemble survival supplies for your wedding day.

Attiring the Bride's Attendants

The more attendants you draft for your bridal platoon, the harder it's going to be to find a dress that all of them like. You have two choices: Be Miss Congeniality and give them general parameters (shades of pink, above the knee, strapless, and so on), and leave them to their own devices; or embrace your role as Dictator for a Day and tell them exactly what to wear.

Start shopping with the wedding Web sites listed at the beginning of this chapter. You may also go to a decent search engine and type in "bridesmaids' dresses" or the name of your favorite designer. Nicole Miller, ABS, and Heidi Weiss are but a few whose reasonably priced and tasteful lines have become popular among the bridal set; by going to their Web sites, you can see current collections and find store information.

Then it's time to round up the attendants and go on a trying-on spree. Record their votes on Form 14-4 (available on the CD-ROM). In the end, however, remember that you are the bride and reserve the right to cast the tie-breaking vote or to exercise veto power.

The Bid Picture: Bride's Attendants' Clothing

Store and Contact Info	Possible Dresses	Price	Notes and Votes
Name: Phone: Address: E-mail:			
Name: Phone: Address: E-mail:			
Name: Phone: Address: E-mail:			
Name: Phone: Address: E-mail:			

Form 14-4: Compare attendants' preferences before deciding on their attire

For attendants who live far away and can't join the posse, try to find the dresses you like on the Web and send them the URL. Then they may be able to locate them in their town and try them on.

If you're ordering all the dresses at once, you need everyone's measurements in one convenient location. Use Form 14-5, the Bridal Attendant Size Chart, which is on the CD-ROM, to record all the pertinent statistics and make ordering a breeze.

Bridal Attendant Size Chart

Person	Normal Clothing Size	Height	Shoulders	Bust	Waist	Hip	Sleeve	Inseam	Shoe Size
Maid of Honor									
Bridesmaid									
Bridesmaid									
Bridesmaid									
Flowergirl									
Flowergirl									

Form 14-5: Size up your bridal attendants.

After the selections are made, it's follow-up time. You need to make sure that all the dresses are fitted properly and picked up on time. Enter Form 14-6, the Bride's Attendants' Clothing Worksheet (on the CD-ROM). Give it to your maid of honor and other attendants. You may also delegate someone to be the "pick-up artist" — that is, to pick up the garb from the store on the appointed day.

Bride's Attendants' Clothing Worksheet

Item	Details	Cost	Fittings and Alterations	Pick-up Date	Picked Up
Maid/Matron of Honor Dress	Color/Fabric: Size: Designer: Style #:				
Bridesmaids' Dresses	Color/Fabric: Size: Designer: Style #:				
Bridesmaids' Dresses	Color/Fabric: Size: Designer: Style #:				
Bridesmaids' Dresses	Color/Fabric: Size: Designer: Style #:				
Flowergirl's Dress	Color/Fabric: Size: Designer: Style #:				

Form 14-6:
Stay on top
of the attire
for the
bride's
attendants.
(Page 1 of 2)

Item	Details	Cost	Fittings and Alterations	Pick-up Date	Picked Up
Flowergirl's Dress	Color/Fabric: Size: Designer: Style #:				
Shoes	Style: Color: Sizes:	$ Dye fee:			
Stockings	Manufacturer: Style: Color: Sizes:				
Accessories	Hat: Gloves: Handbag: Other:				
Hair	Stylist: Contact #: Style: Be sure to bring:				
Makeup	Artist: Contact #: Be sure to bring:				
Other					

Form 14-6:
Stay on top of the attire for the bride's attendants. (Page 2 of 2)

Getting the Guys' Garb Together

Generally, narrowing down the groom's choices entails less drama than finding and fitting the bridal gown. But there are still several elements to pull together depending on how dressy a wedding you're having. See Chapter 4 of *Weddings For Dummies* for some tips on sorting out all of the options. (We also list plenty of Web sites later in this section where you can shop for the groom's attire as well as for his attendant's clothes.)

If you need to purchase or rent garb for the groom, use Form 14-7 when you go to check out what various shops have to offer. A version of Form 14-7 appears on the CD-ROM.

The Bid Picture: Suits and Tuxedos

Store and Contact Info	Possible Styles and Designers	Cost Estimate	Notes
Store: Salesclerk: Phone: Address: E-mail:			
Store: Salesclerk: Phone: Address: E-mail:			
Store: Salesclerk: Phone: Address: E-mail:			
Store: Salesclerk: Phone: Address: E-mail:			

Form 14-7:
Compare the groom's garb offered at different stores.

After you decide on where to buy or rent a suit or tuxedo, you must accessorize — waistcoat or cummerbund? Bow tie or Windsor knot? Belt or suspenders? Form 14-8, which is on the CD-ROM, can help you sort out these accessories.

Groom's Clothing Worksheet

Item	Details	Cost	Pick-up Date	Picked Up
Tuxedo or Suit	Manufacturer/Designer: Style #: Fabric: Color: Store: Contact #: Fitting date/time: Final fitting: Tailor:			
Waistcoat (vest)	Manufacturer/Designer: Style #: Fabric: Color: Store: Contact #:			
Shirt	Manufacturer/Designer: Collar: Cuff: Store: Contact #:			
Cufflinks	Manufacturer/Designer: Store: Contact #:			
Bow Tie	Manufacturer/Designer: Style #: Fabric: Color: Store: Contact #:			

Form 14-8: Get an at-a-glance record of the groom's ensemble. (Page 1 of 2)

Item	Details	Cost	Pick-up Date	Picked Up
Cummerbund	Manufacturer/Designer: Style #: Material: Color: Store: Contact #:			
Suspenders or Braces	Manufacturer/Designer: Style #: Fabric: Color: Store: Contact #:			
Socks	Manufacturer: Style: Color: Store: Contact #:			
Shoes	Manufacturer/Designer: Style: Color: Store: Contact #:			
Other	Manufacturer/Designer: Style: Color: Store: Contact #:			

Form 14-8:
Get an at-a-glance record of the groom's ensemble.
(Page 2 of 2)

Besides the nice selection of tuxedos you can find on modernbride.com, you'll do well to scope out these online resources:

- ✔ **eTuxedo.com:** The "Web's largest discounter of fine men's tuxedos" is a division of Baron's Wholesale Clothiers in Detroit. This friendly, clever site earns high marks from Bizrate.com for its service, prices, and content, which includes fitting tips and sample toasts.

- ✔ **tuxedos4u.com:** The Men's Apparel Group Web site features styles by Oscar de la Renta, After Six, and Raffinati. There's also a store locator (so ushers who live in other cities can find a store nearby and get fitted) as well as Q&A on some burning tuxedo issues.

- ✔ **blacktie.ie:** If you're up for something really different, try a kilt. For some reason, the Scottish take their formalwear very seriously, and even if you pass on the "Highland Wear," you may pick up a style pointer or two from their other snazzy tuxedos.

When you head out to try on some penguin suits, take Form 14-9, which is on the CD-ROM, as you scope out the options.

And now for the rest of the guys. Once the groom decides what he wants to wear, the other fellows are supposed to follow suit, so to speak. You probably don't have to put them through the whole shop-and-vote ritual that's practically obligatory for brides and bridesmaids. Still, you may want to comparison shop for the best price.

The Bid Picture: Groom's Attendants' Clothing

Store and Contact Info	Styles and Manufacturers	Price	Notes and Votes
Name: Phone: Address: E-mail:			
Name: Phone: Address: E-mail:			
Name: Phone: Address: E-mail:			
Name: Phone: Address: E-mail:			

Form 14-9:
Keep score of the guys' duds.

After you figure out where to get the gear, you need to do more than tell your ushers and best man. Fill out Form 14-10 (on the CD-ROM) and give a copy to each male in the wedding party. They'll have no excuse for not knowing exactly what's expected of them in the wardrobe department. If they need to pick up their own clothes, make that clear. Otherwise, designate someone (such as the best man) to carry out this detail.

Groom's Attendants' Clothing Checklist

For the wedding of

_____ & _____

Date of wedding: _____ at _____ o'clock

Place of wedding: _____

Dear Honored Friend (and, boy, are you lucky):

As you are one of the chosen for our wedding day, please be so kind as to attire yourself with the following checked items:

❑   Tuxedo: color: _____   style: _____   designer: _____

❑   Suit: color: _____   style: _____   designer: _____

❑   Shirt: color: _____   style: _____   designer: _____

❑   Cufflinks: your choice

❑   Waistcoat: color/fabric: _____   designer: _____

❑   Cummerbund: color/fabric: _____   designer: _____

❑   Bow tie: color/fabric: _____   designer: _____

❑   Tie: color/fabric: _____   designer: _____

❑   Suspenders: color/fabric: _____   manufacturer: _____

❑   Belt: color: _____   style: _____   designer: _____

❑   Shoes: color: _____   style: _____   designer: _____

Form 14-10:
Keep the best man and ushers posted on the wardrobe front. (Page 1 of 2)

Item	Sizes	Cost	Store Information	Pick-up Date	Picked Up
Best Man	Suit: Shirt: Shoe:		Shop(s): Salesclerk: Phone: Tailor: Fitting date(s):		
Ushers	Suit: Shirt: Shoe:		Shop(s): Salesclerk: Phone: Tailor: Fitting date(s):		
Ringbearer	Suit: Shirt: Shoe:		Shop(s): Salesclerk: Phone: Tailor: Fitting date(s):		
Fathers	Suit: Shirt: Shoe:		Shop(s): Salesclerk: Phone: Tailor: Fitting date(s):		
Other					

Form 14-10: Keep the best man and ushers posted on the wardrobe front. (Page 2 of 2)

Forms on the CD-ROM

Form 14-1	The Bid Picture: Wedding Gowns	Compare bridal gowns store by store.
Form 14-2	Bride's Clothing Worksheet	Organize your bridal wardrobe.
Form 14-3	Bridal Emergency Kit Checklist	Assemble survival supplies for your wedding day.
Form 14-4	The Bid Picture: Bride's Attendants' Clothing	Compare attendants' preferences before deciding on their attire.
Form 14-5	Bridal Attendant Size Chart	Size up your bridal attendants.
Form 14-6	Bride's Attendants' Clothing Worksheet	Stay on top of the attire for the bride's attendants.
Form 14-7	The Bid Picture: Suits and Tuxedos	Compare the groom's garb offered at different stores.
Form 14-8	Groom's Clothing Worksheet	Get an at-a-glance record of the groom's ensemble.
Form 14-9	The Bid Picture: Groom's Attendants' Clothing	Keep score of the guys' duds.
Form 14-10	Groom's Attendants' Clothing Worksheet	Keep the best man and ushers posted on the wardrobe front.

Chapter 15

Focusing on Photos

Ah yes, photography: the hard copy memories you have after your feet have healed and your dress has been put in storage. The proof that there actually was a cocktail hour — and you were there.

Hiring a decent wedding photographer used to be a no-brainer. Then you needed just someone who would pose the two of you on a staircase — looking deeply into each other's eyes, the wedding dress cascading artfully down the steps — and who would ensure that your albums looked the same as those of your parents and everyone else you knew. Now, of course, there are myriad possibilities of photographic styles to choose from. (Check out Chapter 12 in *Weddings For Dummies* to get ideas on what your options are before you embark on your interviewing process.)

In this chapter, we provide the tools to help you select the photographer and videographer you want — and to have them capture your wedding on film the way you want to remember it.

Finding Your Own Prints Charming

Most of the decisions you make about hiring the team for your wedding will be based solely on your judgement of their talent and professionalism. It doesn't matter, for example, that you can't bear the whiny speaking voice your flutist has, or the peculiar perfume the caterer wears. It's a different story with the photographer; if you don't like the photographer, it will show up in the photographs. Even Richard Avedon can't turn a quivering grimace into a radiant smile on film.

As you interview prospective shutterbugs, consider not only the questions listed in Form 15-1, the Photographer Interview Checklist, but also how well you and your fiancée interact with the photographer.

Photographer Interview Checklist

❏ Ask to see entire wedding albums, not just individual photos or albums of their favorite shots. Look at a variety of candids as well as "formals." Look for crispness of the images, the quality of the lighting, the presence of shadows, and the way the story of the day is told.

❏ Ask about their favorite wedding photographs. How do they think a wedding should be covered? Do they take a traditional or photojournalistic approach? What aspects of a wedding do they think are important? These kinds of questions will give you valuable insight into whether the photographer is right for you.

❏ Is the person you're meeting with the actual photographer who will be at your wedding? Are the photographs you're looking at ones that he or she has actually taken rather than a compilation of work from the studio?

❏ Is the photographer familiar with your site(s)? If not, will she visit it or speak to the person in charge at the church or synagogue and/or the site director at the reception venue?

❏ Does the photographer come with an assistant? Does the assistant take photos as well?

❏ In what format does the photographer shoot — 35 mm or $2^1/_4$? Does the photographer also shoot digitally?

❏ What sort of lighting equipment does the photographer use?

❏ Approximately how many and what sort of proofs or contact sheets will you get to choose from?

❏ Who owns the proofs? Who owns the negatives?

❏ What is the photographer's cost structure?

❏ What are the additional costs for albums or reprints?

❏ Are there other expenses such as parking or travel? How many hours are included? What are overtime charges? What would the photographer charge for shooting the rehearsal dinner as well?

❏ Are the final prints chosen for your album custom cropped and colored? Is retouching provided?

❏ When can you expect to get proofs after your wedding? How long will it take to get the finished product after you make your selections? Will the photographer help you map out your album?

❏ Do they offer many kinds of albums? How many pages do they consist of? Are different layouts and formats available such as panoramic, color-toned, or progressive action frames?

Form 15-1:
Ask the right questions and get the best photographer.

Some photographers work on an hourly fee or flat fee. In such case, you negotiate for a specific number of hours. The entire package would include contact sheets, proofs, and perhaps an album.

With all the photographers you evaluate, jot down their name, estimates, and
other notes for future reference. Form 15-2, which can be found on the
CD-ROM, helps you keep all this information organized.

The Bid Picture: Photography Worksheet

Photographer and Contact Information	Cost Estimate	Package Includes	Notes
Name: Phone: Address: E-mail:	$	# hours: _____ B/W:_____ Color:_____ Proofs:_____ Contact Sheets:_____ Retouching: _____Albums: _____ Finished prints: $_____	
Name: Phone: Address: E-mail:	$	# hours: _____ B/W:_____ Color:_____ Proofs:_____ Contact Sheets:_____ Retouching: _____Albums: _____ Finished prints: $_____	
Name: Phone: Address: E-mail:	$	# hours: _____ B/W:_____ Color:_____ Proofs:_____ Contact Sheets:_____ Retouching: _____Albums: _____ Finished prints: $_____	
Name: Phone: Address: E-mail:	$	# hours: _____ B/W:_____ Color:_____ Proofs:_____ Contact Sheets:_____ Retouching: _____Albums: _____ Finished prints: $_____	

Form 15-2:
Compare
wedding
photog-
raphers.

Getting your pics online

You may wish to ask a friend to shoot some pictures at the rehearsal dinner or wedding. It's now easy to share these photos with friends and family via the Web. They can also order prints for themselves without waiting for you to get around to sorting out the negatives. Try these sites:

✔ **Kodak.com:** Photo giant Eastman Kodak Co. offers a series of services including Picture CD, Kodak PhotoNet Online, and You've Got Pictures, which is a partnership with AOL.

✔ **Photoworks.com:** When you mail in your film, this company (formerly Seattle Film Works)

scans and archives it on the Net for free. The site also offers online reprint ordering.

✔ **Snapfish.com:** This site, which has strategic relationships with Eastman Kodak and District Photo, the nation's largest mail-order photo finishing lab, allows you to send in your film or upload your digital images, share them online, receive prints, and shop for photo gifts such as mugs and T-shirts.

✔ **Zing.com:** Top rated by PC Data Online, Zing Network offers free image storage and sharing online, although it charges for prints and other merchandise.

Casting the Perfect Videographer

Videography has come a long way since the blinding lights, boom microphones, and mortifyingly adorable guest interviews that used to keep most sane people from even considering it for their wedding. The most expensive services now provide a finished product that is virtually newsreel quality, and even the less costly companies use advanced equipment and deliver a polished chronicle of the event.

As with a photographer, your videographer will be with you a great portion of your wedding day — and will interact with your guests. Hire someone who impresses you with both skill *and* personality. Even a spectacular Cecil B. De Mille-esque result will not dissolve the memory of someone wrestling your grandmother out of the way to video the cake cutting.

The information you need to assess a videographer differs in some ways from that concerning a photographer. Use Form 15-3, the Videography Company Interview Worksheet, which is on the CD-ROM, as a crib sheet during interviews.

Videography Company Interview Worksheet

❏ Ask to see videos of entire weddings. You'll fast forward through them, but they're preferable to seeing a video montage of "hits."

❏ Focus on the quality of the images, the lighting, the special effects, and the way the story of the day is told. Is the sound clear? Are there a variety of images that make it interesting to watch? Don't get dazzled by beautiful flowers or an opulent site — that's not a function of the videography.

❏ Do they shoot in Betacam or digital camera (both broadcast quality), SVHS (the next best), or VHS (consumer quality)?

❏ What kind of equipment do they use? What sort of microphones? Lighting?

❏ How many cameras do they use?

❏ How many people are in the crew?

❏ What is the editing process? What equipment is used? Is digital editing included?

❏ What special effects are available?

❏ Can you be involved in the editing?

❏ How do they charge?

Form 15-3:
What to ask prospective videog-raphers.

❏ When will you receive the final product? Who owns the master tape?

❏ How much do copies of the tape cost?

❏ How much of a deposit is required to hold the date? Is the deposit refundable? How much notice is required?

Depending on how many video companies you check out, you'll need a way to keep track of them. Use Form 15-4, which appears on the CD-ROM, to help you track all the information you get from various companies.

The Bid Picture: Videography Worksheet

Videography Company and Contact Information	Cost Estimate	Package Includes	Notes
Name: Phone: Address: E-mail:		# of cameras: Type of equipment: Special effects:	
Name: Phone: Address: E-mail:		# of cameras: Type of equipment: Special effects:	
Name: Phone: Address: E-mail:		# of cameras: Type of equipment: Special effects:	
Name: Phone: Address: E-mail:		# of cameras: Type of equipment: Special effects:	

Form 15-4:
Compare
videography
companies.

Cutting the Deal: Contracts

After you select the photographer and/or videographer for your wedding, it's best to get the arrangement in writing. The following two contracts are typical of what you might encounter. In real life, these would have actual numbers next to dollar signs, but we omit this information because those figures vary so widely depending on the professional involved and the location and scale of the event.

Forms 15-5 and 15-6 show what contracts may look like when hiring a photographer and videographer.

Wedding Photography Contract

This letter of [date], will serve as an agreement between [Wedding Photographers, Address] and [Customer Name], as it relates to the marriage of [Bride] and [Groom].

1. [Wedding Photographer] will attend [Bride and Groom's] wedding on [Date], beginning by setting up the wedding and reception room at the [Venue, Address], and continuing with the bride getting ready at a place to be determined and continue with the ceremony at the [Venue]. He will photograph the couple, families, friends, parents, and parents' friends, documenting the events and atmosphere of the event in both black and white and color. *Start times will be worked out within four weeks of the event when a schedule of events and a formal list will be provided by the bride or planner.*

2. A package price of [$amount] will cover the following services and expenses: _____ hours from set up to breakdown, film, and processing of _____ rolls of film, gas, tolls, parking, two assistants, color proofs, a leather-bound color proof book, 11 x 14 enlarged black and white sheets, and title to negatives.

3. [Wedding photographer] will make all color proofs (with reverse-side numbering), leather proof book and enlarged black and white contact sheets with photographer's edits available to the couple four to six weeks after the wedding. The Client agrees to pick up all photographs at the [Wedding Photographer] studio at [Address] or, at the Client's option, authorize the Photographer to deliver the photographs, by messenger or otherwise, at the Client's expense. All risk of non-delivery or damage in such event shall be with the Client. The couple owns all proofs and contact sheets. The photographer and Couple share ownership of the negatives, which can reside in the couple's home, the lab, or the photographer's studio. [Wedding Photographer] will be allowed unlimited access to the negatives. Extreme care will be taken by all parties in the handling and storage of the negatives.

4. [Wedding Photographer] hereby acknowledges receipt of deposit of [$amount]. In the event of postponement or cancellation of the wedding the deposit will be retained by [Wedding Photographer] and become the cancellation fee. Shooting beyond the (n amount) of rolls allotted will be charged at ($n amount) per roll (film, developing and proofs). Hours beyond the allotted (amount) will be charged at $_____ per hour for the three person crew. *Any over charges will be paid upon presentation of the proofs.*

5. The balance [$amount] is paid one week prior to the wedding day. Checks should be made payable to ["Wedding Photographer"]. Prints and/or albums are billed separately once selections are made.

6. With consent of the couple, the photographer may print a selection of photos for his own use.

7. Prints are ordered and billed at a later date, once selections are made. Due to the volatility of the market, prices for printing are subject to change without prior notice.

Form 15-5:
A typical
photography
contract.
(page 1 of 2)

8. Provisions for hot meals will be arranged by the client and facilitated by the planner for the photographer and his assistant.

Arrange with maitre d' in advance to serve photographers meals while guests are eating theirs.

9. If [Wedding photographer] cannot fulfill his commitments due to circumstances beyond the photographer's control, the couple in their total discretion may use another of the photographers employed by [Wedding Photographers] as his replacement (at their going rate) or be refunded the deposit.

10. [Wedding Photographer] shall not be liable under the terms of the Contract for its failure to perform under this Contract if its failure is a direct result of an act of God, personal harassment by individuals connected with this occasion, picket line, or any act on the part of a union employee which makes it impossible for the Photographer to take, process, or deliver photographs. Should any of these events occur, it is agreed that the photographer shall be relieved and released from any and all obligation and liability under this Contract.

Don't let "picket line" jargon throw you—it's boilerplate in many contracts.

11. The Client understands and agrees that photography is not an exact science and that on occasions, film or other photographic instruments and material may be proven to be defective. The Client agrees that if any of the photographic film or equipment is defective or if any photographs cannot be developed, or if the total order is undeliverable because of a defect in materials, equipment or and/or chemicals, the liability of the Photographer will be limited to at most the amount paid by the Client under this Contract. The Client specifically waives any claim for breach of any warranty, mental harm, or emotional distress because of failure of the photographs to be resulting from any defective material, chemical, equipment, or procedures.

12. It is the Client's option to use [Wedding Photographers] printing and album services. [Wedding Photographers'] printing and album policies will be provided with the delivery of the proofs. Please initial the appropriate box:

Get the reprint and album prices during the preliminary interview.

I _____ wish to use [Wedding Photographers] services for prints and or albums.

I _____ do not wish to use [Wedding Photographers] services for prints and or albums. All negatives should be made available to me 24 hours after the wedding.

I _____ am undecided whether I wish to use [Wedding photographers] services for prints and or albums.

Agreed to _____

Date

_____   _____
PHOTOGRAPHER   CLIENT

Form 15-5: A typical photography contract. (page 2 of 2)

Video & Film
Production & Post Production

XYZ VIDEOGRAPHERS, INC
123 ANY STREET
ANYTOWN, US 11111

CONTRACT

The following constitutes our understanding
and can only be modified in writing and if signed by both parties.

Name: **Jane Doe & John Anyone**

Address: **321 The Street, Anytown, US 11111**

Phone: **(555) 555-5555**

Date of production: **00/00/00**

Location: **Holy Venue & Beautiful Reception Hall**

Time of production: **1:00 p.m.**

Description of services to be performed:

The shooting and editing of Jane Doe and John Anyone's wedding at the Holy Venue & Beautiful Reception Hall with our state of the art wedding package.
$_____

ADDITIONAL CHARGES:

1) **Overtime will be charged after the (n)th hour at a rate of $_____ per hour.**

2) **x(amount) copies of the party will be delivered at completion. Additional copies will be charged at a rate of $_____ per copy.**

NOTE: Due to the Artistic choices involved in the production of your video, XYZ Videographers, Inc. can only accept responsibility for editing repairs resulting from editor's errors. (Names misspelled, improper date, etc.). Any requested change of a subjective nature (i.e. selection of a certain type of special effect, etc.) will be billed to the client at a rate of $_____ per hour. XYZ Videographers, Inc. retains the right to use edited copy of tape as a sample of our work.
TERMS:

$_____ **upon signing of contract. Balance upon delivery of tape.**

AGREED AND ACCEPTED :

_____
XYZ VIDEOGRAPHERS INC.   (DATE)

AGREED AND ACCEPTED :

_____
Jane Doe   (DATE)
& John Anyone

If you want footage of pre-ceremony events, indicate those times and locales.

If more than one camera is to be used, indicate so.

Form 15-6:
This is what a video contract might look like.

Give the photographer and videographer a copy of your wedding-day schedule, which you can find in Chapter 8. That way, they'll know exactly where to position themselves and record the action as it happens.

Picture This: Creating the Shot List

You will save yourself and your photographer a great deal of time and trouble during your formal photo session if you compile two lists — a who's who list and a list of the combinations you want shot for the formal photographs.

Figure 15-1 shows you how to organize the first of these necessary lists. Figure 15-2 gives an example of how to assemble the information for the second type of list.

Type up a photo shoot list and send it to the photographer a few weeks before the event. Follow up with a call to confirm that the photographer has received the list. Then print out two copies of each list to have with you on your wedding day — one for the "director" and an extra for the photographer. Designate someone in advance, such as the photographer's assistant, your wedding planner, or a member of the wedding party, to call out the names of the people in each shot.

When deciding on picture combinations, keep in mind that in a 30-minute period, approximately ten different group arrangements can be shot. Organize the various groupings so they can be changed by adding or subtracting one or two people rather than the entire line-up. (Your photographer can help you with this.)

If you are taking your formal photographs after the ceremony, keep the posed photos to a minimum so your guests don't think you've left for your honeymoon without saying goodbye!

When creating a list like Figure 15-2, include short notes that will help make the photographer's job easier, such as "Never include bride's stepmother and mother in the same photo."

Also make a list of people and specific photos that you want the photographer *not to miss* during the rest of your wedding day. Assign someone to point out to the photographer who these people are. Figure 15-3 shows you how you can present this information to the photographer. Make sure to supply this list to the photographer, along with the other two lists shown in Figures 15-1 and 15-2, a few weeks before the event.

Sample of Subjects for the Photographer to Shoot

Bride: Constance B. Goode (C.B.)	Groom: Russell Katz (Russ)
Mother: Mrs. Gayle Wind	Mother: Mrs. Donna Katz
Stepfather: Gus Wind	Father: Eric Katz
Father: Robert Goode	Brother/Best Man: Paul Katz
Father's Significant Other: Anna Craft	Sister-in-law: Alice Katz
Brother: John Goode	Niece/Flower Girl: Cheryl Katz
Sister-in-law: Sarah Chase (Goode)	Nephew/Ring Bearer: Teddy Katz
Sister/Maid of Honor: Lynn Goode	Sister/Bridesmaid: Alison Katz
Grandmother (mother's side): Mrs. John (Celia) Davenport	Grandmother (mother's side): Mrs. Bella Gross
Grandfather (mother's side): John Davenport	Grandfather (mother's side): n/a
Grandparents (father's side): n/a	Grandmother (father's side): Mrs. Rose Katz
Bridesmaids: Alison "Ali" Katz (groom's sister), Lisa Cox, Antonia (Tony) Anderson, Sarah Chase (sister-in-law)	Grandfather (father's side): Arthur Katz
Flower Girl: Chery Katz (groom's niece)	Ushers: John Goode (bride's brother), Arthur Harris, Leon Jones
Others for formals:	Ring bearer/nephew: see above
Aunt Sally and Uncle John Goode	Aunt: Renee Katz
Aunt Eunice and Uncle Lester Davenport	Aunt Barbara and Uncle John Katz
	Aunt Marie and Uncle Steven Gross

Figure 15-1:
Tell the photographer who is to be shot on your wedding day.

Sample Formal Picture Combinations

1. Bride and groom
2. Bride and groom with her parents
3. Bride with her parents
4. Bride and groom with his parents
5. Groom with his parents
6. Bride and groom with her sister, brother, and their spouses
7. Bride and groom with his sister
8. Bride and groom with their attendants
9. Bride and groom with their attendants and both families

Figure 15-2:
Have a concise list of who should appear in each picture.

Sample List of Random Shots for the Photographer

Please be sure to take these photographs:

Bride with college roommate Sara Baum

Groom and his Uncle Casper

Bride and groom with bride's cousin Harry

Bride and groom with their volleyball friends: Herman, Myrna, Tod, Jinx, and Sally

Bride and groom under willow tree in back garden

Figure 15-3:
Tell the photographer what random shots to get.

Forms on the CD-ROM

Form 15-1	Photographer Interview Worksheet	Ask the right questions and get the best photographer.
Form 15-2	The Bid Picture: Photography Worksheet	Compare wedding photographers.
Form 15-3	Videography Company Interview Worksheet	What to ask prospective videographers.
Form 15-4	The Bid Picture: Videography Worksheet	Compare videography companies.

Chapter 16

Nitpicky Tips for the Taking

. . . .

In This Chapter

▶ Making the wedding pages

▶ Licensing your nuptials

▶ Forecasting your wedding-day weather

▶ Changing your name

. . . .

*T*his is the chapter where we shoehorn all of the hopelessly arcane but nonetheless useful information that doesn't fit in anywhere else in this book. For example, this is where we explain how to do niggling tasks like placing your wedding announcement in the local paper, applying for a marriage license in your state, and notifying every last account, colleague, and friend that you have a new name. Last but not least, we give you a few ideas for witty and heartwarming toasts. These are toasts to make to each other when you slice the cake; all the other toasts at your wedding will be made by other folks in your honor, and they can buy their own books to figure out a few memorable lines.

News of the Wed

Many newspapers have ceased devoting newsprint to engagement announcements, but if you still live in a town where the local fish wrapper adheres to this quaint custom, call to see if there's a form you need to fill out. In some cases, a simple letter from the bride's parents will suffice.

If the local newspaper doesn't have its own form for you to supply, you can simply fill out Form 16-1, the Sample Engagement Announcement, which you can find on the CD-ROM, and send it in.

> ### *Sample Engagement Announcement*
>
> | Use full names in all cases. | Date to be published:_____ |
> | --- | --- |
>
> Mr. and Mrs. _____
> of _____ announce the engagement
> of their daughter _____
> to _____, the son of
> Mr. and Mrs. _____
> of _____.
> No date has been set for the wedding.
> The wedding will take place in the month of _____.
> Contact information:
> Name:_____
> Address:_____
> City, state, zip:_____
> Phone:_____
>
> *Labels:* Use full names in all cases. · Indicate the wedding date, if known. · Bride's parents' information.

Form 16-1:
Start spreading the news through your local paper.

Most town newspapers publish wedding announcements as a free service to readers. They usually have a form you must print or type out. If your paper has a Web site, you may find the form there. Otherwise, call to find out the procedure, deadline, and photo specifications.

Form 16-2, a Sample Newspaper Wedding Announcement, shows you what to expect when filling out a wedding announcement form.

Papers like to publish wedding announcements the day of the wedding or shortly afterward, which means there usually isn't time to develop a photo from the wedding to run with the announcement. If you want a formal portrait to appear with your announcement, schedule a session with your photographer several weeks ahead of time. Many newspapers have relaxed the rules and run candid photos of the grinning bride and groom together. Make sure to inquire about the paper's photo policy.

Large-circulation newspapers usually have specific information and date of submission requirements, but they often don't have forms to be filled out. They might want you to submit only a few pieces of information in the form of a letter; read current wedding notices to get the hang of what they're looking for before sending in your pertinent data. Doing so can increase your chances of being one of the lucky chosen.

Sample Newspaper Wedding Announcement

Indicate when a middle name is used as a first name, such as Mary Margaret Jones (known as Margaret) or Thomas Edward Smith (known as Edward). For names like Maryanne and Mary Anne, make clear whether the name is one word or two and which letters are capitalized.

Bride's Full Name:_____
Address:_____
Community/Town:_____
Phone:
(Home)_____ (Business):_____

Bride's Parents' Full Names: _____
Address:_____
Community/Town:_____
Phone:_____

Specify whether parents are deceased, stepparents, divorced, or separated, and where each lives.

Bridegroom's Full Name:_____
Address:_____
Community/Town:_____
Phone:
(Home)_____ (Business):_____

Bridegroom's Parents' Full Names:_____
Address:_____
Community/Town:_____
Phone:_____

Phone numbers are critical for clarifications under deadline. Numbers should be "good" 9 a.m. to 5 p.m. so that responses are not delayed by answering machines or voice mail.

CEREMONY

Place of Ceremony: _____
City:_____ State: _____
Date, Hour: _____
Mass?_____
Ceremony performed by: _____
Of: (church, affiliation, location)_____
Place of Reception: _____
City:_____ State:_____
Honeymoon: _____
Future Address: (will publish community only)
_____

WEDDING PARTY

Escorted to the altar by (full first name):
_____ Relationship:_____
( )Maid ( ) Matron of Honor:_____
Relationship:_____
Best Man:_____ Relationship:_____
Bridesmaids:_____
_____
Ushers:_____
_____
Flower Girl:_____
Ringbearer:_____

Even though they might be your oldest friends, use formal first names such as Antoinette (not Toni), Suzanne (not Sue or Susie), Robert (not Bob or Rob), Anthony (not Tony), and so on. Include last names.

Form 16-2:
Make clear the pertinent details of your wedding.

Making It Legal

Every state has a different protocol for getting married. Some require blood tests, and others make you wait a certain number of days after you get a license. To find out the particulars of getting married in your state, contact the Registrar or Vital Statistics Office of the county of the state where you plan to get hitched.

You can also get some of this information on the Web. For a general overview, check out the charts on the following Web pages:

- www.1800bride2b.com, then click on Marriage Laws
- www.weddingdetails.com/questions/license.htm

 The information on these sites is general, and you should still check with your local government agency.

Non-religious ceremonies — called *civil ceremonies* — must be performed by a judge, justice of the peace, notary public, or court clerk who has legal authority to perform marriages, or by a person given temporary authority by a judge or court clerk to conduct a marriage ceremony.

Religious ceremonies must be conducted by a clergy member (a priest, minister, or rabbi). Native-American weddings may be performed by a tribal chief or by another official, as designated by the tribe. To find out the specific requirements for officiants where you're getting married, check with the county clerk.

 You can also get a copy of your state's marriage license form on the Web by going to www.fileamerica.com, clicking on your state, and downloading the form using Adobe Acrobat Reader (a copy of which is available on the CD-ROM).

 Also use Form 16-3, the Documents and Tests Worksheet, which you can also find on the CD-ROM to keep track of what you need to do in order to make sure your marriage is legal.

 A marriage *license* is the piece of paper that authorizes you to get married and a marriage *certificate* is the document that proves you are married. When you get your marriage license, be sure to order a couple extra copies of the certificate because you have to include the real McCoy (not a photocopy) when applying for a new social security card and driver's license.

Because most states have a cooling off period (a few days) between the time the license is issued and when the wedding may take place, don't put off getting the license until the last minute. However, sometimes it doesn't pay to be super-efficient and ahead of schedule. In some places, a marriage license is good for only a certain number of days. Time your trip to the county clerk's office so your license is still valid by the time you actually get married.

Documents and Tests Worksheet

Required	Item	Bride Needs	Groom Needs	Taken Care Of
	Proof of age			
	Proof of citizenship			
	Doctor's certificate			
	Venereal disease blood test			
	Rubella, sickle cell anemia blood test			
	AIDS blood test			
	AIDS counseling			
	Proof of divorce			
	Parental consent for marriage of minors			

Form 16-3:
Make sure you're legal in the state of your marriage.

To get a copy of a marriage license, birth certificate, death certificate, or divorce record, contact the Office of Vital Records in your state. You can go to `www.fileamerica.com` or `www.vitalrec.com` for such information.

Changing Names

One or both of you may change your name after the wedding. (See Chapter 16 in *Weddings For Dummies* for a discussion of the eponymous permutations to consider.) And you may be moving to a new pad. If so, you need to inform a few parties of your post-marriage changes.

To help you sort out the name-change game, fill out Form 16-4, the Change-of-Data Worksheet, which you can find on the CD-ROM. Make sure that both you and your spouse fill out this form. You can use the form letter Form 16-5 to impart the necessary new information, or you can call, if appropriate.

Change-of-Data Worksheet

DONE	Company	Account or Policy Number	Phone and Address	Date of Call or Letter	Change Name/ Marital Status	Change Address
	Bank loan(s)					
	Business cards and stationery					
	Cable company					
	Car insurance					
	Car registration					
	Charities					
	Checking account					
	Club membership					
	Credit card: Amex					
	Credit card: Mastercard					
	Credit card: Visa					
	Credit card: Other					
	Dental insurance					
	Dentist					
	Doctor					

Form 16-4: Alert pertinent parties of your new name, address, phone number, and so on. (Page 1 of 3)

DONE	Company	Account or Policy Number	Phone and Address	Date of Call or Letter	Change Name/ Marital Status	Change Address
	Driver's license					
	Employer					
	Frequent flier clubs					
	Gift registry					
	Gym					
	House or renter's insurance					
	Internet service provider					
	IRA accounts					
	Leases					
	Life insurance					
	Long distance carrier					
	Magazine subscription(s)					
	Medical insurance					
	Mutual fund(s)					
	Newspaper subscription(s)					
	Passport					
	Pension					

Form 16-4: Alert pertinent parties of your new name, address, phone number, and so on. (Page 2 of 3)

DONE	Company	Account or Policy Number	Phone and Address	Date of Call or Letter	Change Name/ Marital Status	Change Address
	Phone company					
	Post Office					
	Property title					
	Savings account					
	School records					
	Social Security					
	Stocks and bonds					
	Subscriptions					
	Taxes					
	Utilities					
	Voter registration					
	Wills/trusts					
	Other					

Form 16-4: Alert pertinent parties of your new name, address, phone number, and so on. (Page 3 of 3)

After you've stuffed, stamped, sealed, and mailed a few hundred invitations, announcements, and thank you notes, you're in great shape for another mass mailing: letters to all the businesses and institutions that need to be apprised of your new name, address, or marital status (the ones that you have listed in Form 16-4). Print out a few dozen copies of Form 16-5 from the CD-ROM, fill them out, and send them off.

Many companies allow you to update your information by phone or e-mail. However, others, such as banks and credit card companies, require a written request and, in some cases, a copy of your marriage certificate.

Be sure to sign each letter and, if circumstances require it, have your spouse sign as well.

Form Letter for Updating Your Personal Information

Date:

To: _____

_____

_____

To Whom It May Concern:

Re: Account Number _____

Social Security Number _____ - ____ - _____ (if applicable)

I would appreciate your updating your records to reflect my change of:

____ Name _____ Address _____ Phone _____ Marital status

Old information

Name: _____

Address: _____

_____

_____

New information

Name: _____

Address: _____

_____

Phone: _____

If necessary, I enclose a copy of my marriage certificate. Please contact me if you need more information or if there are any additional forms or requirements.

Thank you in advance for your prompt attention to this matter.

Sincerely,

Form 16-5:
Update your
personal
information.

If you're moving to a new house, you may want to send out at-home cards to your friends and family. You can order these from a stationer when you order invitations, or make your own. See Chapter 4 of this book for more information about at-home cards.

Weather Thou Goest, I Will Go

You planned the picture-perfect wedding, and every possible contingency has been thought of, arranged for, and reckoned with. Now, if only someone could accurately predict whether the sun's going to beam down as you recite your vows or whether you're going to have to rent snowmobiles to ferry your guests from the ceremony to the reception. If the forecast is looking gloomy, remain optimistic and remember what they say in New England, "Wait five minutes and the weather will change."

Remember that you're not just concerned with the weather the day of your wedding. If you have events planned before the wedding or people flying in from hither and yon, you'll want to keep an eye out for the weather on the days of those events as well.

The following list gives you some sources of weather information that will either alleviate or heighten your anxiety depending on the results:

- Got cable? Try the good old Weather Channel. These guys and gals are the pros. Best of all, it's all weather, all the time; you can get a fix or fulfill your neurotic craving to know at any moment. They also have a comprehensive Web site with seven-day forecasts at www.weather.com.

- The National Weather Service is responsible for much of what you see — such as satellite imagery — in all the other forecasts. When you hear that the "National Weather Service has issued a storm warning," these are the folks doing the issuing. At http://weather.gov, you can use their clickable map to zero in on the weather information for the area of your wedding. A link on the home page takes you to current warnings and watches across the country.

- America Online users can get to weather information right from the AOL Welcome page. Click on the "My Weather" link and get five-day forecasts. You can also search for forecasts by city and zip code. (Note: They get all their information from weather.com.)

- Just nailed down a date ten months from now and want a forecast? Try logging onto www.weatherplanner.com. They provide long-range forecasts — and we mean really long-range: from five days ahead to one year for all parts of the country. This company uses sophisticated computer modeling, historical data, and 30 meteorologists to create the forecasts they claim are 83 percent accurate. An excellent source of information if you're having a destination wedding and want to let your guests know temperature ranges so that they can pack properly, or if you're looking for a place that may have 75-degree weather in January.

And Now a Word from (Or to) Our Sponsors . . .

Even if you are both so painfully shy that the wedding dress and tux had to be thrown into the dryer after your first dance, you will really miss out if you don't muster the courage to say a few personal words to your guests. Right before the cake cutting, a few well-chosen words serve as the closing punctuation to the reception.

Your toast should be short and heartfelt (without being maudlin) or humorous (without being vulgar). Include thanks to your parents, if appropriate, and any special recognitions that may apply (such as guests who traveled by snowshoe from outer Slobovia to be with you). Refer to the Academy Awards acceptance speeches as the "Don't" model.

Save the closing words of your toast for each other. Some ideas for words to each other include the following:

- If you've written your own vows, reprise that theme for your toast.

- Quote a favorite romantic book, such as *Like Water for Chocolate*, *Love in the Time of Cholera*, or *A Girls' Guide to Hunting and Fishing*.

- Recite some lyrics from your first-dance song.

- Create a ritual and announce it, such as "We will never drink wine together without my proposing a toast to my husband."

- Say a David Letterman-esque list of Top Ten Reasons Why I Love You.

When you can't think of what to say, let someone else do the thinking for you. Here are a few bon mots for posterity — just add your personal touch:

- "Love does not consist in gazing at each other, but in looking outward together in the same direction." — *Antoine de Saint-Exupéry*

- "My most brilliant achievement was my ability to persuade my wife to marry me." — *Winston Churchill*

- "To my wife, my bride and joy." — *anonymous*

- "The supreme happiness of life is the conviction of being loved for yourself, or more correctly, being loved in spite of yourself." — *Victor Hugo*

- "Marriage is not just spiritual communion and passionate embraces, marriage is also three-meals-a-day and remembering to carry out the trash." — *Dr. Joyce Brothers*

- "Marriage is our last best chance to grow up." — *Joseph Barth*

- "Marriage is the alliance of two people, one of whom never remembers birthdays and the other who never forgets." — *Ogden Nash*

You can find more inspiration on the Web from sites such as these:

- ✔ www.tpub.com/Quotes/: A quirky site by a group called Integrated Publishing where you can search by keyword or author's last name.

- ✔ www.famous-quotations.com/: The Famous Quotations Network allows you to search for quotes by category or author, and alphabetically.

- ✔ www.startingpage.com/html/quotations.html: Links to dozens of quotations, pages, and sites.

Still stuck? Try these online resources, some of which can write your toast for you for a fee. These places either send you an appropriate toast via e-mail in 60 seconds or pen a customized toast for you in a few days:

- ✔ **rhymelines.com:** Send in "one-liners" about the person or occasion, and Rhyme Lines will create personalized toasts.

- ✔ **speech-writers.com:** Get an instant speech or toast from this site's $25 Ready-to-Go section. Speechwriters also offers "personalized" speeches, which are based on traditional formulas, and "tailor-made" speeches, which are bound only by your imagination. They also write poems for special occasions.

- ✔ **truly-yours.com:** This site offers unique "poetic" toasts for $50 as well as customized poems and songs — complete with sheet music, and song-books. If you're not on the Information Highway, you can call 800-544-1767 or 877-42-TRULY.

What *did* we do before the Internet?

Forms on the CD-ROM

Form 16-1	Sample Engagement Announcement	Start spreading the news through your local paper.
Form 16-3	Documents and Tests Worksheet	Make sure you're legal in the state of your marriage.
Form 16-4	Change-of-Data Worksheet	Alert pertinent parties of your new name, address, phone number, and so on.
Form 16-5	Form Letter for Updating Your Personal Information	Update your personal information.

Part VI
The Part of Tens

The 5th Wave   By Rich Tennant

@RICHTENNANT

"Would you ask the men with the pink 'Simplicity' boutonnieres not to group around the 'Butterscotch' rose bush. It plays havoc with the entire color scheme of my garden."

In this part . . .

*1*t wouldn't be a *For Dummies* book without a few of these top-ten type chapters. First we help you get the most out of the technology available to you for planning your wedding — the World Wide Web and the Excel spreadsheets on this book's CD-ROM, to be specific. We give you our favorite tips for maximizing both of these powerful tools. Then it's onto the fun stuff: a whirlwind tour of some of our favorite spots for honeymoons and destination weddings. As Carl Sandburg wrote, "Nothing happens unless first a dream."

Chapter 17

Ten Ways to Use the World Wide Web to Plan Your Wedding

*T*he World Wide Web is revolutionizing the way people communicate, shop, gather information, and travel. And now add getting married to that list. No, we don't think you'll be reciting your vows via real-time e-mail to a virtual officiant, but Webcasting your nuptials for everyone who can't be there in person is already technologically possible, so who knows what the future will bring?

At this writing, we are generally not impressed with event-planning Web sites — the ones that claim to send out your invitations, gather RSVPs, and so on. However, these are not to be confused with wedding-planning sites, such as The Knot and Weddingchannel.com, which provide innovative services, scads of information, and wedding-related infotainment. But these sites are just the tip of the iceberg when it comes to using the Web as a wedding resource. In this chapter, we don't review the best sites, but rather explain how to use various kinds of sites as tools to save you time and money, find vital information, shop, plan, and pay for your wedding.

The world of e-commerce is changing rapidly. As we write this, new Web sites are launching even as others are going belly up or consolidating. Shopping on the Web is generally safe, but you need to be a savvy consumer. Before buying anything on the Net, make sure that the site uses encryption software for credit cards, guarantees it won't sell or divulge your personal information, and has a good track record. You can get a read on a site's reputation through consumer ratings services such as Gomez Advisors (www.gomez.com), Bizrate (www.bizrate.com), the Better Business Bureau (www.bbb.org), consumeraffairs.com, and consumerama.com and not to mention print magazines such as *Yahoo! Internet Life* (www.yil.com). You may also want to start reading the business section of the newspaper or watching CNBC to make sure the site where you register isn't going out of business any time soon!

Also look for icons on the site from the BBB and Verisure. If you click on the symbol and it takes you to the watchdog organization's Web site, then it's legitimate.

If you plan to use the Web extensively, you should have as fast a connection to the Net as possible. Otherwise, you may still be waiting for pages to download on your first anniversary. A 56K modem is ideal. You may want to consider upgrading to broadband such as DSL or cable modem.

Targeting Your Search — and Saving Time

The good thing about the Web is the millions of sites, vendors, and services vying for your patronage. You get incredible variety, but how do you find the best of the bunch?

Search engines are the backbone of the Web. You type in a keyword, and these powerful programs scour the Web for matches with the content of sites. Good search sites are Yahoo! (www.yahoo.com), Snap (www.snap.com), Google (www.google.com), and Copernicus (a software download called Copernic 2000 that's available at www.copernicus.com, which enables you to employ a dozen search engines at once). Some of these services function as yellow pages that can help you drill down to the businesses — on and off the Web — that suit your needs.

Just because a Web site turns up at the top of a search list, don't assume that it's the best. On some search engines, companies pay to be placed at the top of a search list, and they may also pay the search engine a fee every time someone clicks through to their site. You still need to do your homework and make sure you're dealing with a reputable firm.

Want to search for a deal? Try adding the word "coupon," "sale," or "discount" to your search criteria. For example, you could type in "tuxedo sale" or "wedding ring discount."

A major way the Web can save you time is through e-commerce sites. You can order almost anything via the Internet, from dresses to stockings to flowers to postage stamps. In fact, there are even e-mail-order bride and groom sites if you're ready to get married but need that crucial component — a spouse to be!

Caveat emptor! A Web presence is no guarantee that you'll be a happy customer. Before hiring vendors you find online, ask them for references and check them before contracting for services site-unseen.

Using All-In-One Wedding Sites

Web sites that deal exclusively with weddings have exploded as a major dot-com category. The best offer a full range of content and products, from budget planners and invitation management to gift registries and gown showrooms.

Many sites have relationships with retailers for registries and bridal magazines for editorial information. These sites compete for a limited market, so they constantly offer incentives like sweepstakes, contests, and discounts.

Sites that fit this all-in-one category include the following: The Knot (www. theknot.com), *Town & Country* Magazine (tncweddings.com), Wedding Channel (weddingchannel.com), Wedding Network (weddingnetwork.com), Martha Stewart (marthastewart.com), and Modern Bride (modernbride.com).

Several sites, such as The Knot and Wedding Channel, offer local vendor referrals and will host your personal wedding Web page on their site.

Exploring a Diamond's Many Facets

If you have yet to seal your engagement with a ring or are shopping for wedding bands, you can find out a lot about the options — and even buy rings — over the Net. Several jewelry sites offer a build-your-own-ring feature where you can click on various menus to choose the stone, cut, clarity, price, and so on. The better sites guarantee your purchase and have customer service representatives who can guide you through the process online or by phone. (You can also find a primer on the subject in Chapter 15 of *Weddings For Dummies*.)

Of course, there's nothing like checking out the fire of a diamond in person, so you might want to do a little field work, or make your final purchase at a bricks-and-mortar jeweler.

The biggest online jewelry companies at the moment are Miadora (www.miadora.com), Mondera (www.mondera.com), Adornis (www.adornis.com), Ashford (www.ashford.com), and Blue Nile (www.bluenile.com). Or do a keyword search for jewelry or diamonds. Another informational site worth looking at is www.adiamondisforever.com, the Diamond Information Center sponsored by De Beers, the world's leading diamond mining company. The site features more than 75,000 ring designs, although it has no links to diamond e-tailers.

Registering Online

As we discuss in Chapter 13, online registries are growing more popular because they offer convenience. You can peruse — and register for — countless items without making a single trip to the store; your friends and family can access your list from anywhere; and you can log on to check on whether anyone has sprung for the Calphalon yet.

However, we recommend that you force yourself out of the house at least once to inspect prospective wares in person. Don't you want to know how that flatware feels in your hand before you commit to owning a dozen place settings?

Saving Moola

Although in many instances e-commerce caters to people who don't mind paying a premium for convenience, there are also ways you can save money through the Web. Here are some ways to get the most for your money:

✔ **Compare prices:** It's always a good idea to know what something is worth — and what the going rate is. Take the time to check prices on several comparable sites, especially for big-ticket items like jewelry and travel. Or use a comparison-shopping bot such as DealTime.com (www.dealtime.com), Cnet.com (electronics only, www.cnet.com), mysimon.com (www.mysimon.com), and clickthebutton.com (www.clickthebutton.com), which search for the best deals for you.

✔ **Watch shipping costs:** Plan purchases ahead of time so that you can avoid overnight or rush shipping charges. And beware of sites — especially fly-by-night discounters — that charge exorbitant shipping. Any e-tailer worth its salt will clearly state the shipping charges on the site and ask you to agree to those costs before charging your credit card. Check out sites like Freeshipping.com (www.freeshipping.com) that direct you to sites where vendors provide free shipping. Sometimes it's not free — you're just quoted an all-inclusive price — but you at least get the full picture right away.

✔ **Pay by credit card:** Don't send cash through the mail and try to avoid paying by personal check. If something goes wrong, you have a better chance of recouping your money through a credit card company.

✔ **Save on sales tax:** To facilitate the growth of e-commerce, Congress has exempted Web purchases from sales tax. However, some sites are required to collect tax if they do bricks-and-mortar business in your state. If you order goods from out of state, keep an eye on the shipping. By the time you send a heavy package across the country, you may have been better off buying from a local merchant.

✔ **Earn frequent-flyer miles:** Use a credit card that gives you frequent-flyer miles for every dollar spent, and patronize Web sites that participate in your miles-with-purchase program. Some sites that participate in these programs include clickrewards (www.clickrewards.com), Mileage Plus Shopping (for United Airlines, www.mileageplus-shopping.com), SkyMiles Shopping (www.skymilesshopping.com), and redtag.com (for Northwest Airlines, www.redtagoutlet.com). You may not save a lot, but you'll be able to plan that second honeymoon before you even get done with the first one.

Booking Travel and Lodging

Whether booking a flight, scouting a hotel, or searching for a vacation rental, the Web can be your personal travel agent. For complicated travel — such as multiple destinations — it's probably best to use a travel agent. They often know the ins and outs of various destinations.

Even when you use a travel agent, the Web can help focus your search through informational sites. For example, after you book a hotel, use MapQuest.com (www.mapquest.com) to show exactly how to get there from the airport or the location of potential hotels in relation to attractions you want to visit.

Decide to venture out and buy your honeymoon on your own? Many sites sell discounted travel. You can even bid auction style at some sites and win the trip of a lifetime at substantial discounts. Check out Expedia.com (www.expedia.com), Travelocity.com (www.travelocity.com), luxury4less.com (www.luxury4less.com), SkyAuction.com (www.skyauction.com), and cheaptickets.com (www.cheaptickets.com). For specialized sites try VillaNet (www.rentavilla.com), VacationRentals.com (www.vacationrentals.com), or VacationCoach.com (www.vacationcoach.com).

Be aware that discount sites have restrictions. Keep an eye out for the following:

- **Black-out dates:** Some trips are sold for only specific dates; others can have limits on seasons or dates of arrival and departure.

- **Cancellation penalties:** Many companies, especially discount sites, have strict cancellation policies, non-refundable costs, and steep fees for changes. For example, Cheaptickets.com charges up to $150 to change a ticket. Lesson: Don't buy unless you are 100 percent certain of travel dates and times.

- **Airline limitations:** If you're bidding on a trip, make sure the carriers or companies are ones you want to use. If the sales description just says a "major airline," you better inquire before bidding.

- **Hidden clauses:** Many travel sites require you to sign a user agreement. This document contains legal mumbo jumbo that you might be tempted to skip over. But read it carefully before you click "I agree." If you have any questions, contact the site before signing.

- **Auction frenzy:** Know what something is worth to you — what you're really willing to pay — before making an impulse bid. Take a few days to track the ending prices of similar trips that appeal to you. By doing so, you get an idea of how much you need to bid to win, and you can price the trip through other travel sites and vendors.

Figuring Out the Flowers

Although it's easy to order bouquets via the Internet, there are many advantages to working with a local florist for your wedding flowers. By developing a relationship with a local florist, you'll have a better chance of getting a good deal, more personalized arrangements, and better service.

The Web, however, can help you find a local florist — use theknot.com, usabride.com, the Web yellow pages, or your favorite search engine. You can also use the Net to research the kinds of flowers you want. If you don't know a petunia from a peony, a good place to start is the Society of American Florists' site, www.aboutflowers.com.

Performing Thoughtful Gestures

Gifting your attendants — male and female — is a must. What to give? You want to make it something that shows how much you appreciate their time, effort, expense, and, depending on your selection of bridesmaid dresses, the embarrassment they endured to be a part of your wedding.

From attendant gifts to welcome baskets (see Chapter 5 on destination weddings for more information on welcome baskets) to party favors, you can find darling keepsakes and hospitality items on the Web. Do a search for "gourmet foods," "gift baskets," or simply "gifts." You can shop a la carte or at sites that do it all for you.

A few sites that specialize in these kinds of items are:

- **Things Remembered** (`www.thingsremembered.com`): A great spot for engraved gifts of all kinds.
- **Eluxury.com** (`www.eluxury.com`): Despite the name, you can find decent gifts here for under $50. Use their gift finder feature or click on Executive Style.
- **Ashford.com** (`www.ashford.com`): A huge selection of watches, often at a discount, and other items, such as jewelry, accessories, and desk accessories.

Finding Vital Documents

A wedding is a celebration, but marriage has legal implications as well. You'll need a license (no driving test required), and you may need to change your name and address with a gazillion companies and organizations. There are now Web sites to help with these life events. (Please see Chapter 16 for the names and addresses of these sites.)

Before you can get married, you may need to track down a few key pieces of paper such as birth, death, or divorce certificates. This can be difficult if you no longer reside in the city or state where these events took place. Try a site like FileAmerica.com (`www.fileamerica.com`), which provides procedures and fees for getting copies of documentation on a state-by-state basis with links to the appropriate sites.

Building a Nest Egg

Although most of what follows applies after the wedding, you can use the Web to set up and manage your wedding account, start saving for the future, and consolidate your finances once you're married.

Internet banking and investing are two hot areas, and they're not just for crazy day traders. Opening a money market account with access to trading stocks and mutual funds can be a money saver as well as a good way to get good interest rates. Money market funds tend to pay significantly greater interest than regular savings and checking accounts, and many offer services such as check-writing (paper and electronic) and debit cards. When you're ready to make the leap into stocks and mutual funds, all your accounts will be under one roof, and you can oversee your vast financial empire in one place on the Internet. eTrade, Charles Schwab, Fidelity Investments, DLJ Direct, Muriel Siebert, Ameritrade and many others offer these services.

Perhaps your current bank offers online banking services. Shop around because fees vary and so does customer support and service. Magazines such as *Smart Money* (Web site www.smartmoney.com) provide regular rankings of the best online brokers. Some brokers — Fidelity and Schwab — have branches where you can walk in and talk to a real person (yes, it's still possible in this electronic age!) and make deposits and trades.

Chapter 18

Ten Tips for Finessing Your Wedding Spreadsheets

. . . .

In This Chapter

▶ Inputting formulas and other tricks

▶ Alphabetizing and sorting names

▶ Undoing mistakes

. . . .

*I*f you've turned to this chapter in a blind panic (having flipped out over the budget and guest list spreadsheets in Chapters 2 and 3), we include the following step-by-step guide to using Microsoft Excel spreadsheets.

If it seems that these spreadsheets are something only Bill Gates could appreciate, give them another try. Trust us: Spreadsheets (and Excel) are really very user friendly. Breathe slowly, take it one step at a time, and you'll be zipping along from cell to cell in no time.

If you've ever used any kind of database, most of these maneuvers will seem rudimentary. If you need a more detailed primer, we suggest you invest in a copy of *Excel 97 For Windows For Dummies* by Greg Harvey.

Before we get into specifics, take a moment to familiarize yourself with the parts of the Excel screen, which you see in Figure 18-1.

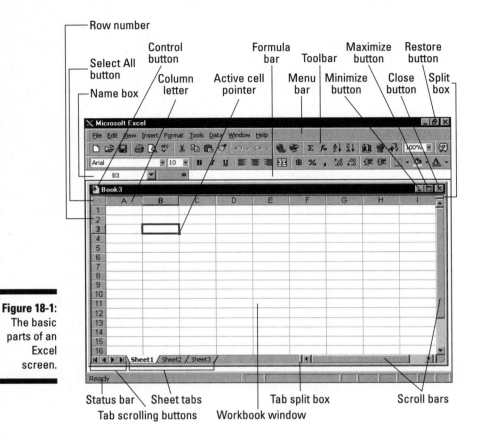

Figure 18-1:
The basic
parts of an
Excel
screen.

Plugging in the Numbers

You talked with a photographer on the phone, and she gave you a rough idea of what it's going to cost to preserve your wedding for posterity. Now you want to input those estimated costs into your budget spreadsheet — the basic skill of working with any spreadsheet.

First you need to find the appropriate cell. In Worksheet 2 of the Budget Template, scroll down to the row that says *Photographer's Fee*, and then over to the *Estimated Cost* column. Click on that cell. You should see the cell bordered on all sides by a double line. Type in the number (say, $1,500). That number then appears in the cell as well as on the formula bar above the columns on the spreadsheet. Hit enter or use the arrow key to move the cursor out of the cell, and your spreadsheet updates itself based on this new information.

By the by, unplugging numbers is pretty easy too. If you get a revised estimate, return to the cell and just type in the new number to overwrite the old one, as shown in Figure 18-2.

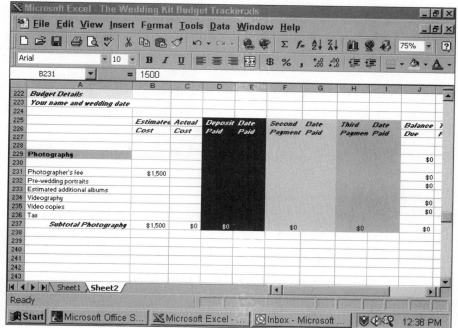

Figure 18-2:
Updating cells as new information comes in.

The Beauty of Natural Selection

The *Select* function is used in performing a number of operations, such as moving (cutting and pasting) information from one cell to another, inserting new rows or columns, and deleting rows or columns.

As you refine your wedding plans, you'll want to customize the budget and guest list spreadsheet to suit your needs. You may want to put in or take out certain line items in your budget. Or you may wish to invent your own system for keeping track of RSVPs, such as bolding the names of people who are coming. But before you get too fancy, you must first master the most basic and useful of Excel functions: selecting the cells you want to change.

First, scroll to the spot on the spreadsheet where you want to, say, insert a new budget line. Click on the row number on the left-hand side. You see the entire row bordered by a double black line and blacked out. (see Figure 18-3). This is known as *selecting* cells; it's similar to when you select or highlight text in a word-processing document in order to bold, italicize, or delete text.

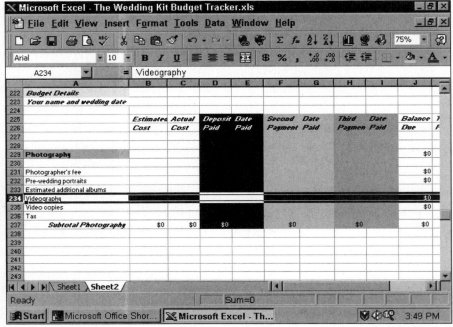

Figure 18-3:
"Selecting"
a group of
cells, as in
row 234,
tells Excel
which cells
you want to
work in.

To select the entire spreadsheet, use Control A, or click on the uppermost cell in the left-hand corner — the cell above row 1 and to the left of column A.

Inserting — and Deleting — Rows

Although it's hard for us to believe, your wedding may entail an expense that's not included in the spreadsheet we provide for you. No problem. Adding budget lines is easy.

First, select the row beneath the spot where you want to insert a new budget line. Then insert a row by using the Insert menu option or by clicking the right mouse button and picking Insert from the dialog box that pops up (see Figures 18-4a and 18-4b).

To insert several rows at once, you can save a few steps by holding down the mouse button and dragging the cursor down the row numbers where you want to insert blank rows. The number of rows you select sends a signal to Excel about the number of rows to insert. Select three, and Excel adds three. Rows get added above the first selected row and columns get inserted to the left of the first column selected.

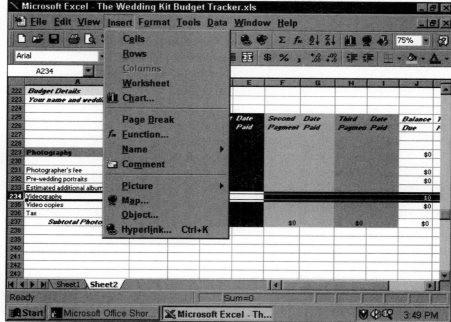

Figure 18-4a:
To add a row in a spreadsheet, you must first select a row and click on the Insert menu, and then on Rows.

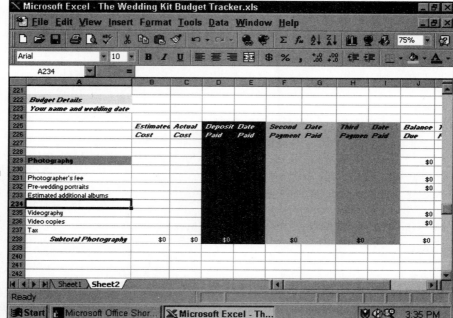

Figure 18-4b:
The spreadsheet now has a blank row above the row that was highlighted.

Deleting rows is just as easy. Select a row(s) as described in the previous section and choose delete from the Edit menu or from the menu that appears when you click the right mouse button.

Formulating a Formula

Suppose you want to figure out the cost of centerpieces for your wedding. With Excel, you don't have to whip out our calculator. You can program a cell to calculate the cost per centerpiece times the number of tables you have. Excel has the capacity to conduct complex mathematical calculations — even though it's nice to know that wedding budgets are mostly a matter of simple addition, subtraction, and multiplication. With this time-saving feature, you can input formulas to tally per head food and beverage costs, invitations, and so on.

All formulas begin with an = sign. Formulas are typed into the cell where you want the results to appear (normally the total or subtotal row).

The formula for adding two numbers together is one cell address + another cell address (for example: =C8+C9 or =C8+D10). For adding several numbers from multiple cells in a row, the formula is =Sum(D8:D25). This will add together all the cells between D8 and D25 (parentheses are required).

You are not limited to vertical formulas. You can also create formulas that go across the spreadsheet horizontally (the columns), such as =sum(C8:G8). *Note:* Formulas don't have to be in cells contiguous with the rows or columns you are trying to add.

When creating formulas, remember the use of the following punctuation marks:

- To subtract, use – (example: =C8-C9). (See Figure 18-5.)
- To divide, use / (example: =C9/C8).
- To multiply, use * (example: =C8*C9).

Calculating the Tax and Tip

As you've heard us say, sales tax and gratuities are two of the most common hidden costs that can throw a budget or the final expense of a wedding out of whack. Many of the quotes and estimates you get from vendors might say "plus applicable sales tax and gratuities" without providing a firm number.

As you estimate costs, figuring in the tax and tip produces a more accurate budget. On the budget spreadsheet, we include expense and gratuities lines in various categories where they apply. These amounts vary depending on local sales tax rates and the amount you wish to tip. You can calculate these percentages in Excel using the multiplication formula.

To calculate the tax or a tip of an item in your budget, multiply the cost of the item by the appropriate percentage. For example, say you want to figure out the tax on the limousine service. Let's say that on your spreadsheet, the cost of the limo service is in cell C9. You know that the sales tax where you're holding your wedding is 6.25 percent. Go to the cell where you want to insert the tax and type:

=C9*6.25%

To figure out a gratuity for the driver, the formula might be:

=C9*.20%

In some instances and categories, you need to add several costs together and figure out the tax on that total. Here's an example:

=sum (C9:C15)*8.25%.

Taxes vary by purchase. For example, hotel stays are frequently subject to a tax higher than the local sales tax, so double check with vendors to find out the applicable tax.

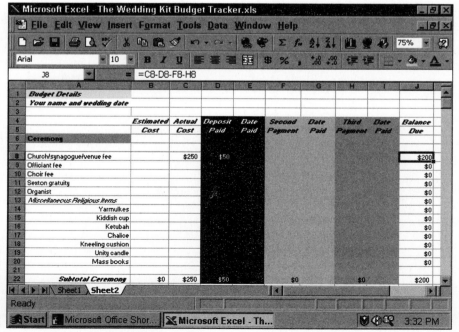

Figure 18-5:
Subtract
using
formulas.

Sorting and Filtering a Guest List

Sorting, or reordering, data in a spreadsheet reorganizes your work or data for a new use, such as alphabetizing the names of prospective guests for your mother to compare against her address book or sorting RSVPs by the yeas and nays. A *sort* involves rearranging data into ascending (1 to 10 or A to Z) or descending (10 to 1 or Z to A) order. It's also possible to sort by the data in any column of either text or numbers.

The first step in sorting is selecting the area of the spreadsheet to be reorganized. It's best to select the entire table, starting at the header row. Click on the number to the left of the header row, and hold your mouse button and drag it down to the bottom row of your table. Anything you leave unselected will not be included in the sort. Then click on the *Data* menu and the *Sort* option. A dialog box appears with pull-down menus that have the names of your columns in them. ***Note:*** Make sure that you have selected: *My list has header rows* at the bottom of the box or you will get column letters — A,B,C, and so on — not names.

For example, in the Master Tracker sheet, you can see all the people attending your wedding grouped by the table they've been assigned, by sorting by two columns: the *RSVP Yes/No* with a descending sort (you want the Y's to come before the N's) and the *Table* number column with an ascending sort (tables listed starting with #1). If you want to make the nays disappear altogether without actually deleting them, read on.

Filtering a spreadsheet is a way of looking at data that meets specific criteria. On your master guest list, you indicate who's on the A List (definitely invited) or B List (invited space permitting). You'll want to separate those lists when it comes time to prepare a final invite list. This is accomplished using Excel's *AutoFilter*. This capability redisplays a spreadsheet based on the criteria you select. When AutoFilter is on, a drop-down menu appears at the top of each column. By clicking on the down arrow, you get a selection of criteria to filter by. In this case you would see A's and B's. If you want to see the invitees, click on the A, and the B's disappear. Switch back by selecting All from the menu.

The AutoFilter function can easily be turned off and on. To turn it on, select the column(s) that you want to filter. On the menu bar click on the Data menu, then Filter, and then select AutoFilter. A drop-down menu appears with options for you to sort by. AutoFilter provides options based on what you have used when inputting data. For example, if you have used codes to distinguish those guests needing special meals, such as K for kosher, V for vegetarian, and ND for no dairy, the pull-down menu shows K, V, and ND as choices for filtering your list.

Don't forget to use this function when you are ready to make lists for your reception. By filtering out the nays from your RSVP list, you then have a list that can be sorted by table number or alphabetically (see Figure 18-6).

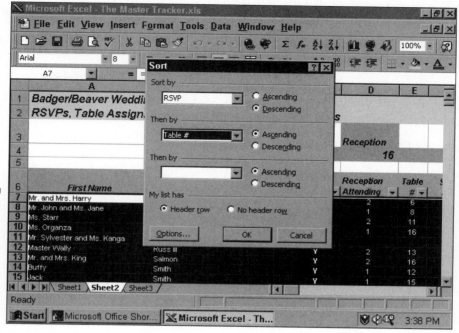

@#%&, I Hit the Wrong the Button!!!

It happens to the best of us — erasing something by mistake, sorting by the wrong criteria, deleting the wrong row, cutting rows instead of copying them. Don't worry. Excel has a great undo function.

Go to the menu bar, where you find the Undo option — the down-facing triangle with a curved arrow on either side. When you click on the arrowhead, a drop-down menu appears listing your most recent actions. Drag the cursor down the list till you reach the one you want undone and click.

The list is sequential, so if the action you want to undo is four actions before, you have to undo all four actions to make the change. However, reconstructing your last few moves this way is often faster than correcting a really big boo-boo.

Printing Only What You Need

Say you're going to meet the caterer and just need to bring your reception budget. Select the rows and columns you want to print — using the instructions in "The Beauty of Natural Selection" in this chapter. Go to the file menu and click on Print Area, then Set Print Area. Then click Print. Just the portion of the budget you highlighted should print.

Copying All or Part of a Spreadsheet

If you're juggling names and numbers "just to see," you may want to make a copy of the original file for safekeeping. To do this, open the spreadsheet and click on Save As under the File menu. Give your spreadsheet a new name and hit return.

It's also possible to copy a smaller section of a spreadsheet to a new spreadsheet or insert the spreadsheet in a different document, such as a word processing document. Simply select the cells to be copied, and then choose Copy from the Edit or type Ctrl + C to copy the area. Then use the menu option to open a new spreadsheet or document and paste the area you copied into the new sheet using either Ctrl + V or the Paste option under the Edit menu.

Protecting Your Data

It's bad enough under ordinary circumstances to hit one wrong button and have your computer stare blankly back at you — all your hard work vanished into thin air! In the midst of planning a wedding, a loss of your data could be just the thing that drives you to elope. Your computer probably does regular saves as you work on files. Play it safe — use the Save option under the File menu, or type Control + S, to save your current work every so often. And back up your files on floppies, of course.

Chapter 19

Ten Amazing Places for Destination Weddings and Honeymoons

Destination weddings are becoming increasingly popular — up 63 percent in the last five years according to statistics compiled by *Modern Bride* magazine. The travel industry categorizes destination weddings as honeymoon travel, and they are, in fact, closely related.

In this chapter, we present a very subjective, personal, and eclectic list of our favorite destination sites. We include some sites because they are particularly nurturing of TATBW's (those about to be wedded) and other sites because the setting is perfect for a stellar destination wedding or awesome honeymoon or both. We list all the sites in alphabetical order so as not to show favoritism.

As we mention in Chapter 5, many countries have prohibitive residency requirements. One way to get around this is to have a ceremony at home and a blessing away from home. If this doesn't appeal to you, head for a country such as Scotland, Italy, Austria, or the Czech Republic, which have no minimum residency requirements.

Beaches, Turks, and Caicos Resort and Spa, Providenciales, Turks and Caicos

Sandals Resorts finally answered the "what-about-the-rest-of-us?" question a few years ago and opened Beaches, which are all-inclusive resorts that welcome singles and children as well as couples. The Beaches location on Turks and Caicos, a chain of islands located between Florida and Puerto Rico, is particularly beautiful and easily accessible.

The rooms are lovely and there's a dance club, a mega water park called Pirates Island, and an "Ultra Nannies" program to supervise the kiddies. In addition to a comprehensive spa, the resort offers five restaurants, a 4,000-square-foot swimming pool, and all the ocean sports you can dream of.

Both Sandals and Beaches are designed to be the ultimate party atmosphere, and if you have an upbeat group of guests, they will have a wonderful time here for your island nuptials.

All Beaches resorts have a dedicated WeddingMoon coordinator plus an assistant on-site. They meet with the couple, plan all the intricate details of the day, and are on-site during the wedding. Four guests are included free for the wedding ceremony and celebration itself, and guests who come solely for the wedding day are given a very fair day rate.

A standard room costs approximately $350 to $600 per person per night; deluxe two-bedroom suites that offer concierge service are more expensive. For more information, call the Beaches folks at 1-888-BEACHES or check out their Web site at www.beaches.com.

Beaulieu Garden, Napa Valley, California

Because of its scenic beauty, the hospitality of the winemakers, and the abundance of wonderful places to eat and drink, Napa Valley has become an especially popular wedding and honeymoon destination.

One exquisite site is Beaulieu Garden, a privately owned residence in Rutherford, in the heart of the Napa Valley. Smaller than the original Beaulieu Vineyards, the grounds feature 90 acres of family-owned, Cabernet-growing vineyards, and 20 acres of lush gardens.

Elaine Bell, a respected local caterer, is the in-house caterer at Beaulieu Garden. Her menu selections comprise creative melanges of California and

International cuisine. The possibilities for your wedding feast in this extraordinary venue range from a "Rutherford Wedding" Sit-down Menu to a "Calistoga Heritage" Wedding Station Buffet. Elaine Bell Catering Company also acts as a full-service wedding planner, employing a staff of party directors, waiters, and chefs.

Weddings must have a minimum of 100 guests. The fee for using the site (not including any food or beverage) is $7,500. Food and beverage prices vary. For more information, contact Elaine Bell Catering Company at 707-963-5299 or on the Web at www.elainebellcatering.com.

The Breakers, Palm Beach, Florida

After undergoing a five-year, $75-million-dollar overhaul in 1995, this once-stodgy Florida resort now exceeds its legendary grandeur. True, the brochures for this "Italian Renaissance Palace on the ocean" seem geared to aristocrats looking for a respite from the strains of feudalism, but don't let that put you off — especially if you want to get married in grand style and honeymoon in a cloud of mega-pampering.

Consummate hoteliers run the resort, and the staff seems trained to psychically divine guests' wishes. The wedding department is not only knowledgeable about food, beverages, ceremonies, and all things wedding, but they are also very caring and committed to making their couples happy.

The food is fresh and innovative — a nice contrast to the magnificent, traditional ballrooms — and the oceanfront property is so sweeping that you can spend a week just enjoying the state-of-the-art, European-style spa, two 18-hole golf courses (the 90-acre Ocean Course is the oldest 18-hole golf course in Florida), four pools, 14 tennis courts, and seven restaurants.

Room rates run from $250 to $800 per night; suites go from $485 to $2,700 per night. Wedding banquets range from $140 to $250 per person, plus tax and gratuity. For more information, contact The Breakers at 561-659-8415 or on the Web at www.Thebreakers.com.

Disney Fairy Tale Weddings, Orlando, Florida

If you're a Disneyphile, there's no greater thrill than saying "I do" in Cinderella's castle or having Goofy as Master of Ceremonies. More than 15,000 couples have tied the knot at Disneyworld since 1991, and Disney's wedding program is getting bigger all the time.

The popularity of this site is due in part to the staff. The women who run the wedding department, JoAnn Rahill and Rebecca Grinnals, take weddings seriously; there are few places to host a destination wedding where you can get such meticulous attention.

Another reason people like this venue is because you can use the park to plan the mother of all theme weddings. For example, you can get married in China, have your reception in France, and then finish with dessert in Morocco. Just head to Epcot Center, where the staff can easily arrange your around-the-world wedding.

If you want a fantasy wedding, there is no shortage of lavish ballroom space complete with props, spectacular floral arrangements, sound, lighting, and other magical enhancements. (This is Disney, after all.)

The umpteen-million-dollar Disney Wedding Pavilion on an island that was built for it, adjacent to the upscale Grand Floridian Hotel, was designed as a perfect ceremony space. Wherever you hold your reception on the property, you can get married in this chapel. The right mix of guests will never be at a loss for things to do at Disneyworld, and there are great possibilities for other wedding events such as an elaborate treasure hunt. The two Disney cruise ships, *Disney Magic* and *Disney Wonder*, host small weddings and vow-renewal parties with ceremonies on the Disney-owned private island, Castaway Cay. Disneyland California is also under the Fairy Tale Weddings umbrella and holds weddings at the Disneyland Hotel and in the Disneyland Park.

Weddings start at a minimum of $10,000 for weekends for 100 guests, and the average price is $25,000. For more information on Disneyworld weddings, call 407-828 3400; for Disneyland weddings, call 714-956- 6527. Or check out Mickey's Web presence at www.disneyweddings.com.

Jumby Bay Resort, Antigua

On this private 300-acre island off Antigua, each well-appointed suite, West-Indian inspired in design, has an ocean view. You can also rent private manor houses suitable for wedding parties. This is the choice for an intimate mellow wedding away, where you and your guests are free to practice the art of relaxation. (However, plans are under way for a new fitness center for Type A's who have to do something.)

The large rooms are outfitted with sumptuous four-poster beds, showers are built into the gardens, the lush island abounds with tropical flowers, and exquisite birds alight in the trees. Oh, and the beaches are incredible.

While Jumby Bay doesn't have an on-site wedding coordinator, it is quite simple to marry legally on Antigua, and there are no residency requirements.

Rates range from $950 for a junior suite to $5,000 for a four-bedroom villa. For more information, call 800-237-3237 or visit the Jumby Bay Web site at www.jumby-bay.com.

L'Auberge de Sedona, Arizona

Ah, Sedona — the resort where Aquarius dawned and where there are more psychics and Chakra adjusters per square foot than any other place on the planet. Even though it has been overbuilt in the last few years, Sedona still feels enchanted. A sunset ceremony in a clearing on a bluff overlooking red rock formations makes all those present feel as if they've witnessed a miracle. The natural beauty has drawn spiritual seekers — and, interestingly, a fair number of wedding planners who can arrange all the details.

The tiny L'Auberge de Sedona welcomes weddings. The service is laid back (if you're looking for a your-wish-is-my-command experience, look elsewhere), and the setting is charming. There are romantic cottages overlooking a lovely creek — all with fireplaces — a good restaurant, many outdoor spots on the property that seem naturally designed for weddings, as well as small banquet rooms.

L'Auberge de Sedona has a competent food and beverage department that is well versed in arranging weddings on the property. Sedona offers fascinating day trips, including deep-woods *vortex tours* (showing energy centers in the earth) via jeep for you and your guests, as well as great hikes.

Rates are from $175 to $345 per night for accommodations; wedding banquets vary. For more information, call 520-282-1661 or visit them on the Web at www.lauberge.com.

Rancho la Puerta, Baja California, Mexico

Mexico is an easy place to get married because there are no residency requirements. Only civil ceremonies are official, and specific legal requirements vary state-by-state, so check in the particular state where you are getting married. One important caveat: Divorced people can't marry in Mexico until one year after their finalized divorce.

Now, why have we explained all of this? Because for a wedding and honeymoon (with no drinking or partying but with both spiritual and physical benefits) for just the two of you, nothing we can imagine compares to Rancho La Puerta, in Baja California, Mexico. The Baja Peninsula is an eclectic mix of deserts, mountains, semi-tropical areas, and hundreds of miles of pristine beaches and coastline. At Rancho La Puerta, you can get married in one of the small towns within a short distance of the resort and have your honeymoon at Rancho's spa. You can luxuriate in an environment filled with wildflower gardens, where the food is truly delicious and all natural — the organic produce is grown at the ranch's six-acre garden.

All stays are arranged from Saturday to Saturday, and there are a variety of accommodations, each decorated in vibrant Mexican colors and each one different. There are no cars allowed on the property and no phones in the rooms, which makes one even more attuned to the flora and fauna.

The ranch also offers classes on topics that range from yoga to Pilates to meditation, and there are invigorating early morning hikes every day. The gyms are state of the art, and dance, stretch, and exercise classes are often held in an open-air gazebo at the foot of a mountain.

There are special programs during some weeks as well as those weeks designated for couples. Nobody leaves this small paradise without feeling they are rejuvenated and ready to return to their world with a renewed sense of purpose.

The trip to Rancho la Puerta is made by flying into San Diego Airport; you are met at the airport and taken by private bus to the ranch. Per-person rates range from $1,500 in the summer to $2,600 in the winter. For more information, check out the ranch's Web site at www.RanchoLaPuerta.com.

Round Hill, Jamaica, West Indies

Round Hill is very Old World and terribly tasteful. Both Bob Pittman and Ralph Lauren own cottages here, and Lauren designed several of the public areas.

The resort comprises luxury cottages with private pools, and most cottages have several bedrooms and breathtaking views of the ocean. Each cottage has an in-residence housekeeping staff who prepares scrumptious breakfasts for you on your private terrace/dining room. (The blueberry pancakes alone are worth a week's stay.)

Katrin Casserly, the wedding guru at Round Hill, is open to any ideas a bride and groom may propose. They also offer a simple wedding package that includes the marriage officiant, photography, flowers, and a video for $750.00.

The site features five tennis courts and a rotating list of U.S. tennis pros, an okay fitness room, and a small but pristine beach. This destination is perfect for a wedding of close friends and relatives who want only to spend time together relaxing and celebrating in a special place. Room rates run from $240 to $750 per couple. For more information, call 800-330-8272 or visit www.roundhilljamaica.com.

Sandals Royal Bahamian Resort and Spa, Nassau, Bahamas

This gem in the Sandals Resorts Signature Spa Collection is a perfect fit for a WeddingMoon (Sandals lingo for destination wedding/honeymoons). If your guest list doesn't include singles or children (they are persona non grata at Sandals resorts), this is a dreamy place to hold your nuptials, and it's plenty romantic enough for a wonderful honeymoon.

The Sandals resorts are all-inclusive, which is a major convenience (and relief) for you and your guests since there are no surprises on the final bill. This particular property is very luxe: ten bars, eight restaurants, seven pools with towering waterfalls, and a gym spiffy enough to let you train for the Olympics. The cherry on the sundae is that unlike many island resorts; it contains a convention center large enough to hold a large wedding.

For rate information check online at www.sandals.com or call 1-888-SANDALS.

The Westin William Penn, Pittsburgh, Pennsylvania

Huh? Pittsburgh? That's what Marcy thought when she was asked to plan a three-day destination-wedding extravaganza here. But — surprise, surprise — the city not only has a plethora of fabulous off-premise spaces, such as the Frick Art Museum, The Andy Warhol's Museum, and the Phipps Conservatory (all available with caterers for rehearsal dinners or weddings), but also is filled with interesting cultural exhibits to entertain out-of-town guests.

Of course, one wouldn't necessarily pick Pittsburgh without a reason (you hail from there or are addicted to Heinz ketchup, for example), but by any measure, the Westin William Penn, affiliated with the Starwood Hotel Group, is an excellent venue. Robert Slick, a wedding specialist extraordinaire, as well as every other special-events person at this nicely restored landmark, makes the event go smoothly, from setting up a welcome desk in the lobby for arriving wedding guests to keeping the hospitality suite stocked to the gills.

Their hotel offers many nice spots for photos and special rooms for the next-day brunch, and the cozy lobby works perfectly as an almost-private club for your guests. On the private banquet floor, a vast black and gold Art Deco room is ornate enough to serve as a ceremony space. It adjoins an equally impressive formal ballroom, an efficient space to hold a large wedding.

Room rates run between $99 and $130 dollars. Weddings are between $65 and $150 per person, plus tax and gratuity. For more information, call 412-553-5000. For reservations, call 412-553-5100.

Appendix

About the CD

$\bullet \bullet$

*H*ere's some of what you can find on the *Wedding Kit For Dummies* CD-ROM:

- Commercial versions of Internet Explorer, MindSpring, and Netscape Communicator
- Evaluation version of Acrobat Reader
- Worksheets, checklists, contracts, and spreadsheets to help keep all your wedding details organized

System Requirements

Make sure your computer meets the minimum system requirements listed below. If your computer doesn't match up to most of these requirements, you may have problems in using the contents of the CD.

- A PC with a Pentium or faster processor, or a Mac OS computer with a 68040 or faster processor.
- Microsoft Windows 95 or later, or Mac OS system software 7.5.5 or later.
- At least 16MB of total RAM installed on your computer. For best performance, we recommend at least 32MB of RAM installed.
- At least 50MB of hard drive space available to install all the software from this CD. (You'll need less space if you don't install every program.)
- A CD-ROM drive — double-speed (2x) or faster.
- A sound card for PCs. (Mac OS computers have built-in sound support.)
- A monitor capable of displaying at least 256 colors or grayscale.
- A modem with a speed of at least 14,400 bps.

If you need more information on the basics, check out *PCs For Dummies,* 7th Edition, by Dan Gookin; *Macs For Dummies,* 6th Edition, by David Pogue; *iMacs For Dummies,* by David Pogue; *Windows 95 For Dummies,* 2nd Edition, or *Windows 98 For Dummies,* both by Andy Rathbone (all published by Wiley Publishing, Inc.).

Using the CD with Microsoft Windows

1. **Insert the CD into your computer's CD-ROM drive.**

2. **Open your browser.**

   If you do not have a browser, we have included Microsoft Internet Explorer as well as Netscape Communicator. They can be found in the Programs folders at the root of the CD.

3. **Click Start⇨Run.**

4. **In the dialog box that appears, type** D:\START.HTM

   Replace *D* with the proper drive letter if your CD-ROM drive uses a different letter. (If you don't know the letter, see how your CD-ROM drive is listed under My Computer.)

5. **Read through the license agreement, nod your head, and then click the Accept button if you want to use the CD — after you click Accept, you'll jump to the Main Menu.**

   This action will display the file that will walk you through the content of the CD.

6. **To navigate within the interface, simply click on any topic of interest to take you to an explanation of the files on the CD and how to use or install them.**

7. **To install the software from the CD, simply click on the software name.**

   You'll see two options — the option to run or open the file from the current location or the option to save the file to your hard drive. Choose to run or open the file from its current location and the installation procedure will continue. After you are done with the interface, simply close your browser as usual.

 To run some of the programs, you may need to keep the CD inside your CD-ROM drive. Otherwise, the installed program would have required you to install a very large chunk of the program to your hard drive space, which would have kept you from installing other software.

How to Use the CD Using the Mac OS

To install the items from the CD to your hard drive, follow these steps.

1. **Insert the CD into your computer's CD-ROM drive.**

   In a moment, an icon representing the CD you just inserted appears on your Mac desktop. Chances are, the icon looks like a CD-ROM.

2. **Double-click the CD icon to show the CD's contents.**

3. **Double-click the Read Me First icon.**

   This text file contains information about the CD's programs and any last-minute instructions you need to know about installing the programs on the CD that we don't cover in this appendix.

4. **Open your browser.**

   If you don't have a browser, we have included the two most popular ones for your convenience — Microsoft Internet Explorer and Netscape Communicator.

5. **Click on File⇨Open and select the CD entitled Wedding Kit FD. Click on the Links.htm file to see an explanation of all files and folders included on the CD.**

6. **Some programs come with installer programs — with those you simply open the program's folder on the CD, and double click the icon with the words "Install" or "Installer."**

   Once you have installed the programs that you want, you can eject the CD. Carefully place it back in the plastic jacket of the book for safekeeping.

What You'll Find

Author-Created Files

The forms that are shown in the book are also available on the CD. Here you'll find worksheets to keep yourself on track and to give to your vendors so they know precisely what is needed when. There are checklists to help keep you focused when interviewing vendors and contracts to fill out in case a particular vendor doesn't have one available. Track your budget and create a guest list with the Excel spreadsheets provided. Links are also available on the CD to take you to the exact locations that are discussed in the book.

The forms appear on the CD in various formats for your convenience. Go to START.htm to view the forms given in the book in Acrobat format. Here you can click on the name of the form and the form pops up in an Acrobat window. You can print the form from this location if you wish. When you're ready to manipulate the forms, go to the Author folder, where you'll find the forms in a folder labeled RTF. The RTF format allows you to type, delete, create, or do anything else you want with the forms. The forms are listed according to their form number that is given in the book. You can activate the self-extracting file, WedKitFD.exe also located in the RTF folder, to place all the RTF files on your desktop in a folder called Wedding Kit FD. The two tracking spreadsheets are available in an Excel format, also located in the RTF folder. You will need to have Excel loaded on your machine in order to use these spreadsheets.

Commercial Software

Shareware programs are fully functional, free trial versions of copyrighted programs. If you like particular programs, register with their authors for a nominal fee and receive licenses, enhanced versions, and technical support. Freeware programs are free, copyrighted games, applications, and utilities. You can copy them to as many PCs as you like — free — but they have no technical support. GNU software is governed by its own license, which is included inside the folder of the GNU software. There are no restrictions on distribution of this software. See the GNU license for more details. Trial, demo, or evaluation versions are usually limited either by time or functionality (such as being unable to save projects).

Here's a summary of the software on this CD.

Acrobat Reader 4.0

For Windows and Mac.

Evaluation version. Limitation: view and print PDF files only. (Use RTF files to manipulate documents).

In order to view and print Portable Document Format (PDF) files (like the ones on this CD), you will need to use this program. To learn more about using Acrobat Reader, choose the Reader Online Guide from the Help menu, or view the Acrobat.pdf file installed in the same folder as the program. More information is available by visiting the Adobe Systems Web site, at www.adobe.com.

Internet Explorer

For Windows and Mac.

Commercial product.

Microsoft Internet Explorer provides the best support to date for Dynamic HTML and CSS. This browser from Microsoft enables you to view Web pages and perform a host of other Internet functions, including e-mail, newsgroups, and word processing. Be sure to check out the Microsoft Web site at www.microsoft.com regularly as it is updated often.

Netscape Communicator

For Windows and Mac.

Commercial Version.

Netscape Communicator also lets you browse the Web like Internet Explorer. It's up to you which browser to use. Check them both out and see what you like. For updates and information about Communicator, see Netscape's support site at www.netscape.com/browsers/index.html.

MindSpring Internet Access

For Windows and Mac.

Commercial version.

In case you don't have an Internet connection, the CD-ROM includes sign-on software for MindSpring, an Internet service provider (ISP). This ISP lets you connect to the Net for a fee on a monthly basis.

If you already have access to the Internet, then don't install this software.

Also, when you install MindSpring on the Mac, the installation program asks you for a keycode. Enter **DUMY8579** into the dialog box. Be sure to use all capital letters, just as it's shown here.

For more information, check out `http://www.mindspring.com/`.

Windows Media Player

For Windows.

Freeware version.

The Microsoft Windows Media Player is an alternative to RealPlayer. Like RealPlayer, Windows Media Player plays streaming media files, both in the Windows Media format and the RealMedia format.

These days, sites tend to offer both Windows Media and RealMedia versions of streaming media files. So you may want to install both programs so that you're equipped to handle whatever files you may come across on your journeys. For more information, see `www.windowsmediaplayer.com`.

My Wedding Organizer

For Windows.

Trial version. Limitation: 45 days to use product.

My Wedding Organizer takes the worry out of wedding planning. The program allows you to do guest lists, to-do lists, invitations, and more. For more information, visit `www.weddingsoft.com`

The Complete Wedding Publisher

For Windows.

Trial version. Limitation: 30 days to use product.

With over 600 paper stock designs to choose from, The Complete Wedding Publisher gives you everything you could want for all your wedding printing needs. For more information, `www.ed-it.com/p_wedsoc.htm`

If You've Got Problems (Of the CD Kind)

We've tried our best to compile programs that work on most computers with the minimum system requirements. Alas, your computer may differ, and some programs may not work properly for some reason.

The two likeliest problems are that you don't have enough memory (RAM) for the programs you want to use, or you have other programs running that are affecting the installation or running of a program. If you get error messages like `Not enough memory` or `Setup cannot continue`, try one or more of these methods and then try using the software again:

- Turn off any anti-virus software that you have on your computer. Installers sometimes mimic virus activity and may make your computer incorrectly believe that it is being infected by a virus.

- Close all running programs. The more programs you're running, the less memory is available to other programs. Installers also typically update files and programs. So if you keep other programs running, installation may not work properly.

- Have your local computer store add more RAM to your computer. This is, admittedly, a drastic and somewhat expensive step. However, if you have a Windows 95 PC or a Mac OS computer with a PowerPC chip, adding more memory can really help the speed of your computer and allow more programs to run at the same time. This may include closing the CD interface and running a product's installation program from Windows Explorer.

If you still have trouble with installing the items from the CD, please call the Wiley Product Technical Staff phone number: 800-762-2974 (outside the United States: 1-317-572-3994).

Index

• E •

Wiley Publishing, Inc.,
End-User License Agreement

READ THIS. You should carefully read these terms and conditions before opening the software packet(s) included with this book ("Book"). This is a license agreement ("Agreement") between you and Wiley Publishing, Inc. ("Wiley"). By opening the accompanying software packet(s), you acknowledge that you have read and accept the following terms and conditions. If you do not agree and do not want to be bound by such terms and conditions, promptly return the Book and the unopened software packet(s) to the place you obtained them for a full refund.

1. **License Grant.** Wiley grants to you (either an individual or entity) a nonexclusive license to use one copy of the enclosed software program(s) (collectively, the "Software") solely for your own personal or business purposes on a single computer (whether a standard computer or a workstation component of a multiuser network). The Software is in use on a computer when it is loaded into temporary memory (RAM) or installed into permanent memory (hard disk, CD-ROM, or other storage device). Wiley reserves all rights not expressly granted herein.

2. **Ownership.** Wiley is the owner of all right, title, and interest, including copyright, in and to the compilation of the Software recorded on the disk(s) or CD-ROM ("Software Media"). Copyright to the individual programs recorded on the Software Media is owned by the author or other authorized copyright owner of each program. Ownership of the Software and all proprietary rights relating thereto remain with Wiley and its licensers.

3. **Restrictions on Use and Transfer.**

   (a) You may only (i) make one copy of the Software for backup or archival purposes, or (ii) transfer the Software to a single hard disk, provided that you keep the original for backup or archival purposes. You may not (i) rent or lease the Software, (ii) copy or reproduce the Software through a LAN or other network system or through any computer subscriber system or bulletin-board system, or (iii) modify, adapt, or create derivative works based on the Software.

   (b) You may not reverse engineer, decompile, or disassemble the Software. You may transfer the Software and user documentation on a permanent basis, provided that the transferee agrees to accept the terms and conditions of this Agreement and you retain no copies. If the Software is an update or has been updated, any transfer must include the most recent update and all prior versions.

4. **Restrictions on Use of Individual Programs.** You must follow the individual requirements and restrictions detailed for each individual program in the Appendix of this Book. These limitations are also contained in the individual license agreements recorded on the Software Media. These limitations may include a requirement that after using the program for a specified period of time, the user must pay a registration fee or discontinue use. By opening the Software packet(s), you will be agreeing to abide by the licenses and restrictions for these individual programs that are detailed in the Appendix and on the Software Media. None of the material on this Software Media or listed in this Book may ever be redistributed, in original or modified form, for commercial purposes.

5. **Limited Warranty.**

   (a) Wiley warrants that the Software and Software Media are free from defects in materials and workmanship under normal use for a period of sixty (60) days from the date of purchase of this Book. If Wiley receives notification within the warranty period of defects in materials or workmanship, Wiley will replace the defective Software Media.

   (b) **WILEY AND THE AUTHOR OF THE BOOK DISCLAIM ALL OTHER WARRANTIES, EXPRESS OR IMPLIED, INCLUDING WITHOUT LIMITATION IMPLIED WARRANTIES OF MERCHANTABILITY AND FITNESS FOR A PARTICULAR PURPOSE, WITH RESPECT TO THE SOFTWARE, THE PROGRAMS, THE SOURCE CODE CONTAINED THEREIN, AND/OR THE TECHNIQUES DESCRIBED IN THIS BOOK. IDGB DOES NOT WARRANT THAT THE FUNCTIONS CONTAINED IN THE SOFTWARE WILL MEET YOUR REQUIREMENTS OR THAT THE OPERATION OF THE SOFTWARE WILL BE ERROR FREE.**

   (c) This limited warranty gives you specific legal rights, and you may have other rights that vary from jurisdiction to jurisdiction.

6. **Remedies.**

   (a) Wiley's entire liability and your exclusive remedy for defects in materials and workmanship shall be limited to replacement of the Software Media, which may be returned to Wiley with a copy of your receipt at the following address: Software Media Fulfillment Department, Attn.: *Wedding Kit For Dummies,* Wiley Publishing, Inc., 10475 Crosspoint Boulevard, Indianapolis, IN 46256, or call 800-762-2974. Please allow three to four weeks for delivery. This Limited Warranty is void if failure of the Software Media has resulted from accident, abuse, or misapplication. Any replacement Software Media will be warranted for the remainder of the original warranty period or thirty (30) days, whichever is longer.

   (b) In no event shall Wiley or the author be liable for any damages whatsoever (including without limitation damages for loss of business profits, business interruption, loss of business information, or any other pecuniary loss) arising from the use of or inability to use the Book or the Software, even if Wiley has been advised of the possibility of such damages.

   (c) Because some jurisdictions do not allow the exclusion or limitation of liability for consequential or incidental damages, the above limitation or exclusion may not apply to you.

7. **U.S. Government Restricted Rights.** Use, duplication, or disclosure of the Software by the U.S. Government is subject to restrictions stated in paragraph (c)(1)(ii) of the Rights in Technical Data and Computer Software clause of DFARS 252.227-7013, and in subparagraphs (a) through (d) of the Commercial Computer–Restricted Rights clause at FAR 52.227-19, and in similar clauses in the NASA FAR supplement, when applicable.

8. **General.** This Agreement constitutes the entire understanding of the parties and revokes and supersedes all prior agreements, oral or written, between them and may not be modified or amended except in a writing signed by both parties hereto that specifically refers to this Agreement. This Agreement shall take precedence over any other documents that may be in conflict herewith. If any one or more provisions contained in this Agreement are held by any court or tribunal to be invalid, illegal, or otherwise unenforceable, each and every other provision shall remain in full force and effect.

 FOR

DUMMIES®

The easy way to get more done and have more fun

PERSONAL FINANCE

0-7645-5231-7

0-7645-2431-3

0-7645-5331-3

Also available:

Estate Planning For Dummies
(0-7645-5501-4)
401(k)s For Dummies
(0-7645-5468-9)
Frugal Living For Dummies
(0-7645-5403-4)
Microsoft Money "X" For
Dummies
(0-7645-1689-2)
Mutual Funds For Dummies
(0-7645-5329-1)

Personal Bankruptcy For
Dummies
(0-7645-5498-0)
Quicken "X" For Dummies
(0-7645-1666-3)
Stock Investing For Dummies
(0-7645-5411-5)
Taxes For Dummies 2003
(0-7645-5475-1)

BUSINESS & CAREERS

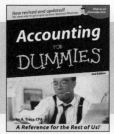

0-7645-5314-3

0-7645-5307-0

0-7645-5471-9

Also available:

Business Plans Kit For
Dummies
(0-7645-5365-8)
Consulting For Dummies
(0-7645-5034-9)
Cool Careers For Dummies
(0-7645-5345-3)
Human Resources Kit For
Dummies
(0-7645-5131-0)
Managing For Dummies
(1-5688-4858-7)

QuickBooks All-in-One Desk
Reference For Dummies
(0-7645-1963-8)
Selling For Dummies
(0-7645-5363-1)
Small Business Kit For
Dummies
(0-7645-5093-4)
Starting an eBay Business For
Dummies
(0-7645-1547-0)

HEALTH, SPORTS & FITNESS

0-7645-5167-1

0-7645-5146-9

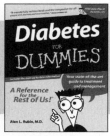

0-7645-5154-X

Also available:

Controlling Cholesterol For
Dummies
(0-7645-5440-9)
Dieting For Dummies
(0-7645-5126-4)
High Blood Pressure For
Dummies
(0-7645-5424-7)
Martial Arts For Dummies
(0-7645-5358-5)
Menopause For Dummies
(0-7645-5458-1)

Nutrition For Dummies
(0-7645-5180-9)
Power Yoga For Dummies
(0-7645-5342-9)
Thyroid For Dummies
(0-7645-5385-2)
Weight Training For Dummies
(0-7645-5168-X)
Yoga For Dummies
(0-7645-5117-5)

Available wherever books are sold.
Go to www.dummies.com or call 1-877-762-2974 to order direct.

 WILEY

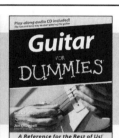
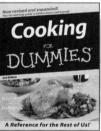

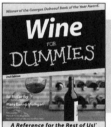

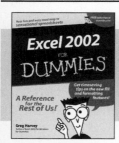  

FOR DUMMIES®

Helping you expand your horizons and realize your potential

TERNET

0-7645-0894-6

0-7645-1659-0

0-7645-1642-6

Also available:

America Online 7.0 For Dummies
(0-7645-1624-8)
Genealogy Online For Dummies
(0-7645-0807-5)
The Internet All-in-One Desk Reference For Dummies
(0-7645-1659-0)
Internet Explorer 6 For Dummies
(0-7645-1344-3)

The Internet For Dummies Quick Reference
(0-7645-1645-0)
Internet Privacy For Dummies
(0-7645-0846-6)
Researching Online For Dummies
(0-7645-0546-7)
Starting an Online Business For Dummies
(0-7645-1655-8)

GITAL MEDIA

0-7645-1664-7

0-7645-1675-2

0-7645-0806-7

Also available:

CD and DVD Recording For Dummies
(0-7645-1627-2)
Digital Photography All-in-One Desk Reference For Dummies
(0-7645-1800-3)
Digital Photography For Dummies Quick Reference
(0-7645-0750-8)
Home Recording for Musicians For Dummies
(0-7645-1634-5)

MP3 For Dummies
(0-7645-0858-X)
Paint Shop Pro "X" For Dummies
(0-7645-2440-2)
Photo Retouching & Restoration For Dummies
(0-7645-1662-0)
Scanners For Dummies
(0-7645-0783-4)

APHICS

0-7645-0817-2

0-7645-1651-5

0-7645-0895-4

Also available:

Adobe Acrobat 5 PDF For Dummies
(0-7645-1652-3)
Fireworks 4 For Dummies
(0-7645-0804-0)
Illustrator 10 For Dummies
(0-7645-3636-2)

QuarkXPress 5 For Dummies
(0-7645-0643-9)
Visio 2000 For Dummies
(0-7645-0635-8)

Available wherever books are sold. Go to www.dummies.com or call 1-877-762-2974 to order direct.

Here Come the Savings!

Congratulations…And Here's Our Gift To You

It's the Day of your Dreams.
Fill it with Unforgettable Sentiments

Unique Bridal Party Gifts and Wedding Day Accessories
Personalized to Commemorate your Special Day

Things Remembered is Convenient

- Shop any of our 800 stores located in just about every mall in America
- Order directly through our catalogs 1.800.274.7367
- Shop online at www.thingsremembered.com

Things Remembered is Fast

- Call ahead to any store and we'll have your gifts ready when you are
- Catalog and online orders are shipped in 3-5 business days (7 days for embroidered gifts)

Things Remembered Guarantees Your Satisfaction

- If you're not 100% satisfied, we'll take back your personalized gift for an exchange or full refund